BOB MARLEY

BOB MARLEY
HIS MUSICAL LEGACY

JEREMY COLLINGWOOD

CASSELL ILLUSTRATED

First published in Great Britain in 2005
by Cassell Illustrated, a division of
Octopus Publishing Group Limited
2-4 Heron Quays, London E14 4JP

This paperback edition published in 2006
by Cassell Illustrated

A CIP catalogue record for this book is
available from the British Library.

ISBN-13: 978-1-844035-05-2
ISBN-10: 1-844035-05-0

10 9 8 7 6 5 4 3 2 1

Printed in China

Designed by Design 23
Edited by Clare Flowers and Karen Dolan

Page 1: Bob in Jamaica, 1979.
Page 2: The iconic 'spliff' portrait that launched a thousand posters. Blackpool, 1973.
Above: Bob in the yard of Dynamics Studio, 1969.

CONTENTS

Foreword

FINDING THE TRUTH IN MUSIC HISTORY IS ALWAYS A difficult task, but when that history is rooted in the ghettos of Kingston, such a task becomes nigh impossible. The old dictum that 'failure is an orphan but success has many parents' is doubly true when the history of Bob Marley is attempted. Just like the first Sex Pistols gig, where the handful who were actually there has since mutated into several thousand people 'who really were there!', huge numbers of people claim to have worked with, written with and guided Bob.

I have used the vinyl releases of Bob Marley & The Wailers to trace Bob Marley's career path. There is a truth to be told in the singles and albums that Bob Marley & The Wailers released, as their career moved from Kingston to London and then on to the global stage.

Illustrated with contemporaneous adverts, reviews and little-known pictures of the group, *Bob Marley: His Musical Legacy* is the most complete musical history of Bob Marley ever written. For his dedicated fans the book will serve as a complete discography of all Jamaican, UK and US releases of Bob Marley & The Wailers. It does not cover the solo work of Peter Tosh, Bunny Wailer or Rita Marley unless distributed by Tuff Gong at 127, King Street and 56, Hope Road.

The UK releases by Island records were mirrored around the globe and do not form part of this project. The Island releases from France, Holland, Germany, Spain, Mexico, the US, Australia, Japan, Korea, and so on were identical in musical content to the UK releases – the only differences being various singles' picture covers.

Side 1 follows Bob from birth to Jamaican fame, and 'feature' sections convey the wider context in which the music was created and how the Jamaican experience influenced Bob & The Wailers. Their music didn't come out of a vacuum, rather from an area that had seen some of the greatest movements and mixings of cultures that have ever taken place in the world. The Caribbean's history was very much shaped by the slave trade and the massive economic boom brought about by sugar production.

Most crucially, Jamaica had its own music and arts scene. Following Independence in 1962, music and the arts began to find international markets and in the late 1960s through to the mid-1970s Kingston had a vibrant cultural scene, with its own magazine, that was strongly influenced by the Black Power movement in the US. Bob was one of the key players on this scene.

Side 2 follows Bob Marley & the Wailers on the path to international success, from uncomfortable jaunts in old, cold vans to massive stadium sell-out tours. As in Side 1, 'feature' sections give a flavour of the context in which all this was happening. At the peak of reggae's time on the international stage, Bob Marley was truly its king.

Every record mentioned in this book I have actually seen. If I have been unable to track down copies of certain records said to exist, such as 'Thank You Lord' coupled with 'This Train' on Dynamic, then such records are not included in this listing. I'm sure, given the nature of Jamaican releases, that there are one or two that have been missed or releases that appeared with one-off label designs or different-coloured vinyl.

Similarly, I have not attempted a 'Sessions' history with a track-by-track listing of musicians and studios. This is for two reasons: firstly, attempts to garner such information frequently end up with several contradictory stories and, secondly, I feel it would add little to the picture being painted.

I have given each item a year of release but not necessarily by date within that year. For Studio One (1) I have run 1963 into 1964 as The Wailers only began recording there late in that year, meaning that a track like 'Simmer Down' may have been recorded in 1963 but was released as a single in December of that year and was a hit for several months in 1964. Likewise, other singles may have been recorded in one year, but released the next.

Left: On stage in Paris, 1978.
Following pages: On stage in Paris, 1977.

Introduction

The release of the *Exodus* album in 1977 gave Bob Marley his first UK Top 10 and his first US Top 20. For the next four years he would tour the world and live life as one of the rock world's élite, before his death in 1981, at the tragically early age of 36, robbed us all of this extraordinary man.

Chris Blackwell's Island records released *Catch A Fire* in 1972, by which point the 27-year-old Marley had already released over 90 singles and some four albums over the previous ten years. Bob Marley had no illusions about how the music business worked and what it took to achieve success; Blackwell was backing someone who had earned his chance, not some young buck looking for a lucky break.

Yet much of how we remember Bob Marley comes from his final years, and those earlier days when he was a star in Jamaica, and a hero to the cognoscenti of the Western world, have been overlooked, largely owing to the lack of images (both moving and still) from the time; the music itself has been buried under the weight of legal and in-fighting since Bob's death.

As with other music greats, such as Elvis Presley and The Beatles, Bob Marley's career went through several phases and his music changed and developed over the years, yet for many he is remembered simply for having long locks, smoking weed and dating beautiful women. This, at best, is a tabloid short-hand and, at worst, seems to be uncomfortably close to the 'happy dancing native' colonial view of the Caribbean population, an image that Hippies, both in the USA and the UK, were happy to take on board.

My aim is to tell the full story of Bob Marley through the vinyl that he released over the years and to shine a light on some of the artistic peaks of his career: the sublime rocksteady of the Wail 'N Soul 'M years, The Rebel Sound of Lee Perry & Marley and the peerless tunes that flowed from 127, King Street, the first HQ of Marley's Tuff Gong label.

Many commentators ignore or are unaware of the vastly impressive canon of Marley's work. I believe that these early writings/recordings form an integral and pivotal part of how Bob developed and honed his ability to reach out and communicate on a worldwide scale.

Equally, the role of Rita Marley is often buried beneath the events that followed Bob's death, but a look at the Discography will show her to be a prolific artist, who occasionally paid for the mastering of Wailers' records and who, together with two other already established female stars, Judy Mowatt & Marcia Griffiths, provided Bob with killer harmonies as his songs conquered the world. She was also, of course, a supportive wife to Bob, mother to several of his children and the focal point of his family.

Naturally, our story begins in Jamaica and only moves to the

UK in 1973 when the focus began to shift to the world stage following the breakthrough concert at the Lyceum in London. By the time of the success of the *Live!* album in 1975, Bob had moved to a large house in Kingston's suburbs (56, Hope Road). This marked the end of Bob's time in Downtown Kingston and was a powerful symbol of his rise to stardom.

The Discography section of the book covers all vinyl released in the UK during the years 1962 to 1974, and conversely all the vinyl released in Jamaica during the International years, so collectors have a complete listing of all vinyl released in Jamaica, the UK and the US & Barbados. For the first time ever, all Bob's releases are catalogued to the best of current knowledge.

Above: Bob in London, with Gold Discs from Island, 1980.

Jamaica: A Brief History

WHEN CHRISTOPHER COLUMBUS 'DISCOVERED' JAMAICA IN 1494, and brought its existence to the attention of the Western world, the island had an indigenous population of around 60,000 Arawaks. Originally from Venezuela, the Arawaks had been on Jamaica for some 800 years but were being threatened by the warlike 'Caribs' tribe from Guyana that was slowly conquering parts of the West Indies. The Arawaks were a peace-loving agrarian people who cultivated crops such as cassava and cotton. They exported cotton and gave the world the hammock.

In 1509 Spanish colonists arrived on Jamaica and Spanish Town was established. This was only ever intended as a base for supporting the Spanish conquest of the Americas, but by 1517 the first black slaves were imported from Africa to Jamaica. This was necessary because the Arawak workforce was declining rapidly, owing to imported European diseases and the harsh treatment meted out by the Spanish.

After several decades of attacks from the British, Jamaica finally came under British control in 1655. By then the island had become a base for the 'privateers' or 'pirates' that raided shipping

across the West Indies. The town of Port Royal had by now become the place were the loot was sold and the money spent on all kinds of indulgences. Jamaica could name Henry Morgan and Blackbeard as one-time residents; this was to be the start of Jamaica's reputation as the Island of the exciting and exotic. In 1692 an earthquake caused much of Port Royal to crash into the sea. This event was seen by god-fearing folk as divine retribution on the evil and licentious town.

The British soon found themselves at war with escaped slaves known as 'Maroons', whose name comes from the Spanish 'Cimarron', meaning wild or untamed. In 1690 these Maroons joined up with a force of slaves from Clarendon, mainly Coromantes who were a warlike people from the African Gold Coast. Together they set up a form of rural guerrilla warfare, which kept the British troops in check. They used the 'abeng', which was a cow's horn bugle, to warn of approaching troops. This war was long (over 70 years) and costly, but eventually a truce was signed and the Maroons agreed to cease hostilities and hand back any new runaway slaves for a cash reward.

The English had first planted sugar cane in Barbados where, over a ten-year period, the wealth of the planters multiplied hugely. Jamaica was 26 times the size of Barbados, so predictably a 'sugar cane rush' began in Jamaica that saw the number of plantations or estates rise from 57 (in 1673) to 430 (in 1739). In their 18th century heyday these estates became the world's largest producer of sugar and Jamaica became the most profitable colony in the British Empire. The plantations made a few British élite extremely rich, built beautiful towns and cities back in the home country, and cost millions of lives.

A huge labour force was required to run these estates, so many slaves were brought to the island from Africa. The regime in Jamaica was very brutal, with slaves often worked to death then replaced by new ones, unlike in parts of the deep South in the US where many plantation owners preferred their slaves to breed to provide the future workforce. Some 5 million slaves were brought to Jamaica over a 150-year period, of whom 250,000 survived. The estates were like small villages where the owners ruled absolutely. It was not unusual for there to be a small settlement that housed children the owner had sired by slave women: indeed the offering of sexual favours was an option that

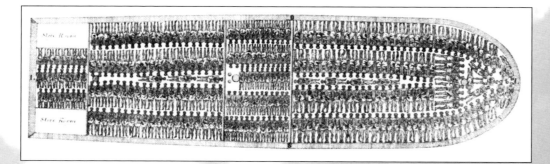

some slaves took. The predatory sexual behaviour of the estate owners was just one facet of this brutal economic model. Clearly little, or no, slave 'family' life took place on plantations. For the sailors on the slave ships, Jamaica was a very welcome rest from the rigours of life at sea. It was also where they got paid and this created a demand for the services of prostitutes (female & male).

The Slave Trade was abolished in Britain in 1807 but the final emancipation from slavery didn't happen until 1838. Jamaica remained a country controlled by a very small élite who tried to continue running the estates by importing indentured workers from East India. However, although the estate system continued to decline, social conditions remained more or less the same for the ex-slaves. The population became increasingly dissatisfied and in 1865 Paul Bogle and George William Gordon led what became known as the Morant Bay Rebellion. Although this revolt was put down with terrible brutality, it did bring about some gradual changes and improvements in Jamaica.

Over the coming years, Jamaica attracted people from many countries looking to build a new life – Chinese, Lebanese, Irish and Germans joined the population of African slaves and East Indian labourers. There had been a Jewish presence on the Island from the days of Spanish rule. Jamaica's economy moved to the production of bananas, bauxite (the raw material of aluminium) and tourism. By the 1920s the New Orleans Jazz scene was buying its 'viper' (weed) from sailors who had called in at Jamaica. It was the first sign of a business that would bring new (illegal) wealth to the country. By the 1930s Jamaica had become a favourite playground of the rich and famous, especially among members of the new filmmaking industry. A study in 1942 found that there were certain towns (often by the sea) that were well known for the sexual services available. There were even towns that specialized in homosexual services. The survey also found that the sexual morals of the old plantocracy had been adopted by many visitors, who saw nothing untoward in their behaviour.

Jamaica's various ethnic groups, although often small in number, were to play a major role in post-plantation and modern Jamaica. Many of these groups were entrepreneurs and retailers who came together to build many businesses, including the reggae industry which started up in the late 1950s and early 1960s.

Jamaica's national slogan is 'Out of many, one people', which hasn't applied at all in many areas of life, but the music industry truly drew upon all the peoples of Jamaica, and their spirituality, to create a new musical form.

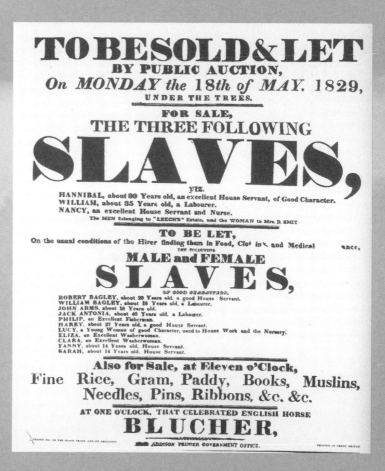

Bob's Early Life, and Jamaica in the 1960s

ROBERT NESTA MARLEY WAS BORN ON 6 FEBRUARY 1945 in the rural village of Nine Mile in the parish of St Ann's. His mother was a Jamaican teenager, Cedella Malcolm, and his father a white man, Captain (from his time in the British Army) Norval Marley, now a local government official. Unusually, for such a liaison, Norval actually married Cedella and gave the baby Robert legitimacy. However he barely played a father's role, although it seems he did arrange for Bob to go to live with relatives in Kingston at the age of five. Shortly afterwards, Cedella tracked her son down and brought him back with her to the village of Stepney where he attended the local school and met Neville (Bunny) Livingston, who was two years younger than him.

In 1957, when Bob was twelve, he and his mother moved to Kingston. Cedella had become romantically involved with Bunny's father, Taddy (Thaddius) Livingston and they had a baby, Pearl. Friends since their Stepney schooldays, Bob and Bunny soon became even closer. Bob's first experience of work was as a welder, but early on he got a piece of metal in his eye and required hospital treatment. Soon after, he and Bunny set out to earn a living as musicians. They started with crude, homemade instruments and had soon hooked up with Peter McIntosh (Tosh) and were receiving guidance from Joe Higgs, who was already a successful singer.

By 1962 Cedella had married Edward Booker and moved to Delaware in the US in1963. A newly married Bob stayed with his mother for a few months in 1966 and worked on the assembly line of the local Chrysler car factory. It was a short and unhappy stay for the introverted musician, who missed his wife, and all his Trenchtown and Studio One friends.

Bob was a teenager in a Jamaica that had gained independence from Britain in 1962 and was already achieving recognition on the international stage, far beyond what one might expect from its size (population circa 2 million).

1962 saw the release of the first-ever James Bond film, Doctor No, which was filmed in Jamaica. The scene where Honey Rider (Ursula Andress) appears from the azure sea, which has frequently been voted the sexiest scene in film, has James Bond singing a Jamaican mento as he spies upon her. The film also provided a young (and well-connected) Chris Blackwell with his first job! Ian Fleming, the author of the Bond books, was a Jamaican resident. In fact, he was part of a triumvirate of famous pleasure-seekers for whom Jamaica was a playground in paradise, Errol Flynn and Noel Coward being the others.

In 1963 Miss Jamaica, Carole Joan Crawford, was crowned 'Miss World' – this was at a time, of course, when such titles received massive news coverage. Sound Systems (mobile discos) crowned their own 'Queens' and beautiful women were featured in every newspaper and in 'street' magazines such as Swing; every Jamaican tourist guide had a chapter on the island's beautiful women. In later years, Bob would famously live with Cindy Breakspeare, who was Miss World in 1976, and who in 1978 gave birth to their son, Damian.

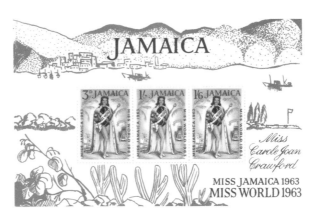

Jamaica also became home to a Playboy Hotel, again reflecting the dangerous and sexually exiting image of the island. Chris Blackwell's fledging Island Records released 'Ska at the Jamaica Playboy Club' (1966), demonstrating early on his flair for marketing. Millie had a hit in the UK with her 'My Boy Lollipop' ska cover of Barbie Gaye's hit (Darl) and Prince Buster's music drove the legendary 'Blue Beat' label forward in the UK.

Ska had hit the international stage via the World's Trade Fair in 1964, where the likes of Prince Buster and Jimmy Cliff had performed. Byron Lee played in New York and got a record deal with US Atlantic, based around the Ska craze.

1966 had also seen the visit to Jamaica of Emperor Haile Selassie of Ethiopia – a massive event in Kingston. Selassie was met by Mortimer Planno (or Planner), described in the newspapers of the time as a 'Ras Tafarian leader'. The capital was brought to a halt as people clamoured to see the Emperor, while drums rolled

and the smell of ganja hung in the air. Selassie met politicians, academics and groups like the Rastafarian Brethren Association and travelled the island during his three-day visit. The Wailers recalled the event with 'Rasta Shook Them Up', which featured Peter on lead vocals, as Bob was away in the US at the time.

There were reports of riots during the visit and police used tear gas to control the crowds. Riots and violence were on the rise during this period and songs such as Higgs & Wilson's 'Gun Talk' (Luxor, '60), The Rehoboth Gospel Singers' 'Crime Is Taking Over The Nation' (Tabernacle, '66) and Count Lasher's 'Peace, Peace, Peace' (SEP, '66) typified the music business's response to society's problems. The outbreak of violence from 'Rude Boys' was the subject of several singles from the likes of Prince Buster, The Clarendonians and Alton Ellis. Wailers' tracks like 'Rude Boy', 'Simmer Down' and 'One Love' are, of course, in the same vein.

The musical influence of the United States, via radio and tours, was still strong. Initially it had begun with R&B from artists such as Fats Domino and Lynn Hope, but as Bob was growing up, the romantic Soul Balladeers also became hugely popular. As Bob recalled, 'And one time me saw a show down here (Kingston) with Brook Benton and Dinah Washington. Like they all show up: Nat King Cole, Billy Eckstine, y'know.' The popularity of such singers has done much to influence reggae and its love of a good ballad.

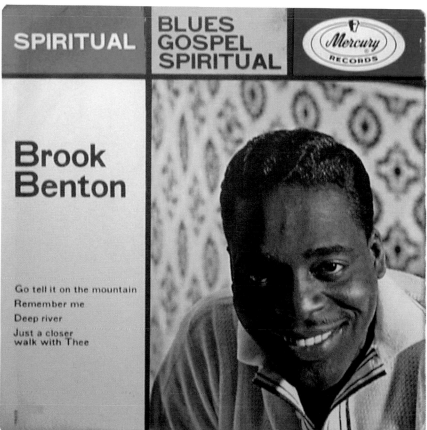

SIDE 1

JAMAICA (JA)

1962 – 1974

'Judge Not' to 'What's New, Pussy Cat?'

ROBERT MARLEY
Judge Not /
Do You Still Love Me?

Judge Not – from the well known 'Judge not, that ye be not judged' from the Bible (Matthew 7:1), Bob creates a song of warning with a moral message. It's ska all the way as Beverly's All Stars provide the musical backdrop to the young Bob's sermon-like composition.

Do You Still Love Me? is a familiar tale of love and loss. Bob's youthful vocal style makes it sound almost like a teen drama song. It's a slower ska, with a strong harmonic line, again from Beverly's All Stars.

BOBBY MARTELL
One Cup Of Coffee /
DON DRUMMOND
Snow Boy

The second single was rather strangely credited to 'Bobby Martell' – and is another song about love gone wrong. It's a slower ska piece but both the lyric and Bob's credit are very American! It's not a cover of Brook Benton's 'Another Cup Of Coffee', as is often cited, though Brook Benton was hugely popular in Jamaica and the song does sound like a cover, despite the Marley writing credit.

Don Drummond was one of the original Skatalites, a band put together by Dodd.

BOB'S FIRST SESSION

A 17-year-old Bob Marley was introduced to Leslie Kong by Jimmy Cliff, with whom Kong had already scored with tunes such as 'Miss Jamaica' and 'Hurricane Hatty'. Bob's first recording sessions were for Kong, a Chinese-Jamaican whose family ran an ice-cream parlour in Orange Street, Kingston; he was just getting into the flourishing domestic music business. The young Marley saw two singles released on Kong's Beverley's Records label (another track, 'Terror', reportedly sits in a vault somewhere). This brief session for the budding producer was to prove a false start for Bob as both singles sank without trace.

Leslie Kong was typical of the Jamaican Chinese community, who were traditionally active in the retail part of the economy. He was one of many of that community who became successful in the emerging music business; others were Thomas 'The Great Sebastian' Wong – operator of one of Jamaica's first Sound Systems, Justin Yap and his Top Deck label, Herman Chin-Loy and his Aquarius Studio and imprint, Byron Lee and his brother Neville who ran Sonic Sounds, Jo Jo and Ernest Hoo Kim and their Channel One Studio and associated imprints, Mickey Chung (of Third World) – the list goes on.

THE WAILERS AT COXSONE DODD'S STUDIO ONE

By the early 1960s, Clement 'Coxsone' (or 'Coxson') Dodd was already a key player in the developing Jamaican music industry and had several Sound Systems that played in Kingston and across the island, as well as his own recording studio (Studio One), his own house band of top musicians and a variety of labels on which he had released Jamaican R&B, calypso, gospel and, of course, ska.

In late 1963, Clement 'Coxsone' Dodd began recording The Wailers, a group headed by Bob that included Bunny Wailer (Neville Livingston), Peter Tosh (Winston Hubert McIntosh), and several occasional members such as Junior Braithwaite, Constantine 'Dream' or 'Vision' Walker, Cherry Green and Beverly Kelso. The Wailers had spent many months rehearsing under the tutelage of Joe Higgs, in the backyard of his home in Kingston. Higgs (as part of duo Higgs & Wilson) was already a star in Jamaica and had

Left: Bob's first-ever singles, recorded by Leslie Kong on his Beverley's Records label.
Above: A young Clement Dodd (on the left) leans on one of his bass bins from his 'Down Beat' Sound System.

Far left: Clement Dodd (Sir Coxson), promoter, musical director and recording engineer, with Roland Alphonso (Mr Versatile), sax player and founder member of The Skatalites, a band that often provided backing for The Wailers.
Left: Bob, Bunny & Peter in their satin suits, circa 1967.

found success on the WIRL label, then owned by the future prime minister of Jamaica, Edward Seaga. Higgs was also an occasional member of The Wailers, and performed with the band when Bunny dropped out on the American leg of the first 'Island' tour in 1973, to promote *Catch A Fire* and *Burnin'*.

During the period at Studio One, the Wailers' line-up varied around the core of Bob, Bunny and Peter. Both Junior Braithwaite and Cherry Green left the group during 1964, with Beverly departing the following year.

It was at Studio One that Bob Marley met the young singer Alpharita Consticia Anderson, who recorded as the lead singer of The Soulettes and later under her own name. 'Rita' was actually born in Cuba but taken to Jamaica as an infant. Dodd appointed Bob as coach to the vocal group. After a brief romance, Bob and Rita were married on February 10, 1966.

THE WAILERS
Climb Up The Ladder /
Straight and Narrow Way
Climb Up The Ladder features music from the top band of the day – The Skatalites – and finds Bob issuing a warning: 'Climb the ladder. Mind you fall back down.' Bob was already ensuring that The Wailers rehearsed and rehearsed, until they had it perfect, so that they kept climbing that ladder.
Straight and Narrow Way features a lead vocal by Junior Braithwaite, whose very young-sounding voice seems to run contrary to the theme of the record. It offers moral advice to all the Rudies (Rude Boys) and their female friends who haven't stuck to the prescribed path.

Right: 'Blanks' sometimes carry Dodd's 'Down Beat' or 'Musik City' stamps.

Bob was away in the US for some eight months immediately following his marriage, staying at his mother's home in Wilmington, Delaware. He worked the night shift in the parts department at the Chrysler car factory to get some money together. Bunny largely covered vocal duties in Bob's absence. Peter also recorded several tracks as the named artist on the label, especially during this period.

The two groups, The Wailers and The Soulettes, became close during Bob's absence in the US, with Constantine 'Dream' Walker joining The Wailers; he was Rita's cousin and a fellow Soulette. The Wailers also appeared on various Soulettes' and Rita Marley singles (see 'Wailers on harmonies & Rita at Studio One' in the Discography).

While signed to Dodd, The Wailers (including Bob) appeared at some of Dodd's Down Beat (and Round Beat) dances across the island and at other venues such as the Ward Theatre, the Palace Theatre and on Vere Johns' *Opportunity Hour* (a talent show). Dodd was commercially highly astute and, with one eye on the success of Motown in the United States, he borrowed the tag line used on their single sleeves and in promotion, 'The Sound of Young America'; Studio One productions duly came to carry the tag, 'The Sound of Young Jamaica'.

Dodd paid his artists day-rate wages only; he might give them a bonus or

(continued on page 28)

THE WAILERS
Destiny / I Am Going Home
Destiny is an upbeat ska number that cautions 'Love one another' and 'Do unto others as they may do to you. The road is rough and you may stumble too'. The Skatalites, with Dizzy Moore on trumpet, provide the music.

I Am Going Home is a ska romp, whose biblical lyrics are the beginning of what Rastas would expound as a return to Africa. It uses the spiritual 'Swing Low Sweet Chariot' as its basis.

Destiny appeared on various coloured vinyl pressings, which seemed to be a Dodd favourite for a short while.

THE WAILERS
Simmer Down /
I Don't Need Your Love
An early release for Dodd was an original composition that Marley had written a couple of years previously. It was to set the style of Bob's work with a direct call to the youth, using a mix of street slang and Jamaican (JA) folklore.

Simmer Down was reportedly a hit as soon as it was played as an acetate, or Dub plate, on Dodd's Sound System: it went on to sell some 60,000-plus copies. Several coloured vinyl pressings have surfaced.

I Don't Need Your Love is another ska piece from The Skatalites, this time with a sax solo from the great Roland Alphonso. Subject matter is standard boy/girl stuff, with strong harmonies from Peter, Bunny, Junior Braithwaite and Beverly Kelso.

THE WAILERS
Tell Them Lord / Christmas Is Here
Tell Them Lord is a gem of a ska tune, with Bob, Bunny, Peter, Junior Braithwaite, Beverly Kelso and even the Wailers' mentor, Joe Higgs, in the vocal mix. 'Can't get no work and can't get no food' sets the tone of this lament of the dispossessed of society, which in Jamaica was a huge underclass. 'So tell them Lord, abolish the book of slavery'. The Skatalites are steaming, with Dizzy Moore providing a top trumpet solo. An early signpost to the mix of music, lyrics and attitude that would fire Bob's career.

Christmas Is Here, aka 'Sound The Trumpet', is a holiday season special with The Skatalites still cooking – they even add a quick musical romp through 'Santa Claus is Coming To Town'! What more could you want?

Above: Dodd's single sleeves owed much to Motown's.

1964

BOB MARLEY AND THE WAILERS
Do You Remember? /
PETER TOUCH & THE WAILERS
Hoot Nanny Hoot
Do You Remember is a rough ska tune that
carries a tuff Bob lead vocal, which contrasts with
the song's subject matter of love. The line, 'How
many times have I told you that I love you?' gives
the track its alternative name ('How Many Times').
Bob re-cut it for JAD (see JAD section) and a fine
dub plate mix of that recording surfaced in the
late 1970s.
Hoot Nanny Hoot takes its name from the US
TV programme *Hootenanny* that showcased the
then upcoming 'radical' folk music of the 1960s.
'I just don't know how to do this dance', Peter
(using his 'Touch' name) sings on this rather odd
ska piece. In the UK, musician Jools Holland has
adopted the name for his now traditional New
Year musical show.

THE WAILERS
Habits /
PETER TOUCH & THE WAILERS
Amen
On **Habits**, Junior Braithwaite takes a rare outing
on lead vocals, on this simple ska song of folk
wisdom. On the chorus The Wailers throw
everything into the vocal mix. Junior's vocal
sounds very much as his name suggests. The
horn line still wins best contribution award.
Amen can be found on many of Curtis Mayfield
and The Impressions' greatest hits collections. The
Wailers' version is a storming ska knees-up with
Peter's lead being answered by Bob, in a call-and-
response style.

BOB MARLEY & THE WAILERS
I Left My Sins /
BOB MARLEY & THE SPIRITUAL SISTERS
Just In Time
Coxsone Dodd ran a gospel imprint, Tabernacle, to
house his output for that market.
Jamaica has the greatest number of
churches per head of population of any country in
the world. The Bible, especially the Old Testament,
was the *lingua franca* for what was then a largely
illiterate population, so it's no surprise to see Bob
recording traditional gospel music: the spirit had
always been part of his life.
I Left My Sins is a gently bobbing, slight ska
tune, on which he sings of leaving his sins down
by the river.
Just In Time, with Rita Anderson (Marley) and
Marlene Gifford (both Soulettes, they were also
fellow Studio One employees) as the Spiritual
Sisters, is a true gospel tune, with Bob as full
baritone. As in everything that they turned their
hands to, they applied themselves admirably.
However, Bob's lack of a pure voice meant this
kind of gospel wasn't for him.

THE WAILERS
It Hurts To Be Alone / Mr Talkative
It Hurts To Be Alone is the last track that Junior
Braithwaite sang lead on before he left for the US.
It's another romantic ballad, which became a
Wailers favourite. The excellent playing of guitarist
Ernest Ranglin comes in on the middle eight.
Mr Talkative warns gossips of the serious
trouble coming their way if they don't keep quiet.

Roland Alphonso on sax makes his musical presence felt. Bob re-cut this in 1970 as 'Mr Chatterbox' for Bunny 'Striker' Lee, as a more light-hearted jibe at fellow producer Niney (Winston 'Niney' Holness).

1965

THE WAILERS
Love & Affection / Teenager In Love
A brace of romantic ballads from The Wailers:
Love & Affection finds Bob cleverly working the titles of previous Wailers' tracks – 'It Hurts To Be Alone' and 'Lonsome Feelings' – into the song. This ability to recycle snatches of previous lyrics would become a trademark of Bob's compositions. 'Love & Affection' was, reportedly, a favourite at The Wailers' live appearances.
Teenager In Love is an adapted version of Dion and The Belmonts' original hit, written by rock and roll writing team Doc Pomus and Mort Shuman. The track's R&D rhythm makes it more homage than new creation.

THE WAILERS & THE MIGHTY VIKINGS
There She Goes / Lonsome Feelings
A couple of tunes that feature musical backing from the show band, The Mighty Vikings. Both tracks also have harmonies from Beverly Kelso, as well as Cherry Green, who would only appear on two more Wailers records.
There She Goes is about heartaches and finds Bob singing at the top of his register, with a very 'girly' chorus and even a cheesy organ break. 'Have you ever had a lonesome feeling?' Bob asks, as this choppy ska tune begins on the flip. Like 'There She Goes', there are lots of high-pitched harmonies on this slight romantic story.

THE WAILERS
Dana / Don't Ever Leave Me
Dana – aka 'Donna' – more romantic lyrics with Bob on lead vocals, which for a short section he shares with Beverly Kelso – the only time that she took lead. Once again, Dizzy Moore's trumpet is to the fore.
Don't Ever Leave Me is another romantic song that harks back to the US of the 1950s. Ernest Ranglin's guitar solo is worthy of note.

Bunny, Bob and Peter pose for the cover of their debut album, The Wailing Wailers, pressed by Studio One.

THE WAILERS
I Made A Mistake /
BUNNY & RITA
The Vow
I Made A Mistake is an early example of the influence of Curtis Mayfield on Bob (and Jamaican music). On this soulful ballad written by Mayfield, music comes from top Studio One session guys, such as Lloyd Knibb, Lloyd Brevett and Lynn Taitt.
The Vow features Bunny Wailer and Rita Marley; originally a JA hit from Sound System favourites Gene & Eunice. This slushy ballad is typical of many that were hugely popular in Jamaica, particularly for dancing close to late at night. Rita recorded 'I Do' for Tuff Gong in 1971, which covered similar territory.

THE WAILERS
And I Love Her / Do It Right
The Beatles were hugely popular with middle-class Jamaicans and it's no surprise that Bob & Co covered **And I Love Her**. Now more of a curiosity than anything else, it's a good example of how Bob was always aware of the mainstream music scene.
Do It Right is a galloping ska that features The Skatalites in fine form with Bunny, Peter and Beverly Kelso providing harmonies. The percussive sound that appears to be empty beer bottles being struck with metal openers is just that!

THE WAILERS
Another Dance /
Somewhere To Lay My Head
Another Curtis Mayfield composition about the simple pleasures of dancing and meeting a new girlfriend, here presented as a rolling ska piece. Originally, The Impressions' track was called 'Just Another Dance' from their *People Get Ready* album. Bob's writing credit is bogus.
Somewhere To Lay My Head (aka 'I Want Somewhere') is a slow ska in which Bob searches … but is it a spiritual or secular quest for a home: Africa, heaven or simply a roof?

BOB MARLEY & THE WAILERS
Cry To Me / Wages Of Love
The lyric 'Walk back through the heartache, shed those lonely teardrops' sets the tone of this proto-rocksteady ballad. Bunny and Peter's harmonies add to the doo-wop feel of the piece. Bob returned to this track with Lee Perry, and for the *Rastaman Vibration* album.
Wages Of Love features Bunny and Rita singing falsetto lead on this gentle ballad of love.

'Skanky Dog'. For Tuff Gong, Peter cut 'Once Bitten', and the first release on his own Intel-Diplo label was 'Dog Teeth', which included more folk wisdom, such as 'If you lie with dog, you must rise with flea.' The first pressing of 'Maga Dog' was on a blank with Roy Richards' 'Fat Dog' on the flip.

BOB MARLEY & THE WAILERS
I'm Gonna Put It On /
Love Won't Be Mine This Way
A hit for The Wailers in 1965, **I'm Gonna Put It On** (aka 'Put It On') is a rocking ska piece that is a spiritual celebration of the power of the Lord. But the line, 'I rule my destiny' again crosses into the real world. The couplet, 'I'm not boasting, I just feel like toasting' is the first vinyl outing for the phrase 'toasting' (talking over a rhythm track – the precursor of rap). Another track that Bob recut later in his career, for Lee Perry, as 'Put It On'.
Love Won't Be Mine This Way finds The Wailers singing this message to an old girlfriend. A slow ballad, which recalls the harmony doo-wop groups of the 1950s, but without any added Jamaican spice. Fine sax work from Roland Alphonso fails to save the day.

THE WAILERS
I Am Still Waiting /
THE SKATALITES
Ska Jam
I Am Still Waiting is a top-drawer soul/reggae ballad that finds Bob in fine vocal and writing form. An exquisite song about the pain of waiting for love, which Bob manages to reflect in his vocal lead. His Island hit, 'Waiting In Vain' returns to the same territory.
Ska Jam is actually 'Ska Jerk' by The Wailers and is another track about the Jerk dance craze that was based on Junior Walker's hit, 'Shotgun'.

THE WAILERS
Jumbie Jamboree /
R ALPHONSO STUDIO 1 ORCH
I Should Have Known Better
Peter takes the lead on this stomping ska tune, telling the story of when 'They mash-up the theatre, 'cause the 'lectricity had a failure' – an actual event that occurred when The Wailers were playing at the Palace Theatre. 'Jumbie' is another folk term for 'duppy' or ghost. The title is reminiscent of the mento/calypso 'Zombee Jamboree' that is an ode to the joys of the Bacchanalia.

(BOB MARLEY) & THE WAILERS
Diamond Baby /
Where's The Girl For Me?
One of a handful of records that now fetch hundreds of pounds is this fierce ska scorcher on which The Skatalites are in fine form. It's a tough adaptation of Mayfield's 'Talking 'Bout My Baby'.
Where's The Girl For Me? is an homage to the doo-wop groups of the 1950s; its saving grace is the guitar playing of Ernest Ranglin.

BOB MARLEY & THE WAILERS
Good Good Rudie /
CITY SLICKERS
Ocean 11
Good Good Rudie became better known as 'Jailhouse' (also called 'Ruddie', 'Ruddie Boy' or 'Rudie Rudie') and is one of Bob's best for Studio One. A perfect mix of street slang and biblical references, it's a plea for restraint and even wisdom, in the face of provocation. 'We're going to rule this land' is the message of victory to come, with a passage from Luke 10:21 closing the

track: 'What has been hid from the wise and prudent is now revealed to babes and sucklings'.
A harmonic cut, over the original rhythm, appeared on the Coxsone label, as Roy Richards' 'Green Callie'.

THE WAILERS
Hooligans /
PETER TOUCH
Maga Dog
Bob, Peter and Bunny reacted to riots at concerts with **Hooligans**: 'Don't be a donkey, if you are really a man'. It sets the tone of the track, whose honking ska beat and horn solo identifies the sound of Studio One. 'Man what do think you are? A leggo (wild) beast to be sure,' sing the Wailers in this anti-riot song. Writing credits of 'BM Burke' on the single have yet to be identified.
Maga-Dog – Peter drives this ska raver that uses a folk saying about 'maga' (skinny, malnourished) dogs with warnings about 'Jumping out of the frying pan'. He returned to the theme with a similarly named track for Joe Gibbs, which gave rise to a whole host of further cuts with names such as 'Boney Dog' and

Above: The Impressions, featuring Curtis Mayfield (left), were a big influence on Bob & The Wailers, and they covered several Mayfield compositions.

THE WAILERS
One Love / Do You Feel The Same Way Too?

The words **One Love** have become synonymous with Bob Marley. It was a remake of this track that brought him huge chart success in the 1980s. This sparkling original has Bob and Bunny swapping vocal lead over a driving ska beat, with the chorus 'One Love, One Heart', becoming a Rasta greeting of unity in the 1970s.

Do You Feel The Same Way Too? is a slight teenage love song with a mid-tempo ska backing and a sharp alto sax solo from Lester Sterling. Bob used the Impressions' 'People Get Ready' as a basis for 'One Love' and the later cut was called 'One Love / People Get Ready'.

THE WAILERS
Playboy / Your Love

Bob sings lead on **Playboy**, a pop/ska tune, which borrows heavily from the Motown group The Contours' hit, 'Do You Love Me?'

Your Love has The Wailers firing on all cylinders, with Bunny, Junior Braithwaite and Beverly Kelso on harmonies. Joe Higgs, The Wailers' mentor, takes on the almost spoken bass part that jumps out of the mix.

THE WAILERS
Rude Boy /
SOUL BROS ORCH
Ringo's Theme

Bob leads on another one of his Rude Boy anthems (also known as 'Rude Boy Ska' and 'Rule Them Rudie'). 'Walk the proud land with me,' urges Bob, as the track ignites. The chorus 'I've got to keep on moving' would reappear as the title of a track for Lee Perry and probably indicates that Bob had been listening to The Impressions' 'I Gotta Keep On Moving' from their *Never Ending Impressions* album.

THE WAILERS
Shame and Scandal /
ROLANDO AL & HIS SOUL BROTHERS
Sca-Balena

This is a classic Jamaican calypso/mento that is a bawdy celebration of the nature of many Caribbean families: the lyrics, 'That girl is your sister but your mama don't know' to 'Your Daddy ain't your Daddy but your Daddy don't know' give the flavour. Probably the most covered song in Jamaica during the 1960s. Peter's vocal leads a fine performance, with The Skatalites driving the ska beat.

Shame and Scandal was released in the UK, on Island, with 'The Jerk' on the flip. I have been unable to find the original Jamaican release of this track, which is one of three, in praise of the dance 'The Jerk', that the Wailers cut. 'The Jerk' was originally a huge hit in the US for The Larks, who used The Impressions' track 'Girl You Don't Know Me' as the basis for their hit.

BOB MARLEY & THE WAILERS
What's New Pussy Cat? /
Where Will I Find

Bob sings Tom Jones! A British journalist, obviously concerned about Bob's street cred, asked him why he had ever sung such a pop song and Bob said it was because he liked it and just began to sing along. Perhaps it was because he empathised with the character from the film or maybe Coxsone Dodd twisted his arm – who knows? Anyway, it's a great version, with fine horns from Tommy McCook and Dizzy Moore. **Where Will I Find** is another ill-advised attempt at a doo-wop-style love song on which everyone seems lost.

BOB MARLEY & THE WAILERS
White Christmas /
BOB MARLEY & THE SPIRITUAL SISTERS
Let The Lord Be Seen In You

Bob tackles an unlikely song for a Caribbean-based musician, but The Wailers make it their own. A nice change to the lyric (reportedly by Peter) finds Bob singing 'I'm dreaming of a white Christmas, NOT like the ones I used to know'.

Let The Lord Be Seen In You is Bob, with Beverly Kelso and Cherry Green as The Spiritual Sisters this time. This spiritual doesn't really work as the female harmonies are all over the place.

The following singles were all recorded while Bob was away working in the US.

1966

THE WAILERS
Dancing Shoes /
PETER TOUCH & THE CHORUS
Don't Look Back

Dancing Shoes is a celebration of Sound System dances. Bunny's sweet tenor proclaims 'We're going skanking all night long' and when he sings 'We won't care 'cause we got the blues when we got on our dancing shoes' a universal truth is spoken. The skanking horn line is by Headley 'Deadly' Bennett. One of Bunny's finest with The Wailers at Studio One. DJ Dennis Alcapone cut an early version with 'Dancing version' that appeared on his classic *Forever version* album (1971, Studio One), with original Wailers' vocals.
Peter tackles The Temptations' hit **Don't Look Back**, with fine harmony support from Bunny and Constantine 'Dream' Walker. At less than two minutes' long, it never really gets going. Peter re-cut it when he signed to the Rolling Stones' label in the late 1970s, when he duetted with Mick Jagger.

THE WAILERS
I Stand Predominate /
NORMA FRASER
Come By Here

A chugging ska, with Bunny taking lead vocal duties. At once a Rude Boy boast and a proclamation of faith with the Rasta 'I & I' patois appearing, along with 'He's always beside me and always to guide me – he's my one and all' which speaks of a deep spiritual faith. The quality playing of Roland Alphonso (sax) and Vin Gordon (trombone) shines through.

THE WAILERS
Lemon Tree /
MARCIA GRIFFITHS
Feel Like Jumping
or Soul Brothers Hot Rod

Peter and Bunny share lead vocals on this slight American folksong that sounds as if Peter, Paul and Mary were the original performers – as indeed they were. Probably picked up as The Impressions covered it on their *Never Ending* album. A nightclub in Kingston called The Lemon Tree was an advertiser in the first copies of *Swing* magazine. It's a rare record for which no label copy has ever appeared.

help with stage clothes if they had a hit. The producer was, and often still is, the person who built a musician's career. Many of the tracks recorded at Studio One were written by Bob but they are frequently referred to as 'R Marley – C Dodd' compositions. This is because the producer often gave himself credit, as a matter of course, as part composer. These credits sometimes appear, even when the track is a cover of someone else's song.

Just like Motown, Dodd used top session men to back his artists, such as The Skatalites, who were the top ska group of the day (members included Roland Alphonso, Lloyd Knibb, Don Drummond, Tommy McCook and Johnny 'Dizzy' Moore). They frequently backed The Wailers, as did a later incarnation of the group, The Soul Brothers.

With Coxsone Dodd, The Wailers had joined the premier division of groups in Jamaica but they wanted greater financial rewards from their success and were clearly all strong characters who liked to be masters of their own destiny. Dodd was reportedly very helpful toward Bob, even giving him somewhere to sleep at the back of the Brentford Road studio, and lending him money so that he and Rita could get married. Yet Dodd's paternalism was not enough for Bob who, although drawn to father figures, was keen to control all aspects of his career and reap the financial rewards.

As *Swing* magazine reported in a survey of the music industry in Jamaica in the late 1960s: 'In 1964 he [Mr Dodd] set up his own studio which at the time was the most successful in the island. But because of what they describe as 'low rewards and chicanery business', artistes such as The Gaylads and The Wailers, Delroy Wilson and others have left the company.'

This period marked a high point in the number of tracks on which Bunny would sing lead vocal. In 1976, Bunny released an album, *Bunny Sings The Wailers* (Island/Solomonic), on which he re-recorded some 10 songs from this period. A dub version of the album, *Dub Disco Vol II* (Solomonic), was released in Jamaica. The albums are well worth checking out. (See CD guide in the Discography).

Above: The Skatalites in the studio, circa 1966. Left to right: Jackie Mittoo, Lester Sterling, Tommy McCook, Roland Alphonso, Lloyd Brevett, Johnny Moore, Jerry Haynes.

Marcia Griffiths, later to be one third of the I-Threes, makes a solo appearance on one of the flips. Generally, she wasn't part of the group but made a ballad with Bob, 'Oh My Darling', that appeared credited to The Soulettes. Griffiths became a star in her own right in Jamaica, before joining Bob & Co in 1975. **Feel Like Jumping** is a great track.

THE WAILERS
Lonesome Track / Sinner Man

Lonesome Track is a driving ska scorcher, with The Skatalites in top gear and Roland Alphonso blowing sweetly. Bob (who recorded this in 1965) uses the traditional gospel image of a train that will take him to the promised land: just as the underground railroad in the slave-owning southern states took those who rode it to freedom. 'Why must man suffer, oh Lord?' cries Bob.

Sinner Man – see below.

THE WAILERS
Let Him Go / Sinner Man

More Rudie business as Bunny takes the lead vocal on **Let Him Go**. 'You frame him, things he didn't do' make it clear where The Wailers' sympathies lie. Bunny's sweet tenor vocals add to the plaintive nature of this rolling track: 'Remember he is young and will live long'.

Sinner Man features Bunny sharing lead vocals with Peter on this traditional gospel that is very Old Testament in sentiment. Peter went on to make it his own (and took composer credits!) and recut it as a solo artist as 'Oppressor Man' (Trans Am); as lead vocalist for The Wailers, with Perry, as 'Downpressor', and later again as a solo artist as 'Downpressor Man'. Nina Simone cut 'Sinner Man' on her 1965 album, *Pastel Blues*.

THE WAILERS
Rasta Shook Them Up /
SOUL BROTHERS
Ringo's ska

'A few days ago we had a wonderful time …everyone was jumping!' sings Peter as he describes the arrival of Emperor Haile Selassie of Ethiopia at Kingston's airport. It was a momentous day for the Rastafarians of Jamaica, but unfortunately for Bob, he was living in Delaware at the time. It was several hours before Selassie could be persuaded to leave the plane as he was frightened by the 'welcome' from the Rastas – with whom he had no connection. The track kicks off with Peter speaking a few lines of Amharic, the

language of Ethiopia and the Bible, and then launches into the first Wailers' full-blown expression of their Rasta faith. Fellow Studio One vocal harmony trio, The Gaylads, provide the splendid harmonies.

PETER TOSH
The Toughest /
MARCIA GRIFFITHS
No Faith

The Toughest is a swaggering statement of belief: 'Anything you can do, I can do better!'. A hit for Peter, with Constantine 'Dream' Walker helping on harmonies. The ghettoes of Kingston were already home to Rude Boys, gangs – some with political connections – and a great deal of violence and crime. Thus, alongside spiritual aspirations there was a street culture that required a 'tough and rough' attitude – which Peter had in spades. This became Peter's theme song.

THE WAILERS
Rock Sweet Rock / Jerking Time

One of the top three Studio One rarities, **Rock Sweet Rock** (aka 'Sweetest Rocker'), is a joyous romp that celebrates the pleasures of the dance. Despite what certain reggae historians claim about the spiritual and rebellious nature of Jamaican music, Sound Systems – even at the peak of Rasta reggae – were all about a good night out. Bunny rides a groove that he returned to on his chart-topping *Rock 'n' Groove* album of 1981.

Jerking Time (aka 'Jerk In Time'), finds Bunny in the same groove as the topside, but here celebrating the current dance craze of the 'Jerk'.

Jackie Mittoo, of The Skatalites, plays piano and there's a terrific organ solo by Richard Ace. Sweetness.

THE WAILERS
Sunday Morning /
He Who Feels It Knows It

Sunday Morning – Bunny's sweet tenor is perfect for this gentle ballad of love. Alongside Peter, Constantine 'Dream' Walker harmonises with Bunny's romantic vocal lead. Strictly for lovers! Gregory Isaacs recut the track for Bunny's own Solomonic label, set up in 1981.

He Who Feels It Knows It: Bunny leads on his own composition, with Constantine 'Dream' Walker on harmonies. Its title is reportedly taken from the Bible and became a Rasta phrase meaning a deep understanding. It was the title of Rita's first solo album (on Tuff Gong). The track is also known as 'Linger You Linger', another line from the lyrics.

Above: Mortimer Planner, friend and mentor to Bob, welcomes the Ethiopian Emperor, Haile Selassie, to Jamaica on 21 April 1966.

THE WAILERS
What Am I Supposed To Do? /
JACKIE MITTOO & THE SOUL BROTHERS
Do The Boogaloo

With Bob still away, Bunny is again in the composer's and lead vocalist's chair. A sweet, swaying love song, whose beat is rocksteady/ska and features a lovely sax solo from The Skatalites' Tommy McCook.

The flip, which features a Jackie Mittoo workout (also of the Skatalites), has suddenly become collectable thanks to the interest in funky reggae.

THE WAILERS
I Need You /
KEN BOOTHE
Don't Want To See You Cry

I Need You (So) features Bunny with mournful doo-wop-style vocals. It's a slow ballad, which looks to the US for its stylistic template – actually The Temptations' 'Baby Baby I Need You'. Peter and Constantine 'Dream' Walker experiment with multiple-part harmonies on 'You'. This is a different song from 'I Need You' (with a Bob lead) that appeared on the *Wailing Wailers* album.

BOP & THE BELTONES
Treat Me Good / Dancing Time

Despite the credit, this is a Peter Tosh track in which he simply asks to be 'treated like a friend'. As with many of Peter's tracks, there's a threat – if you don't do as I say, there will be a price to pay. Musically, it's more reggae than ska.

PETER TOUCH & THE CHORUS
Making Love /
SOUL BROS
Voodoo Moon

Peter and The Chorus – Bunny Wailer and The Soulettes (Rita Marley, Marlene Gifford and Constantine 'Dream' Walker) – deliver a simple pop/ska love song. Lightweight, but nicely executed.

PETER TOUCH & THE CHORUS
Can't You See /
RITA MARLEY
Time To Turn

Can't You See – a real one-off track, with a studied take on British R&B of the period. Could easily have been on a contemporary Rolling Stones album. It's all over in two minutes, as Peter pleads to his girl: 'Can't you see what you are doing to me?' A real oddity, but a track that Peter returned to with Leslie Kong in 1970, when he cut a much more typically reggae version.

Time To Turn was a protest hit for The Byrds and was written by folk revivalist Pete Seeger, who used the Book of Ecclesiastes for inspiration. So, quite a Jamaican vibe to the track. Rita was active at Studio One, with the Wailers, as part of The Soulettes and as a solo artist. Her output is covered in the Discography, and it includes tracks that feature other Wailers in the mix.

ALBUMS

The original release of *The Wailing Wailers* has a cover picture of Bob leaning forward, supported by Bunny and Peter. The silkscreen reissue is often thought of as an original as it looks 'old' but it was, in fact, first produced from the mid-1970s. The astute Coxsone Dodd reissued the Wailers' material from the mid-1970s in various guises but always with added production, usually adding drums to various tracks.

THE WAILING WAILERS
Put It On / I Need You /
Lonsome Feeling / What's New Pussy Cat /
One Love / When The Well Runs Dry /
Ten Commandments of Love /
Rude Boy / It Hurts To Be Alone /
Love & Affection / I'm Still Waiting /
Simmer Down

All the above tracks are as the singles except the following: **I Need You**, which has Bob on lead vocals, rather than Bunny. A slow, thoughtful piece with a rock-style chorus.
When The Well Runs Dry is based on an old folk saying and has Bunny and Peter on lead, with Rita and Constantine 'Dream' Walker providing harmonies. A rather muffled recording masks a lovely little track.
Ten Commandments of Love is a cover of Harvey and the Moonglows' doo-wop harmony classic. It certainly works better than most of the Wailers' tracks that hark back to the US in the 1950s. Of historical, rather than musical, interest.

A few Wailers' tracks appeared only on compilations of the time:

Top right: The cover of the first-ever pressing (by WIRL) of The Wailers' Studio One album.
Below right: An early Wailers promo shot, circa 1966: Bob, Peter and Bunny with Beverly Kelso.

PRESENTING JAMAICA ALL STAR VOL I
(Studio 1, 1966)
Rolling Stone – The Wailers sing Bob Dylan! Here they adapt that classic and Bunny's lead works a treat. The lyric 'Time like a scorpion stings without warning' is something that everyone still feels. The gently rolling, rocksteady beat is the perfect accompaniment.

SKA STRICTLY FOR YOU
(N&D, 1967)
Flying Ska (aka 'Wings of a Dove') is a Jamaican folk and mento standard that has appeared on many, many albums aimed at the tourist market. The Wailers turn it into a lovely gentle ska rocker. A JAD demo of the track exists.

THIS IS JAMAICA SKA
(N&D, 1965)
Go Jimmy Go – a real ska stormer of the Jimmy Clanton rocker, with the band firing on all cylinders. The very young- sounding chorus just adds to the excitement. 'Go Jimmy Go' also surfaced on a blank with 'Do You Remember?' on the flip. The matrix CS 1964B/CS 1964A showed that new stampers were created for 'Do You Remember?' That is most unlike Mr Dodd!

Over the years, Dodd recycled much of the Wailers' material on various compilations. These are listed in the 'Re-presses' section of the Discography and all feature additional production. Several previously unreleased tracks surfaced on these compilations. The original recording of these tracks (sans overdubs) can be found on the Heartbeat CDs.

BEST OF BOB MARLEY & THE WAILERS
(Buddah US)
Where Is My Mother? finds Bunny sharing lead with Bob on a deeply bittersweet ode to family emotions. The intro is shared with 'This Train' and 'Where Is My Mother?' shares that song's gospel sensibilities: 'Is she lost in the world of sin?' Bunny asks.

BIRTH OF A LEGEND
(Calla US/CBS UK)
Nobody Knows is a rocking and rolling (complete with handclaps) ska cover of 'Nobody Knows the Trouble I've Seen'. The excellent trumpet solo from Dizzy Moore fails to lift the track above average.

MARLEY, TOSH, LIVINGSTON & ASSOCIATES
(Studio 1)
Dance With Me – this driving ska starts off with The Drifters' 'On Broadway' and then develops as Dizzy Moore once again lifts the proceedings with a fine solo. It fails to ignite as a song.

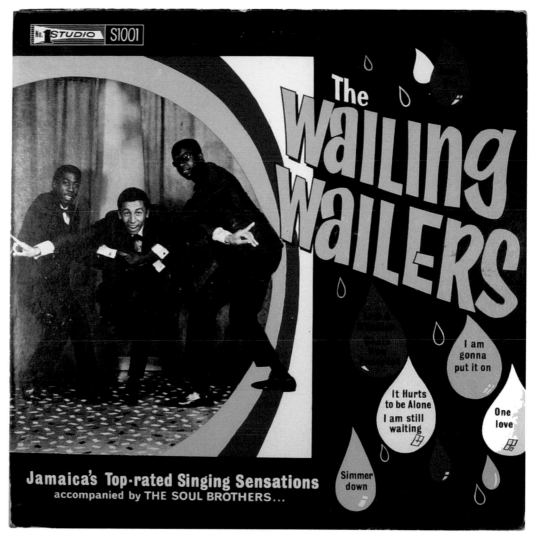

Sound Systems

SOUND SYSTEMS ARE PERHAPS JAMAICA'S GREATEST contribution to global music culture. By the mid-1950s many young Jamaicans were spending nights listening to records imported from the US by artists such as Fats Domino, Lynn Hope and Ernie Freeman, played at deafening volume through PA systems' amplifiers and brightly painted speaker boxes. These Sound System 'Dances' were to become a key element of Jamaican music culture – not only in Jamaica itself but also in places like London and New York where large communities of ex-patriot Jamaicans were living.

From humble beginnings, Sound Systems quickly grew to become one of the main forms of entertainment in Jamaica for 'Downtown' youth. The events were places at which to see and be seen – dressing to impress was a crucial part of the evening: so much so that Sound Systems would crown their own Beauty Queens. Champion Dancers (male & female) would also provide entertainment for the crowds. Providing refreshment was another

source of income for the promoters, so Curried Goat and Red Stripe were sold.

The whole show would be run by an 'MC' who would chat to the crowd while the next 78 was selected. These MCs would use US-style Disc Jockey 'jive talk' between the records and, of course, they became stars themselves – even after the use of twin turntables (during the 1970s) enabled the playing of records back to back. Of the mobile Sound Systems pioneers, Tom 'The Great' Sebastian is a good example, as its MC, Count Machuki, was one of the first MCs to be recorded on vinyl. Duke Vin, Machuki's 'selector' – the individual who selected which tunes to play – went on to set up the UK's first Sound System.

By the late 1950s and into the early 1960s names such as 'V-Rocket', Duke 'The Trojan' Reid, 'Prince Buster' and his 'Voice of the People Sound', Vincent 'King' Edwards and, of course, Sir 'Coxsone' (or 'Coxson') Dodd's 'Round Beat'/'Down Beat' Sound were all fighting (sometimes literally!) for business in a small area of Kingston known as Beat Street. Competition between the Sounds was fierce and each year a King of the 'Sounds & Blues' would be crowned.

As demand grew for local music, these dances became the ideal place to promote Jamaican records, and some of the Sound owners set up their own labels. Bob Marley's early years were spent with the famous Clement 'Coxsone' Dodd, who owned several Sound Systems that toured the island, and who founded the legendary Studio One. Bob & The Wailers even played a few live sets at Coxsone dances.

New recordings would be cut on to acetates (aluminium discs covered with a thin layer of vinyl) that later became known as 'Dub plates'. These would be played at Sounds to gauge the crowds' reaction before being released. Pictured above right is the original acetate of Bob Marley & The Wailers' 'I'm Gonna Put It On' cut for the King Edwards Sound in 1965. For Studio One buffs it also contains the Gaylads' 'Lady With The Red Dress On' and The Skatalites' 'Street of Gold' on the flip side. The labels of these plates typically had little information on, a deliberate ploy to protect the provenance and hence the exclusivity of the recordings.

A whole clutch of tracks that have surfaced since Bob's death in 1981 were only ever released on Dub plates. Tracks like 'Natural Mystic' (original), 'Rainbow Country', 'Pass It On'

(original) and 'Why Should I?' (original) began their life as exclusives at selected Sound dances. By the mid-1970s Dub plates began to feature exclusive mixes of tracks that only certain Sounds owned copies of. The first appearance of the name 'King Tubby', who pioneered the dub mix, was on labels of these plates.

The link to the Street that Sounds provided has given reggae its edge and its ability to express all aspects of everyday life. Bob Marley & The Wailers' first 'hit' record, 'Simmer Down' (during early 1964), was a plea to Sound System 'Rude Boy' crowds to control their temper. Sounds were also great places for people to meet and the music selections reflected this, with certain Sounds specialising in romantic tunes after midnight! One of Bob's remarkable talents was his ability to sing equally expressively about rebellion, spiritual love and secular love.

Sound Systems were a key part of the social fabric for the mass of Jamaican youth and remain so to this day, although the power of MTV is certainly felt in Jamaica! It's amazing how many current Rap and R&B videos owe their dancing style to the culture of Jamaican Sounds.

Left: Original speaker box from the 'V-Rocket' Sound System; original Dub plate of 'Rainbow Culture', circa 1976.
Above: Original Dub plate of 'I'm Gonna Put It On', circa 1966. Right: Original flyer for a Coxson dance.

'Freedom Time'

1967

**BOB MARLEY & THE WAILING WAILERS
WITH THE SOUL BROTHERS**
Bend Down Low / Freedom Time
Recorded at Studio One after the split with Dodd, this was the group's first single to feature the new slower, loping rocksteady beat.

The risqué **Bend Down Low**, full of the joys of love and sex, proved to be a big seller and even had its own dance. The track would be re-pressed for years to come and was re-cut for the *Natty Dread* album. Byron Lee produced a Ken Lazarus cover at the time (on Soul), aimed at the Uptown and tourist markets, and Gregory Isaacs cut a version early in his career.

The politically hard-edged **Freedom Time** – 'Didn't my people before me slave this country?' – finds Bob echoing sentiments from the Black Power movements in the US. This song was to form the basis of 'Crazy Baldheads' from the *Rastaman Vibration* album.

THE SUCCESS BOB MARLEY & THE WAILERS FOUND AT STUDIO ONE HAD TAKEN them into the musical premier league in Jamaica. However, like many before, and since, they found Dodd's practice of treating musicians as day-rate workers without the benefit of royalties somewhat less than rewarding.

By all accounts, the split, when it came, was friendly and the first record that Bob & The Wailers issued on their own 'Wail 'N Soul 'M' imprint was recorded at Studio One and carries a musician's credit to the 'Soul Brothers', and a Studio One matrix.

The imprint's name refers to the 'Wailing Wailers' and to the 'Soulettes' – Rita's group which recorded at Studio One. The classic red, gold & green label, with its famous logo (see page 37), was based at 18A Greenwich Road, Kingston 5, from where records were sold and distributed. Unfortunately, no pictures of this first set-up – located at Rita's family home – appear to exist. A later label stamp gives the address of Wail 'N Soul 'M as 14 Crescent Road, Kingston; there was reportedly a 'Soul Shack' on the corner of Orange Street and Beeston Street and there is also a mention of a shop in the Parade. Whether these were three different places, or one and the same, remains unknown. The 'Soul Shack' may have been an early name for the King Street shop, but that is unclear.

At Studio One, the majority of the group's releases had been as 'The Wailers', yet from the outset of this new 'co-operative' venture, every release was as 'Bob Marley & The

Above and overleaf: Bunny, Bob, Rita and Peter, photographed at The Port Royal lighthouse in 1968.

Wailing Wailers'. This change flagged up who was at the controls and already had the most visible public profile. The group's line-up at Studio One had changed over the years but from this period onwards, the group maintained a stable membership of Bob Marley, Bunny Wailer, Peter Tosh and Rita Marley. Keeping the 'Wailing Wailers' name made sense as it was from their debut album. After this date, any releases carrying a 'Wailers' tag usually meant that Bunny or Peter was singing lead vocal. The label's logo or trademark was of three hands, interlocked, and the names 'Bob, Bunny (Bunnie), Peter' as a signal of group unity. Whether it was also a commitment to sharing profits three ways, as Bunny recounts, is unknown. A stylised version of this logo would appear on the later '56 Hope Road' and 'Tuff Gong' imprints.

The Wail 'N Soul 'M imprint has become legendary, as the music released was top-drawer rocksteady and many of the tunes formed blueprints for later hits. Also, much of this material has not appeared on the endless compilations of Bob's early work. This initial foray into running a label folded after some 18 months but left a fine body of work. Clancy Eccles, who was one of the young up-and-coming artist/producers, lent some production help on some tracks. (Clancy Eccles went on to become Prime Minister Michael Manley's 'right-hand man for music'.)

When interviewed later about this period (*Jamaica Daily News*, 1974), Bob said: 'We had to fight hard. When Christmas come the man say the stamper smashed and all that.' Peter added, 'They were holding us down as little producers. As usual the big guy controls the small guy.' The stamper is the metal mould from which a single is pressed and is an expensive item. Replacing a broken one is costly and may make it uneconomic to re-press old tracks.

As can be seen from the pages of *Swing* (page 43), the group entered the island's annual song contest but didn't make the final:
a decision which, according to the
magazine, was extremely
unpopular.

BOB MARLEY & THE WAILING WAILERS
Stir It Up / This Train
This is the original recording of **Stir It Up**, which would become one of Marley's classics. A song about the joys of sex – 'I'll push the wood, blaze the fire' – needs little interpretation. It was re-cut on The Wailers' Island debut album *Catch A Fire*. The king of rocksteady pop, Johnny Nash, had a hit with the track in 1971. Nash's company JAD had signed Bob & Co as artists and songwriters (to Cayman) in 1967.
This Train is the spiritual evergreen with Bunny's lead vocal reflecting the gospel heritage of the track. He re-cut it on his solo debut album for Island, *Blackheart Man*.

BOB MARLEY & THE WAILING WAILERS
Nice Time / Hypocrite
Nice Time was a hugely popular ode to the joys of dancing and romance which has an almost mento/calypso feel to it. It was covered at the time by Byron Lee, briefly Bob's JAD label mate, and by Lyn Taitt, the extraordinary Trinidadian guitarist, who played on the original. Both of these singles, on JAD and Merritone respectively, were aimed at the tourist market. Top producer Duke Reid cut a version with the 'queen of rocksteady', Phyllis Dillon (Cool Soul label).
Hypocrite is a powerful song that gives full rein to Bob's talent as a potent lyricist, as he casts an eye over the music business, with biblical references to the fore. In 1979 this pairing was re-released on the Tuff Gong label and made it into the reggae singles chart. The rhythm became a standard again during the 1980s dancehall era.

BOB MARLEY & THE WAILING WAILERS
Mellow Mood / Thank You Lord
Mellow Mood is a wonderful love song that is both sweet ('My love, my sweet, my love, darling') and strong ('We can rock it all night long, darling'). A true hymn to the joy of earthly love.
Thank You Lord is in the style of a traditional hymn, with Bob's lyrics sung in loving praise to his then traditional 'Lord'. Biblical references would keep appearing throughout Bob's writing, but by 1968 (and 'Selassie In the Chapel'), Bob's God had clearly changed.

BOB MARLEY & THE WAILING WAILERS
Bus Dem Shut / Lyrical Satirical I
Bus Dem Shut is about working so hard that 'you burst your shirt' while the track's alternative name 'Pyaka' hints at the darker side of the Jamaican (and the human) psyche. There is no direct English translation but a 'pyaka' is a person who is always on the look-out for themselves and envious of others' success and progress.

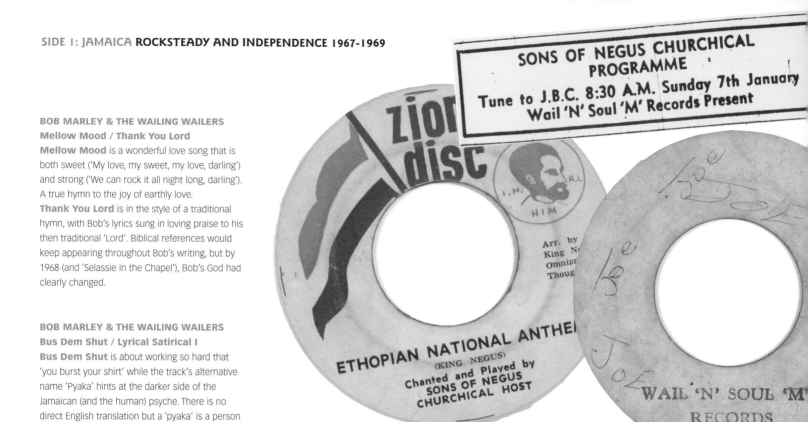

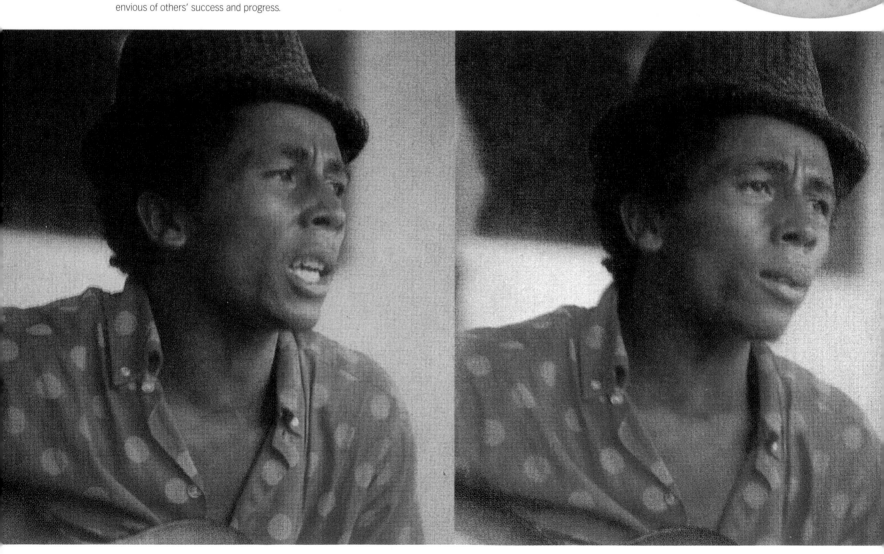

Above: Bob recording at the Russell Heights home of Johnny Nash and Danny Sims in 1968.

Lyrical Satirical I features nyahbinghi-style drumming and is the only instrumental released credited to The Wailers, that was not actually a version of an existing rhythm.

BOB MARLEY & THE WAILING WAILERS
Funeral / Pound Get A Blow
With Peter on lead vocal, **Funeral**, which became better known as 'Burial', is a song of defiance that echoes the biblical theme of 'Let the dead bury the dead.' A 1980s Dub plate from Gemini Sound has this original, together with the Pablo/Tubby 1975 cut 'House Raid', and also, a contemporary DJ piece proclaiming how Gemini will bury all other Sounds. Pablo re-cut it again in the late 1970s as 'Crucial Burial' (Rockers disco 45).
Pound Get A Blow reflects concern over the devaluation of the pound, which reminds us how strong the colonial links were – the British pound sterling was Jamaica's currency.

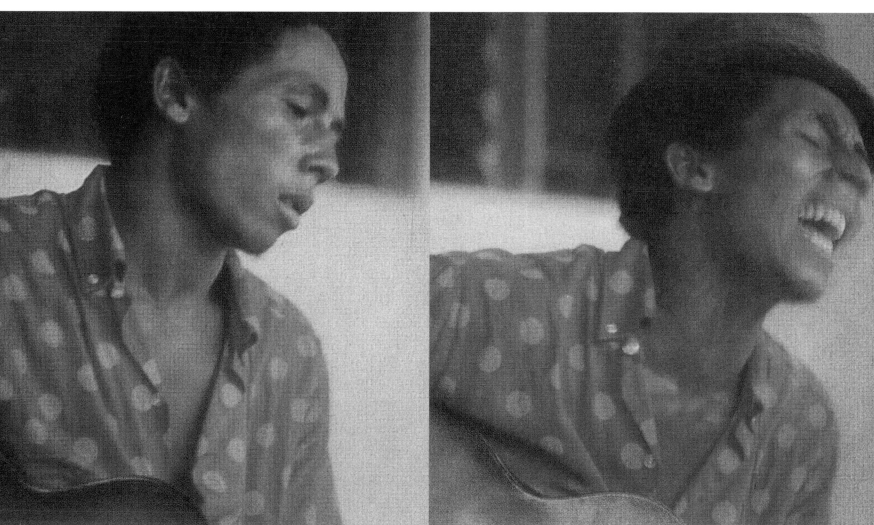

Top left: The fledgling Wail 'N Soul 'M label sponsors, (Ras Michael and The) Sons of Negus Churchical radio programme.
Top right: A 1980s Dub plate with Bob Marley and The Wailers' 'Burial' as 'Burial 1'. ('Burial 2 was from the mid-1970s and 'Burial 3' was a new cut to the rhythm.)

From this point on, the releases from the Wail 'N Soul 'M imprint seem to be on blank labels only. The full-colour labels were undoubtedly not cheap and the cost of being independent was taking its toll. The quality of the music remained incredibly high. All pairings are thought to be original, using the matrix numbers as a guide. There are many other pairings of Wail 'N Soul 'M sides; these are listed in the Reissues section on page 164.

This year was to prove traumatic for The Wailers as all three were to spend periods in jail. Bob and Peter were locked up briefly: for a driving offence and taking part in an anti-Rhodesia protest, respectively. Bunny, however, was convicted of cannabis possession and spent more than a year in prison, from June 1967 until September 1968. The charges, which Bunny has always maintained were bogus, saw him serve time in the General Penitentiary and then cutting sugarcane at the Richmond prison farm. The track 'Battering Down Sentence' (Solomonic, 1974) was inspired by his incarceration. The track also appeared on his classic debut album *Blackheart Man* as 'Fighting Against Conviction'.

BOB MARLEY & THE WAILING WAILERS
Steppin' Razor / Hurtin' Inside
Steppin Razor has become synonymous with Peter Tosh. This is the original, on which the 6-foot 4-inch Peter makes his own the song by The Wailers' Trenchtown tutor, the diminutive Joe Higgs. Peter excelled at these rude boy boasts, as he had shown at Studio One with 'The Toughest': indeed few ever messed with Peter.
Hurtin' Inside is a great contrast: a song that is open and speaks of vulnerability and deep loss. Bob's lead vocal works perfectly with the horns – echoing the plaintive lyrics. Bob's ability to deliver heartfelt songs that manage not to come across as saccharine-sweet is one of his great assets. The track would be frequently re-pressed in Jamaica.

Above and right: Bob Marley & The Wailing Wailers, on the Beach at Port Royal in 1968.

BOB MARLEY & THE WAILING WAILERS
Play Play / Bend Down Low
The often ignored **Play Play** has a Rita Marley
lead vocal, but is clearly a Wailers' tune and now
one of the most valuable on the collectors' scene.
It's a song about accepting love for 'Our Father
and the life of the Lord.' The title refers to those
who just 'Play play' and 'Ray ray ray' – which
means 'Blah, Blah, Blah'
Bend Down Low makes one of its many
reappearances.

BOB MARLEY & THE WAILING WAILERS
Them Have Fi Get a Beatin' / Fire Fire
Them Have Fi Get a Beatin finds Peter
leading another tirade against injustice. His powerful
vocal summons up the retribution promised in the
Old Testament. He would re-cut the track for Joe
Gibbs as a solo artist in the early 1970s.
On **Fire Fire**, Peter co-leads with Bob on a track
that again speaks of divine retribution, this time for
all the non-believers. Bunny Wailer re-cut it as 'Love
Fire' in the late 1970s on a Solomonic disco label
and Simply Red recorded a version in the 1990s.

BOB MARLEY & THE WAILING WAILERS
Don't Rock My Boat / Fire Fire
Don't Rock My Boat is a great example of how
Bob would re-cut and develop a song. He
recorded it for Lee 'Scratch' Perry (two versions),
for his own Tuff Gong imprint (with a DJ version)
and then it resurfaced as 'Satisfy My Soul' on the
Kaya album.

BOB MARLEY & THE WAILING WAILERS
Chances Are /
The Lord Will Make A Way Somehow
The influence of JAD and the US-focused material
that Bob and the band were developing is clearly
heard on these tracks. Both are slow, southern-
soul-influenced ballads. Bob displays the full range
of emotion he could wring out of a song

1969

BOB MARLEY & THE WAILING WAILERS
Trod On aka Tread Along / Version
A Bunny Wailer vocal and song that he later
claimed was a 'conscious' song rather than one
emphasising the more carnal matters that the
line, 'You're like a stick of macaroni in bed'
indicates! Few copies of this surface. It's notable
as the first Wail 'N Soul 'M release to feature an
instrumental, or 'version' on the B-side.

BOB MARLEY & THE WAILING WAILERS
Feel Alright / Rhythm

An early cover of a James Brown track: here Brown's 'There Was A Time' has been adapted. This mix has an irritating percussion sound, which is rather jarring and has been described as like 'cutlery being dropped'. A later Tuff Gong re-press, with the matrix NL 824, happily has a different mix that dumps the 'cutlery' and is by far the superior recording.

The track dubbed **Rhythm** is the backing track to a Wailers' song that has never materialised. The vocals that can be heard breaking through serve to confirm that it is from a Wailers recording, but which one remains a mystery.

SOUL SHOTS

JEFF DIXON

Soul shots are you set — let's zoom off like a jet catering to all human beings on the scene. — It grows.

The atmosphere is filled with hot air cause what they say is that Festival 8 will be great like your soul doc was on stage at State Theatre on Sunday night last, guiding things along on the elimination of 8 finalists for Festival song — everything went wrong — like they advertised 28 contestants, 26 entered — and a very unpopular decision from Judges not including the "Wail 'em' Soul 'em' Wailers" in the finals. But don't watch dat — watch dis y-here — It grows.

Keep on moving for days — that's soul Bro. Desmond Elliott — who walked out of Big 5 and stepped into Macmillan Advertising as a shot. Words also lipped out that he moved from Mona Heights to Beverly Hills. — He grows. It grows.

News to blow your fuse — blue eyed soul bro. Charlie Babcock is off to homeland. It grows.

Look out soul records enthusiasts — very soon you'll be linking your soul stocking feet with soul treat — on Links Label — which incorporates The Gaylads — Melodians — and Ken 'Puppet on a String' Boothe. — It grows.

Guess what soul shot staying at the Sheraton — is the Caribbean's "Yul" Lord Bryner — just released two very soon LPs, all calypso naturally. Leaves on the 12th for London to make a presentation to Her Majesty. It grows.

The Biggest Stage Show ever!

This SUNDAY 2nd June 8.00 p.m.

STATE Theatre

THE BIG FESTIVAL SONG ELIMINATION CONTEST

28 PROFESSIONAL SINGERS

• The Heptones • Alton Ellis • Roy Shirley
• Ernest Soul Wilson • The Blenders • Clancy Eccles
• Al & The Vibrators • The Techniques • The Paragons
• The Sensations • Dawn Penn • Derrick Harriott
• Rudy Mills • Keith & Tex • The Federals
• Bob Marlye & The Wbailers • Hopeton Lewis • Marva Moo
• The Versatiles • Desmond Dekker & The Aces
• The Maytals • Glenmore & Dave • The Three Tops
• Winston Samuels
• Bertie Callan • Patterson & The Silver Tops
• Stranger Cole • Monty Morris

backed by **THE MIGHTY VIKINGS**

GUEST ARTISTES: THE JAMAICANS

8 will be selected from the 28 to vie for the Festival Song for 1968 and the

SPARKLING BEVERAGE CASH

GATES OPEN AT 6 p.m. SHARP

Admission: 10/- All Seats (Childre...

Left: Peter Tosh, 1968.
Above: Bob Marley & The Wailers take part in the Big Festival Song Elimination Contest and lose. Jeff Dixon comments on the outcome in his Swing column.
Right: Some 'blanks' carry a printed address label for 'Wail 'N Soul Records'.

BOB MARLEY & THE WAILING WAILERS
Trouble Is On The Road Again /
Comma Comma

The last single from the Wail 'N Soul 'M set-up. **Trouble Is On The Road Again** is based on an incident when Bob was arrested for allegedly driving without a licence.

Comma Comma was another hit for Johnny Nash in 1972 on his massively successful *I Can See Clearly* album. The Wailers' version has remained a hidden gem in their catalogue. One would have expected Bob to return to such a song during his international years, but he didn't. The stamp 'Tempa' reflects the label that 'The Letter' surfaced on (see page 61).

BOB'S PASSION AND ALMOST shamanic stage presence were his hallmarks on the international stage. They were also elemental aspects of his Caribbean character which he used to full effect. Uniquely, he was able to contain in one person the fire of political rebellion, the fire of spiritual belief and the fire of sensual love .

Since the days of American blues pioneer Robert Johnson during the Depression of the 1930s, the split between these 'fires' had been a key feature of African-American (and its white offspring rock and roll) music: the choice between the Lord and the Devil. Sam Cooke left gospel for pop success, as did Al Green (only to return). Others who switched (often more than once) included: Jerry Lee Lewis, Eddie James 'Son' House and Little Richard. Many of these stars owed a deep debt to gospel, but a life regulated by high moral standards was not for them.

In Caribbean Christian culture, the Old Testament has a starring role, thanks to missionaries who recognized that those

with nature and spirit-based belief systems found its powerful fire-and-brimstone imagery more appealing than the New Testament. Because it linked thunder and lightning, blood and fire with the actions of a vengeful God, the people who listened to its stories came to see fire as a purifier, a theme Bob tackled directly in 'Fire Fire'.

Fire also features in Jamaican gospel music recorded on vinyl.

The fire that burned in the belly of the boxer Cassius Clay was taken to the hearts of many Jamaicans and his most glorious fights were all celebrated on record. The fire-red vinyl single on the Fire label (stolen from a US R&B label noted for Elmore James and Buster Brown) celebrates Clay's defeat of Sonny Liston in 1964. In the mid-1970s, The Soulettes performed at a concert at which Muhammad Ali (as he was now known) was the star attraction. And as the Rasta faith took hold in the ghetto, during the mid-1970s, phrases such as 'Fire-a-go-burn' or 'Blood and Fire' (from a classic Niney tune that gave its name to the top reggae reissue imprint), became part of the language. When the 'New Roots' music movement appeared in the late 1980s, one of the key tunes was 'Fire Pon Rome' (by Anthony B).

But another fire burns in Jamaican musical culture – sexual fire. 'Fire In Ya Wire' was a calypso song whose theme continued to be covered by reggae artists, such as I Roy, with 'Fire Stick'. Calypso was at one time seen in the United States as the 'next big thing' after rock'n'roll, with US-based artists recording the music, various companies releasing the music and even a couple of films being made. Hollywood tackled female sexuality in *Fire Down Below* (1957), a movie set in the Caribbean.

Calypso was risqué, exotic and spoke of a forbidden world. It crystallised the European view of Jamaica, which was based on years of predatory sexual behaviour by the slave owners.

This first flush of Caribbean culture saw the writer Maya Angelou releasing a fine album of calypsos, on which she remodelled such classics as 'Shame & Scandal' to reflect her distinctive view. And Louis Farrakhan, leader of the Nation of Islam, started out in the 1950s as a calypso singer known as 'The Charmer' and released various sides, including a 78rpm that is an ode to the joys of Bacchanalia.

Bob & The Wailers realised the commercial potential of the form at Studio One, where they covered various calypsos. Rita even

SWING
JAMAICA'S WEEKLY ENTERTAINMENT GUIDE.
LABOUR DAY SWINGS ON BACK CO SOUVENIR CENTR 'OS ON 'EAD

SCENE MAY 17—23 (Labour Day Swings)

PUTTING FIRE IN EVERY WIRE.

Born Milicent Todd, (Public christened Patsy) 23 years ago, this young lady has shown what hard work and sincerity can do for the performer. Miss Pata pata as she is now known made her first hit in LOVE NOT TO BRAG with Derrick Morgan and with each succeeding year she has shown that VERSATILITY (an ingredient lacking in most singers) is hers to command.

No one (world-wide) has captured the Miriam Makeba sound with such ease and understanding and Patsy's last 3 hits have been done in this manner. FIRE IN YOUR WIRE has been "taking life" for several weeks now and her latest release: "Hanging On" is destined to do even better. * this song along with several hits will be on Patsy's first Album. VERSATILE PATSY

Yes 'little' Miss Patsy is a sure fine hot with every effort, and SWING wishes to congratulate her on very fine performances everytime. Keeping the good show Patsy — STAY WITH IT!

ACTION CAMERAS AT AKARA FRIDAY

MERRITON

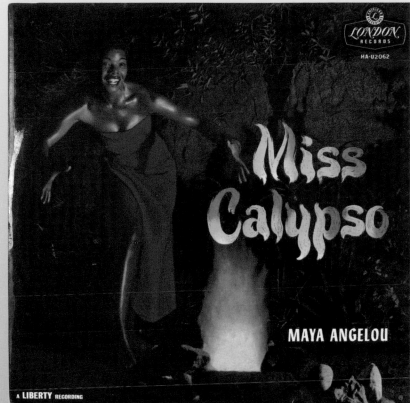

recorded a mento, 'Cutting Wood', as Girl Wonder. Bob remodelled Count Lasher's 'Calypso Cha Cha' as 'Rocking Steady' – an early example of how he was absorbing the music around him as he developed his own style.

Bob managed to switch effortlessly from the burning passion of romantic and sexual love to the fires of spiritual belief and power. The twin Tuff Gong recordings of 'Satisfy My Soul Jah Jah' and 'Satisfy My Soul Babe' illustrate this abilility perfectly.

'Man To Man': Bob Marley and Lee Perry

1970

BOB MARLEY & THE WAILERS
Duppy Conqueror / UPSETTERS – Zig Zag
BOB MARLEY & THE WAILERS
Duppy Conqueror / UPSETTERS – Boss
One of Bob's best ever songs, which he co-wrote with Perry, who said to Carl Gayle (1974, *Black Music*: 'I said to him, "Well, look here, Bob, I want you to write a tune with 'Yes, me friend, we on the street again' in it." He gave me the third line, I gave him the fourth line and so on. We started to work together and the ideas started to flow till we made the tune 'Duppy Conqueror'.'
Duppy (ghost) Conqueror is a powerful statement of self-affirmation, as Bob declares that he is afraid of no one: not even duppies! The lines, 'Bars could not hold me' and 'Me deh 'pon street again' refer to Bob's release after a short jail sentence for a driving violation. It was re-cut on the *Burnin'* album.
Zig Zag is an instrumental 'version' of 'Duppy Conqueror'.
Boss is an unrelated (and unidentified) piece. It was becoming the fashion to have a version on the flip: they were popular at Sound System dances so the DJ could chat over them as he entertained the crowd. These versions were given names, as in this case, and within a few years would be remixed themselves into 'dubs' or dub cuts, with snatches of vocal left in.

IN WHAT WAS TO BECOME ONE OF THE MOST COMMERCIALLY FRUITFUL OF their early partnerships with a producer, Lee 'Scratch' Perry, aka The Upsetter, recorded and released records by The Wailers from 1970 to 1972. Made in Randy's Studio, many of these were immediate local hits – 'Duppy Conqueror', 'Who is Mr Brown', 'My Cup' and 'Dreamland', and later the classic 'Small Axe' and finally 'Kaya'. It's interesting to note that the celebrated tune, 'The Sun Is Shining', never appeared as an Upsetter single.

Now 25, Bob was heavily influenced by America's music and its radical Black movements – he had just returned from visiting his mother in Wilmington, Delaware, with Rita and the children. Perry had likewise long been fascinated by soul and rhythm & blues. He had been producing records for more than two years with his house band, The Upsetters, and had found success in Jamaica and the UK, through a deal with the British-based reggae label Trojan Records. Many of these records had been organ-driven instrumentals inspired by the hugely popular spaghetti westerns that were shown in Kingston's cinemas. Perry's productions were beginning to change and develop and now ranged from the soul styling of artists such as Dave Barker to the deeply Rastafarian-inspired works of Junior Byles. In the three years from 1970 to 1972, Perry released some 154 singles, of which 14 were by The Wailers – fewer than 10 per cent. He also released 15 albums, of which three were by The Wailers – 20 per cent of output. The impression often given in the history of Bob Marley & The Wailers is that their artistic relationship

Above: Mr Lee 'Scratch' Perry, circa 1973.

RECORD SHOP
36 CHARLES STREET KINGSTON

BOB MARLEY & THE WAILERS
Man To Man /
UPSETTERS Necoteen

More folk wisdom from Bob as he warns against some so-called friends: 'Some will eat with you, then behind them su su 'pon you'. Which translates as 'talking maliciously behind someone's back'. One of the lines from the chorus, 'Who the cap fit', gave the name to the re-cut for the *Rastaman Vibration* album.
Necoteen is the version.
(KG's was a shop and distributor which appears to have paid for the stampers for this record.)

with Perry was similar to that between The Beatles and George Martin. It was not – the group was one of many acts Perry worked with. Perry was also building his own 'Upsetter' house band, which Bob would soon appropriate.

In true Jamaican style, Bob & The Wailers were recording with the hitmaking Leslie Kong and others while they also recorded for Perry and his fledging Upsetter and Justice League imprints. Promotional duties in the UK for JAD would also take Bob away at times during this period.

Bob had been developing his production skills on the Wail 'N Soul 'M releases, sometimes alongside Clancy Eccles, and also by working with JAD-imported American session musicians on Johnny Nash recordings.

The music Bob and Lee Perry created was undoubtedly the result of collaboration, and not just a product of Lee Perry's studio skills. As Bob said in 1974 (to the *Jamaica Daily News*): 'We checked out Lee "Scratch" Perry [The Upsetter] and together we wrote "Duppy Conqueror". We found roots again.'

BOB MARLEY & THE WAILERS
Who Is Mr Brown / UPSETTERS – Dracular
BOB MARLEY & THE WAILERS
Mr Brown / UPSETTERS – Dracular

A very odd tune that recounts the story of a coffin travelling around Kingston, driven by three crows, looking for a Mr Brown. Lyrics such as 'Oh, calling duppy conqueror and the ghost capturer' and 'Down in parade, people running like a masquerade' only serve to add to the confusion. Another release of the time, 'Duppy Serenade' by The Innkeepers (Dennis Alcapone), also tells the story.
Dracular is the version.
The promotional card Bob had designed and printed to promote the release is illustrated (overleaf). In the style of a Sound System dance flyer, it is an early example of Bob's innate understanding of the need for promotion – it was the first time such a thing had been done on the Jamaican music scene which, to this day, does little to promote its records.

Above: The Upsetters in Randy's Studio, 1969: The Barrett Brothers, Aston 'Family Man' (left) and Carlton 'Carly' (drums), Alva 'Reggie' Lewis (guitar) and Glen 'Capo' Adams (organ). Below: A couple of Wailers/Lee Perry productions appeared as 'blanks' stamped 'Power Label'.

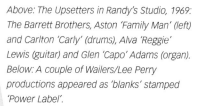

BOB MARLEY & THE WAILERS
My Cup /
UPSETTERS My Dub

Bob pays homage to James Brown in this cover of his 'I Guess I've Got To Cry Cry Cry' which remains too loyal to the original to work in its own right. Brown was hugely popular in Jamaica and had his music pressed on the island, on an under-license 'King' label.

BOB MARLEY & THE WAILERS
All In One / Part Two

There was a short-lived craze for medleys of previous hits. The Wailers re-recorded excerpts from the tracks listed below over a new rhythm track. It is interesting to see which they considered previous hits. Introduced by Perry, the medley consists of:
'Bend Down Low', 'Nice Time', 'One Love', 'Simmer Down', 'It Hurts To Be Alone', 'Lonesome Feeling', and continues on Side 2 with 'Lonesome Feeling' (reprised), 'Love & Affection', 'Put It On' and 'Duppy Conqueror' before returning to 'Put It On'.

THE WAILERS – Dreamland /
UPSETTERS – Good Luck
THE WAILERS – Dreamland /
UPSETTERS – Dreamland version 2

A classic piece from Bunny Wailer, which also appeared on Bunny's seminal *Blackheart Man* album (1975). Bunny's sweet voice makes this the perfect paean to a heaven on Earth where 'We'll get our honey from the bees' and as this **Dreamland** is 'so far across the sea' it seems fair to assume that here Africa is regarded as the homeland. It's actually a beautiful love song which, research has revealed, Coxsone Dodd got Bunny & The Wailers to cover at Studio One, though it was never released. The original was the obscure 'My Dream Island' by El Tempos.
Good Luck is an unrelated instrumental.

BOB MARLEY & THE WAILERS
Small Axe /
UPSETTERS
Down the Road

 1971

A defining recording that strikes a chord with anyone who has ever felt that they were in a David-versus-Goliath situation. In typical Jamaican style, it's a lateral approach to the problem: Perry and Bob wanted to challenge the dominance of the Federal, Dynamic and Studio One operations, so they became the 'Big t(h)ree'. Bob and Perry were, of course, the small axe 'sharpened to cut you down'. Intentions were made clear but names were spared – perfect songwriting!
Perry recounted to *Black Music's* Carl Gayle in 1974: 'One Sunday morning I get up and sort of think over the whole thing and got this idea. I said: "Well if they are the big three, we are the Small Axe," and started to write a song. Then I get stuck at a certain part so I bring it to Bob. Bob read it and started to sing a melody. Bob created the melody for that. We were stuck for about three quarters of an hour and I went for the Bible where of course he found the line "Why boasteth, oh evil men".'
Musically, The Upsetters were creating a strong Jamaican reggae that was a long way from the ska of Studio One.
Down The Road is an unrelated instrumental.

BOB MARLEY & THE WAILERS
More Axe / Axe Man

Bob returned to 'Small Axe' very soon with this nyahbinghi-drum-led cut 'Small Axe' with slight variations on the lyrics and some quite beautiful harmonies. The Rastafarian influence is becoming more and more marked in these recordings.
Axe Man is the bongo version.

Above left: Bob Marley had this promotional card made, in the style of a Sound System Dance flyer, for the 'Mr Brown' single. He realised the importance of promotion.

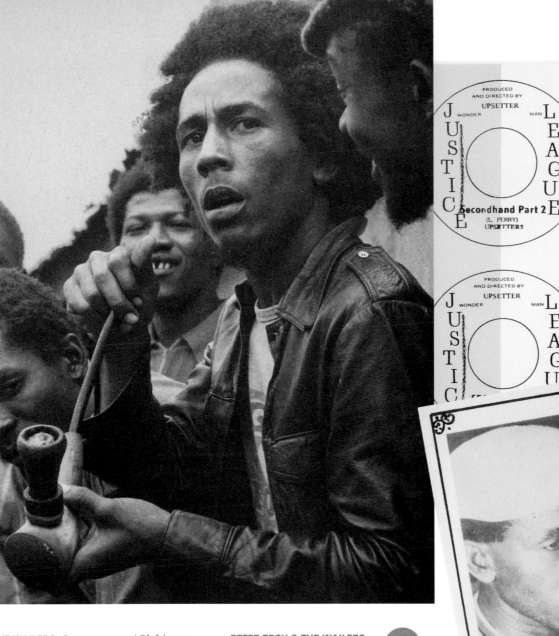

JULY – Lee 'Scratch' Perry
(Sept. '69) hit the big times.

**THE WAILERS –Downpressor / Righteous
UPSETTERS – Downpressor version**
Peter takes lead again, as he did at Studio One,
when the Wailers first cut 'Sinner Man' – a
traditional spiritual. (See Studio One entry in the
Discography).

**BOB MARLEY & THE WAILERS – Kaya /
UPSETTERS – Version**
A terrific ode to weed or ganja (kaya being a
particular high-grade variety) that starts with a
deep intake of breath. Bob's vocals are dominant
in the mix. 'I feel so high, I could touch the sky' is
the feel. There is a terrific version that starts off
with a crazy vocal exchange that has only
appeared on CD. 'Kaya' became the title track of
an Island album and Bob revoiced the track as
'Turn Me Loose', which stayed on tape for years.

**PETER TOSH & THE WAILERS
Secondhand /
UPSETTERS – Part 2**

1972

One of the least pleasant songs in The Wailers'
canon is this Tosh vocal complaining about women
of easy virtue on Kingston's streets. 'If you think it's
the dress that you wear makes you a lady, get that
out of your mind, you must be crazy.'

**BOB MARLEY & THE WAILERS
African Herbsman / Keep On Moving**
African Herbsman is an adaptation of African-
American folk singer Richie Havens' 'Indian Rope
Man' and fits perfectly with Bob's developing
interests because it discusses weed and slavery.
Havens himself was a visitor to Trenchtown and
fully approved of Bob's cover.
Keep On Moving is a cover of a song by The
Wailers' hero, Curtis Mayfield, from The
Impressions' *Never Ending Impressions* album

(1965). A true vocal collaboration, with Bob, Peter
and Bunny taking a stanza each and creating a
masterpiece in the process. The theme is similar to
Bob's 1975 hit, 'I Shot The Sheriff'.
In the late 1970s, Perry remixed this track at his
Black Ark studio and created an extraordinary disco
45, that included a honking sax and DJ Wong Chu.
Bob also re-cut 'Keep On Moving' in London, in 1977.

Above: A ganja moment!

ALBUMS

The initial release of *Soul Rebels* by Perry, via his deal with Trojan in the UK, was allegedly the reason for the breakdown of his relationship with The Wailers – reportedly he forgot to mention the deal to them and even when they discovered its existence, no monies were forthcoming. It was when Bob was in London in 1971, touring and recording with JAD, that he saw *Soul Rebels* in the record shop racks and went nuts. Back in Jamaica a major row erupted and the partnership was dissolved.

The album was released in Jamaica using sleeves from the UK and British-made stampers. The album initially had the vertical Upsetter logo on a yellow and red label; later issues were on a white label.

The timing of the release of the albums that follow has caused much confusion over the years. Here is my best guess:

Perry releases *Soul Revolution Part II* on his Upsetter imprint, with the vertical logo on a plain background, with 'Soul Rebel' seen as 'Soul Revolution Part I'. Later pressings switch to the horizontal Upsetter logo. Housed in a full-colour sleeve from the vocal album, of which a large surplus existed (probably due to a minimum print run). The stampers came from the UK and the matrix indicates the involvement of Trojan.

ALBUM

1970

BOB MARLEY & THE WAILERS
Soul Rebels (Upsetter)
Soul Rebel / Try Me / It's Alright / No Sympathy / My Cup / Soul Almighty / Rebel's Hop / Corner Stone / 400 Years / No Water / Reaction / My Sympathy

Soul Rebel finds Bob on great form – vocally and lyrically – as he captures the growing spirit of the youth of an increasingly 'funky' Kingston.
Try Me is a slighter song, Bob singing: 'If you need satisfaction, listen baby, I'm got the action.' The Upsetters roll along on this rhythm-driven piece. Bob closes with 'One more thing … I'm black!'
It's Alright is more funky fuel from Bob and The Upsetters: James Brown might have written it, but didn't. The song was reworked as 'Nightshift' on the *Rastaman Vibration* album. In **No Sympathy**, Peter returns to the darker themes he often sang about, this time a lack of sympathetic love. A choppy guitar and clunky rhythm add to the gloomy feel. **My Cup** – as single. **Soul Almighty** finds Bob in a funky groove that checks various American dance craze tunes – the 'Funky Chicken' and the 'Mashed Potato' – and is more pastiche than creative. **Rebel's Hop** is similar to the single 'All In One' – it's actually a medley of The Wailers' own 'Rude Boy' mixed with The Temptations' 'Cloud Nine'. Bunny's vocal is lovely. **Corner Stone** goes back to the Bible (Psalm 118) for inspiration, transferring the metaphor – 'the stone the builder rejects has become the cornerstone' – to human relationships. Sweet and mellow. On **400 Years** Peter's unmistakable voice cries out for all 'black and brown' to wake up to reality. The Upsetters' tight rhythm drives forward Peter's question of why, after 400 years, 'they' don't see. Peter re-cut it on *Catch A Fire*. In **No Water** Bob has a thirst that seems to require a nurse! Gregory Isaacs had a hit with the similarly themed 'Night Nurse' in the early 1980s. Bunny and Peter provide harmonies and vocal inflections. **Reaction** has a strangely meditative vocal and finds Bob in a reflective mood. It has a mantra-like chorus, with the lyric 'To every little action, there's a reaction'.
My Sympathy is the slow chugging version of '400 years'.

Above: A travel poster provides the backdrop for this famously tacky album cover.
Left: Peter Tosh, 1969.

Perry then releases the rhythms as *Upsetter Revolution Rhythm* on his Upsetter label with the vertical logo. It's housed in a plain sleeve and also in the vocal *Soul Revolution Part II* sleeve. Later presses use surplus *Soul Revolution Part II* labels (some of which lose their Bob Marley & The Wailers credits) and continue to use surplus vocal sleeves.

The vocal album *Soul Revolution Part II* is released on the Maroon label as *Soul Revolution* and again uses surplus sleeves from the first pressing. Perry has always denied that he released this pressing of the album but it reportedly resulted from a 'lickle bit of business' that Perry did with The Pottingers (who ran the High Note label) to raise some cash. As with the Trojan deal, when Bob found out about this 'business', extremely sharp words were exchanged. The matrix of 'LOP' certainly supports this story, as it stands for Lindon O Pottinger, who ran the label before his wife, Sonia Pottinger, took over after Lindon's early death.

So really there were two vocal and one 'Version' album: *Soul Rebels, Soul Revolution II* and its rhythms as *Upsetter Revolution Rhythm*. All the confusion has arisen from surplus labels and sleeves being used on the 'Version' album and the Maroon pressing of *Soul Revolution* being regarded as the definitive first pressing, which it wasn't.

UPSETTER RECORDS PRESENT
SOUL REVOLUTION PART II
BOB MARLEY and the WAILERS

ALBUM   **1971**
BOB MARLEY & THE WAILERS
Soul Revolution Part II (Upsetter/Maroon)
Keep On Moving / Don't Rock My Boat /
Put It On / Fussing & Fighting / Duppy
Conqueror V/4 / Memphis / Riding High /
Kaya / African Herbsman / Stand Alone /
Sun Is Shining / Brain Washing

Although the stampers have Trojan matrix numbers, this album wasn't released in the UK. The cover shows Bob & Co. as 'revolutionaries' complete with guns, which are clearly toys. Getting involved with real guns in Kingston tended to shorten one's life expectancy!

Keep On Moving – see single.
Don't Rock My Boat is The Wailers' second recording of this song. Here it's been brought into the current reggae style, with Bob's vocal right up in the mix and in sharp relief from the music, which is free of harmonies. The line, 'We feel like sweepstake winners' still has a contemporary feel.
Put It On is another re-cut of a Studio One recording brought up to date. This cut is all harmonies and minimal music backing, with occasional interjections from an impassioned Bob.
On **Fussing & Fighting** Bob is calling for peace: this would become one of his trademarks.The ghettoes of Kingston had been violent for years (and still are) and such calls were heartfelt, as reflected in Bob's almost pleading vocal lead. Glen Adams' organ drives a typically rocking Upsetters rhythm along.
Duppy Conqueror V/4 – see single.
Memphis has Peter Tosh using his melodica skills, more famously heard on 'Sun Is Shining' or to greater effect on 'Anti-Apartheid' (Solomonic 1976).
Riding High, a slight but pleasurable instrumental, has Bunny on lead – an increasingly rare occurrence – on this simple song of the delights of chasing a girl and the pleasure of catching her. Bunny re-cut it during his dancehall phase as a Solomonic disco.
Kaya – see single.
African Herbsman – see single.
Stand Alone is another sweet song of love with Bob's lead vocal beautifully supported by Bunny and Peter. 'How could I be so wrong to think that we could get along?' asks Bob.
Sun Is Shining actually appeared as a Tuff Gong single and its more ethereal content is at odds with the mundane matters that this album covers.
Brain Washing features Bunny singing about the mental enslavement of the oppressed people of the ghetto through nursery rhymes and fairy stories.

Right: Bunny Wailer, 1969.

ALBUM
BOB MARLEY & THE WAILERS
Upsetter Revolution Rhythm (Upsetter)
Keep on Moving / Don't Rock My Boat /
Put it On / Fussing & Fighting /
Duppy Conqueror V/5 / Memphis /
Riding High / Kaya / African Herbsman /
Stand Alone / Sun is Shining /
Brain Washing

This album was a groundbreaker from Perry because it consisted solely of all the instrumental backing tracks to the vocals from *Soul Revolution Part II*. No other such album had previously been released – it was the precursor of dub albums. In 1973 Perry released *Blackboard Jungle Dub* – arguably the first-ever dub album, with special mixes of existing backing music. *Blackboard Jungle Dub* included the remixed rhythms from The Wailers' 'Kaya', 'Dreamland' and 'Keep On Moving'. Dub and sound pioneer King Tubby was at the controls along with Perry.

Perry sold the sessions with The Wailers to Trojan which released two albums and several singles by Bob & The Wailers. Initially, Trojan released *Soul Rebels* (in 1971) but, following The Wailers' Island debut, quickly followed up with *African Herbsman* (1973) and a reissue of *Soul Rebels* as *Rasta Revolution* (1974). This album included two additional tracks: the Tuff Gong singles, 'Trench Town Rock' and 'Lively Up Yourself'. It was the release of these albums that sparked the idea that Bob Marley & The Wailers had been a 'Lee Perry group'.

However, following the split with Bob & The Wailers, Perry did lend some help on early Tuff Gong releases. There is still confusion over how much help might have been given on which records. Many tracks have co-writing credits on the labels.

Although Perry came out of the recording sessions with the monies they generated, he ended up losing the drum'n'bass heart of his Upsetters band to Bob. Aston 'Family Man' Barrett and his brother Carlton began working on the Tuff Gong sessions, with Tyrone Downie on keyboards and the legendary Tommy McCook on saxophone and Vin Gordon on trombone. Perry recruited new musicians into the Upsetters.

Perry went on to become a highly successful producer, first in Jamaica and then in Britain. However, he never nurtured artists – like Phil Spector, he tended to try to mould artists to his vision. It was inevitable that this would lead to tensions with Bob, as he wanted to be in control of his own career.

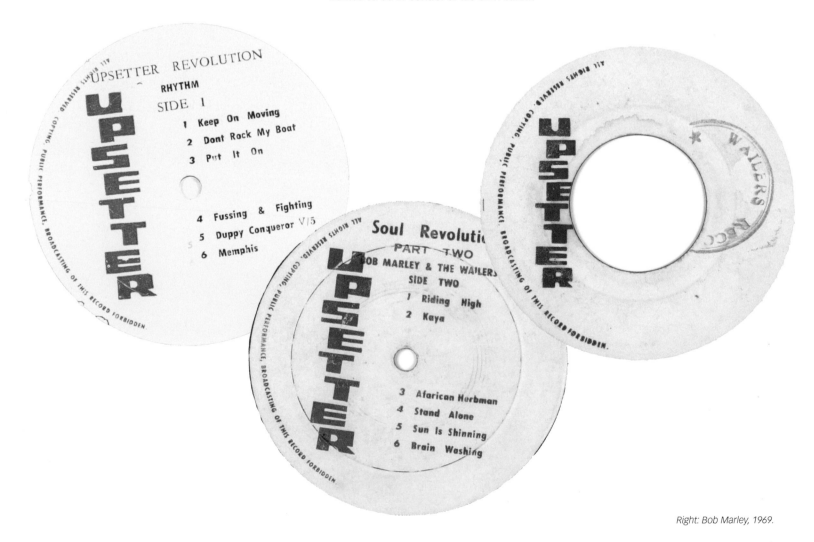

Right: Bob Marley, 1969.

MARLEY OBSERVERS HAVE RIGHTLY COMMENTED UPON Bob's lack of a father as a child and the subsequent importance of several strong male figures in his life. These included Joe Higgs, Coxsone Dodd, Danny Sims, Alan 'Skill' Cole, Chris Blackwell, Lee 'Scratch' Perry and, of course, Haile Selassie. Several of these people became life-long business partners, or friends, and all were important individuals from whom Bob learned.

It was Joe Higgs who took the young Wailers under his wing and put them through their paces until they got it right. He, as half of the duo Higgs & Wilson, was already a star in Jamaica. He remained an occasional member of the group into the 1970s, replacing Bunny when he dropped out of a tour in the US. His belief that practice makes perfect was a lesson that the teenage Marley took to heart as he realised this was crucial to success.

Coxsone Dodd was a paternal entrepreneur who helped out his day-rate musicians with stage clothes and places to stay. Though he wasn't a presence throughout Bob's career, his business sense was not lost on the young musician and that is probably where Bob got the idea from the very beginning of Wail 'N Soul 'M and

ghettoes, and was very supportive of Bob & The Wailers in the Cayman publishing trial (see the section on JAD in the Discography). He remained close to Bob throughout his career and lived with him at Danny Sims' New York apartment, in the fateful months leading up to Bob's death in May 1981.

Chris Blackwell of Island Records was, of course, the person who saw the need for overdubs of the group's music and created the marketing ploys that successfully broke them in the UK and then the US. Blackwell invested serious money in them and Bob stayed with his label, despite overtures from the powerful majors. With Blackwell in the producer's chair, Bob released the albums and singles upon which his international career was based.

The relationship with Lee Perry, which began at Studio One, continued into the late 1970s. Even after assorted rows about money, they worked together on several singles aimed at a Jamaican or dancehall audience, with dub plates. It was the death of Haile Selassie that gave rise to 'Jah Live', a clarion call to faith for all Rastafarians, which Perry produced at Harry J's studio. When Bob was in Jamaica for the 1978 One Love Peace Conference concert, he

The Making of Bob Marley:
THE TUFF GONG

Tuff Gong that all their music should be regularly re-pressed and advertised.

Danny Sims signed Bob to JAD records in 1967 and worked with him in various capacities until Bob's death in 1981. His roles were many and various: publisher, record company owner, tour manager and co-manager were a few of them. Sims' influence on Marley is often underestimated. Sims' line, 'Just because I'm an Afro-American – why should I make protest music? I want to make pop music and get the money and girls!' led many to believe he was a one-dimensional character. Sims was, in fact, politically aware and booked Malcolm X's college gigs in the US; he was also the political rapper Gil Scott-Heron's manager and co-publisher in the early 1970s. It was through JAD that Bob got to work with top African-American session musicians in Jamaica. Bob understood early on that the people who controlled the music business were extremely powerful, and Sims was one of these.

Alan 'Skill' Cole, the former Jamaican soccer centre-forward, was Bob's manager and close friend from the days of King Street Tuff Gong, in early 1970. Aside from his fame as a footballer, Cole was a powerful person in day-to-day dealings in the Jamaican

found time to cut two sides with Perry: 'Blackman Redemption' and 'Rastaman Live it Up'. It was for a similar major concert in 1976 that Bob had gone to Perry's Black Ark studio to record one of two cuts of 'Smile Jamaica'. The other tracks they cut together have only surfaced after Bob's death. These are the two Dub-plate-only tracks – 'Natural Mystic' and 'Rainbow Country' and 'I Know A Place' / 'Who Colt The Game', all of which were recorded at Perry's Black Ark studio.

As the group's Rasta faith grew during the 1960s, it was reflected in Bob's songwriting. The recording of 'Selassie Is The Chapel' in 1968 marked the first recorded hymn to Haile Selassie as a divine figure. Rasta became a great constant throughout Bob's years on the world's stage and he became the faith's best known follower. Before Bob died, he joined the Ethiopian Orthodox Church, as have many other Rastas since. Selassie drew Bob to a culture that can truly claim to be straight out of the Bible, and his global success brought the extraordinary country of Ethiopia to the fore of the Western world's consciousness.

It is a mark of the man that Bob Marley could work and build a career with such powerful men, yet remain true to his vision.

Right: Joe Higgs, Bob's mentor and long-time friend, on stage with him in 1978.   Centre: Chris Blackwell of Island Records.

'Black Progress' to 'Sugar Sugar': On The Kingston Vibe

BOB MARLEY PLUS TWO
Mellow Mood / Bend Down Low (JAD)
Bob re-cut these two Wail 'N Soul 'M rocksteady tunes in an attempt to add soul to the mix, just as Johnny Nash had added pop to rocksteady with massive success. Unfortunately, Bob's effort sank without a trace.

VARIOUS PRODUCTIONS 1968 TO 1971

In the years following the failure of the Wail 'N Soul 'M label, and preceding the productive sessions with Lee 'Scratch' Perry and for their own Tuff Gong imprint, the group recorded a few singles for other producers, as well as several self-produced singles. These provide a snapshot of the material they were recording as an independent group: the music covered a wide spectrum, from the Black Power-influenced 'Black Progress' to the deeply spiritual 'Selassie Is The Chapel' to the reggae/pop of 'Sugar Sugar'.

During this period they also recorded an album's worth of material for Leslie Kong's Beverley's imprint: Kong was by now the most commercially successful producer the Jamaican music business had ever seen. His productions were charting in the UK. Many of the black-and-white photographs of Bob Marley & The Wailers used in this section of the book were taken in the compound of Byron Lee's Dynamic Sounds Studio in 1969. It's known that they recorded the 'Adam & Eve' and 'Wisdom' tracks in that studio at that time, so these pictures probably hail from that session.

Of course, all these small-scale sessions have only served to confuse discographers such as myself and I suspect that what is mapped out below may not be the full story.

JAD PRODUCTION: 1968

Bob Marley and The Wailers remained contracted to JAD throughout this period, until the contract was assigned to Island, from JAD/CBS in late 1971. JAD was keen to break Bob to an Afro-American audience and developed music for that market. On the left is the only record from these sessions that was released in Jamaica. The credit (Plus Two) reflects the fact that Bunny was in jail on a cannabis charge at the time. JAD released the single in the US and France as 'Bob, Peter & Rita'. See 'The Wailers & JAD' section in the Discography.

BOB MARLEY
Selassie Is The Chapel /
MORTIMER PLANNER
A Little Prayer (Mortimer Planner)

A deeply spiritual hymn to Selassie, which marks Bob & The Wailers' growing Rastafarian faith. It's dominated by Rasta-style hand drumming and features Peter on guitar and Rita on harmonies. Bunny was believed to be in jail (see page 58) but he remembers it differently. It's based on the old country & western song 'Crying In The Chapel', at that time most recently recorded by Elvis. The mythology of this record is that only 26 copies were pressed and distributed to associates. The relic-like qualities of this single are heightened by the flip side, which finds Mortimer in full Rasta flow.

THE WHALERS
Adam & Eve / Wisdom (Ted Powder)

An odd brace of tunes for such an Uptown commercial release and the spelling of the group's name only adds to the strangeness.
Adam & Eve, written by erstwhile Lee Perry collaborator Leo Graham, has a biblical root. It's the old 'woman is the root of all evil' nonsense, which surely few can't see reflects a perceived cultural, not spiritual, truth.
Wisdom again looks to the Bible (Proverbs 10:15 and 10:21) but from these passages Bob creates a real beauty: spiritual wealth will always be more valuable than monetary wealth. A demo of 'Wisdom', with just Bob and guitar, has recently surfaced and it's terrific. Bob came back to these lyrics on 'Stiff Neck Fools' and Peter, likewise, on 'Fools Die'.

MORTIMER PLANNER PRODUCTION: 1968

Mortimer Planner, or Planno as he became known, was a Rasta 'elder', who accompanied Bob Marley to Danny Sims and Johnny Nash's Uptown home on their first meeting. He acted as Bob's manager but was more a spiritual 'guide'. He can be seen in the famous photograph on page 29 greeting a very bemused Haile Selassie on the steps of his plane at Kingston airport.

TED POWDER PRODUCTIONS: 1969

Ted Powder was a Dutch engineer at the Dynamic Sounds Studio. He was a mainstream, 'Uptown' producer and engineer. Four tracks were cut that have appeared endlessly on compilations ever since, although only the single on the right ever surfaced – to the best of my knowledge. The other two tracks are uptown re-cuts of Wail 'N Soul 'M gems: 'Thank You Lord' and 'This Train'. Rita Marley, as one of The Soulettes, worked on an album project by Ted Powder aimed at the tourist markets. The Soulettes sang harmonies with Lloyd Wilks on the *Jamaica Magic* album (FRM).

Left: Bob Marley & The Wailers perform in Kingston, circa 1970.
Above: 'Selassie Is The Chapel' – reputedly one of only 26 copies. All have blank labels.

BOB MARLEY & THE WAILERS
Mr Chatterbox /
THE CORSAIRS
Good Night My Love (Bunny Lee)
Bob updates an old Studio One track, 'Mr Talkative', in a friendlier vein. It's a dig at fellow 'rebel' producer Winston 'Niney' Holness (aka The Observer). A great bit of chat from Lee and Bob starts the tune off nicely. Niney was, of course, a pal of Bob's friend, Lee Perry. Someone described the Jamaican music scene as like 'village life in a soap-opera sort of way'.

BOB MARLEY & THE WAILERS
Sugar Sugar /
PETER TOSH & THE WAILERS
Green Duck (Randy's)
Bob tackles the Archies' bubblegum pop smash, **Sugar Sugar**, with huge success. Ignored because of its pop sensibilities, it's actually one of the first recordings on which Bob creates a reggae/pop hybrid successfully. The interplay between Bob and the harmonies (Rita, Bunny and Peter) is very similar to the sound he would create when working with the I-Threes. The lyric, 'Pour a little sugar on me babe', which surfaces during the track, became the basis for a song in its own right that Judy Mowatt (Tuff Gong 1972) and Johnny Nash (CBS 1974) covered.
Green Duck is an instrumental that reportedly features Peter on the piano.

GLEN ADAMS
Rebel version /
BOB MARLEY & THE WAILERS
Nice Time version (Glen Adams)
Adams' **Rebel version** is a piano and horns cut over the original Upsetters 'Soul Rebel' rhythm. Adams also released it as 'Rebel Version (version 3)' on a Capo (JA) single, with a straight version on the flip.
Nice Time version is a real oddity, with Bob and the crew re-voicing just some of the 'Nice Time' lyrics that feature in this mix. Recently the full DJ cut of 'Nice Time' has surfaced. Over the rhythm, U-Roy Junior chats a new lyric that's full of then current favourite phrases. The vinyl 'Nice Time' version is the DJ rhythm track with the Wailers vocals left on.

BUNNY LEE PRODUCTIONS: 1970
Edward 'Bunny' Lee, also known as 'Striker' and 'The Hitmaker' was just that – a highly successful producer. He was one of the new producers coming through and had links with Lee Perry. A real entrepreneur, with fingers in many musical pies, he remains to this day one of the key characters on the Kingston music scene, though not necessarily for his current work. He has a massive catalogue of material from the likes of Johnny Clarke, Delroy Wilson, Cornell Campbell; in fact the list is endless. He is best known for his 'Flying Cymbal' sound of the mid-1970s and his patronage of King Tubby's first dub studio.

CLIVE CHIN RANDY'S PRODUCTIONS: 1970
The Chin family owned Randy's record shop and Randy's studio, both of which were key venues in Kingston. This was the studio Lee Perry used before he built his own. The Chin family moved the business to New York in the late 1970s and Victor and Pat Chin set up 'VP' records, currently home to Sean Paul.

GLEN ADAMS PRODUCTIONS: 1971
Glen Adams had been the keyboard player for The Upsetters, Lee Perry's band, and moved to New York in the early 1970s. He released a few reggae singles on his Capo imprint and later produced music with a rap and hip-hop flavour.

The Hottest Sunday Session ever
TODAY IS SWINGING Ferry Inn WITH THE FESTIVE SOUNDS OF **Fabulous Five** INC
P L U S
● Bob Marley and the Wailers
● The Soulettes ● Eric Donaldson
AND THE ULTIMATE SWINGDISK
The Swinging Starts At 12 Noon Cover $2

WAILERS SELF-PRODUCTIONS: 1970

In between their Wail 'N Soul 'M and Tuff Gong imprints the Wailers cut a few self-produced records as listed below. These appeared on blanks or on the short-lived 'Tempa' label.

LESLIE KONG PRODUCTIONS: 1970

In 1970, Bob went back to the man for whom he had first recorded some eight years earlier. By now, Leslie Kong was a top producer whose international success with Desmond Dekker's singles, '007' (in 1967) and 'Israelites' (in 1969) would have very much interested the sharp and ambitious Marley. Kong was to enjoy further UK chart action with the Pioneers' 'Long Shot Kick The Bucket' and the Melodians' 'Rivers of Babylon' which Boney M took to record-breaking heights a decade later.

The recordings listed on pages 62-63 are often dismissed by purists as lightweight or too 'pop', but this misses the point that Bob was developing his understanding of commercial reggae/pop music which was to serve him well with Island records in the years to come. Some great songs were recorded in these sessions – 'Caution', for example – and Bob was still keeping his mix of protest and love songs going. Also notable is that Peter sings lead vocal on four tracks.

Kong died of a heart attack in 1971, robbing the reggae world of a true hit-producer. The much-reported 'death threats/prediction' made by Bunny (or Bob, or Peter depending

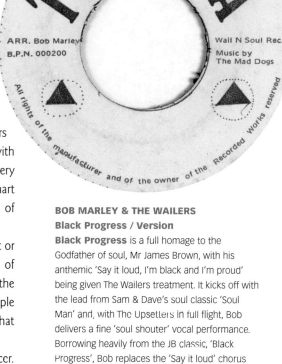

BOB MARLEY & THE WAILERS
Black Progress / Version
Black Progress is a full homage to the Godfather of soul, Mr James Brown, with his anthemic 'Say it loud, I'm black and I'm proud' being given The Wailers treatment. It kicks off with the lead from Sam & Dave's soul classic 'Soul Man' and, with The Upsetters in full flight, Bob delivers a fine 'soul shouter' vocal performance. Borrowing heavily from the JB classic, 'Black Progress', Bob replaces the 'Say it loud' chorus with a 'Black Progress' chorus and starts off crying, 'Down too long, we've got to get strong'. He goes on: 'Brother, like it makes two eyes to make a pair – we won't quit till we get our share.' 'Family Man' Barrett remembers this as the first single he recorded with Bob, who had been impressed with the Barrett Brothers' playing on The Uniques 'Watch This Sound' (Tramp).

RITA MARLEY & THE MAD DOGS
Give Me A Ticket /
PETER TOSH & THE MAD DOGS
Give Me A Ticket
Rita returns to Studio One days of covering US hits as the group record this cover of 'The Letter' (with a different title), the 1967 pop hit by The Box Tops. Bob and Bunny provide the harmonies and the label states 'Arranged by Bob. Marley'. The flip has Peter on lead.

RITA MARLEY & THE MAD DOGS
Give Her Love / Version
Clearly cut at the same time as 'Give Me A Ticket', **Give Her Love** is a Rita solo outing over a rhythm that is strangely familiar – It's a slightly reworked 'Ticket'. The 'RM' and the 'Rita' in the matrix number seems to indicate that this was a Rita-driven project. Rita, who has been with the group since the beginning, continues to be an active member of The Wailers, as well as a singer in her own right, with her group, The Soulettes.

Record producer dies of heart attack

One of Jamaica's leading record producers, Mr. Leslie Kong died of a heart attack at his home at Norbrook Acres Drive on Monday afternoon. He was 38 years old.

Mr. Kong, a former student of St. George's College, entered the recording business in 1962, in the pre-ska era. He had as his top recording stars, Millie Small, Derrick Morgan, Owen Gray, and Jimmie Cliff. It was he who was largely responsible for Millie Small's success in London under the management of Chris Blackwell, who was a business associate of Mr. Kong.

In recent years Mr. Kong, who was managing director of Beverley's Recording Co. and Kong's Real Estate Ltd. had gained international success through his recording stars, Jimmy Cliff, Desmond Dekker, Jackie Edwards, the Maytals, the Pioneers, the Melodians, Ken Boothe, the Gaylads and Millie Small.

His recording company sold one million copies of "Israelites" recorded by Desmond Dekker and the Aces. He was also the producer of this year's Festival Song runner up "Teacher, Teacher," and the previous Festival Song winners "Sweet and Dandy" by the Maytals, and "In-tensified Festival" by Desmond Dekker and the Aces.

Two of his artistes. Millie Small and Desmond Dekker will be coming to Jamaica from London for the funeral service, which will be held at Holy Cross Church on Sunday at 2:00 p.m.

A recording will also be made by these two artistes in memory of their late manager.

Mr. Kong leaves wife, Mrs. Colleen Kong and two children.

MR. LESLIE KONG

Round-the-world flying record?

DARWIN, August 10 (Reuters): Two Australian pilots landed here today after flying around the world in a light aircraft in 125 hours 27 minutes — believed to be a new world record.

The two men, Trevor Brougham, 37, and Bob Dickefon, 31, landed in their Beechcraft Baron twin-engined aircraft after their attempt to better the time set by U.S. Air Force Major Bob Wallick in 1966.

Major Wallick, accompanied by his wife, flew around the world in 126 hours 16 minutes 40 seconds in 1966.

Mr. Brougham said on arrival that he was sure they had broken 26 of 32 existing place-to-place records for general aviation aircraft below 6,500 feet, either single or double propeller.

On the round-the-world record he said: "We will have to contact the Federation International Aeronautique in France, the world authority on these records, to really know."

Above: Leslie Kong's death is reported in the press.

BOB MARLEY & THE WAILERS
Soul Shake Down Party /
BEVERLEY'S ALL-STARS
Shake Down Version (Leslie Kong)
The most successful track from these sessions
sees The Wailers in pop/soul/reggae form. It's a
simple celebration of the pleasures of partying,
with some vocal styling borrowed from the likes
of Edwin Starr or Wilson Pickett. Bob made a
slight return, on Dub plate only, with 'Soul Shake-
Up Party!', that has yet to be released.

THE WAILERS
Stop the Train / Caution (Leslie Kong)
Stop the Train is a powerful lament from Peter,
who 'still can't find no happiness'. The train motif,
commonly used in gospel songs, fits Peter's dark
mood as he sings, 'Stop the train, I'm leaving'.
Later Tosh talked about the song being a
reflection of his thoughts of leaving the group,
although he was still around some three years
later when he re-cut it for *Catch A Fire*.
Caution is the best song from these sessions
and was apparently written after Bob had spent a
night in jail after Mortimer Planner, then 'manager'
and Rasta 'guide' to Bob, was pulled over for
driving without a licence. 'Caution, the road is wet'
is a metaphor for the 'road of life'. Hux Brown
drives the music with splendid guitar-playing and
the vocals are top drawer. Strangely, the line, 'You
crazy mother funky!' is removed on this single
(and the UK single release) but appears in the
album mix.

on which version of the story is told) to Kong over the album title have only served to
further over-shadow the work they did together. The story goes that, upset with Kong's
choice of title for the album – *The Best of The Wailers* – Bunny or Peter or Bob, said to
Kong that their best work was yet to come and that, therefore, if it was the best work that
they were to record with him, he couldn't have long to live.

Kong died shortly afterwards. It seems that he had long suffered from a heart
condition, though many accounts claim that Kong was in perfect health.

Beverley's RECORDS

135ª ORANGE STREET,
KINGSTON, JAMAICA., W.I.

S.R. 165

STOP THE TRAIN
(P. McINTOSH)
THE WAILERS

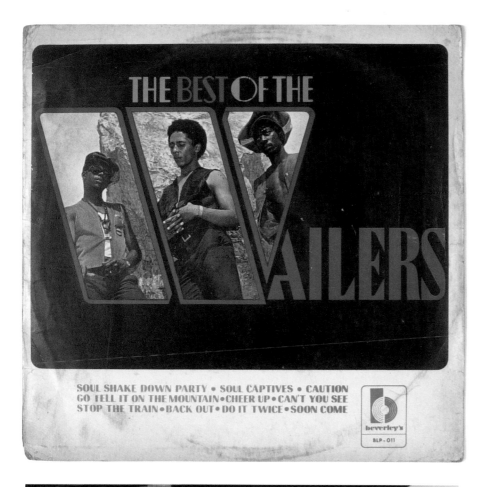

THE WAILERS
Soon Come /
BEVERLEY'S ALL STARS
Version (Leslie Kong) 1970

Tosh is once again bemoaning life's difficulties; this time the non-arrival of a friend, a lover, monies or something. The phrase, 'soon come' became widely used for Jamaicans' very flexible attitude to time, appointments and the like. This was largely thanks to journalists' use of the phrase in the 1970s. Following Kong's death, these tracks were licensed to assorted companies in the West. They have appeared on countless compilations ever since, especially after Bob's death.

ALBUM

THE WAILERS
The Best of the Wailers
(Beverley's Records (Leslie Kong))
Soul Shake Down Party /
Stop The Train / Caution / Soul Captives /
Go Tell It On The Mountain /
Can't You See / Soon Come /
Cheer Up / Back Out / Do It Twice

The second pressing of this album has the black and white pictures on the back printed reversed.

Soul Shake Down Party – see single.
Stop the Train – see single.
Caution – see single.
Soul Captives – an easy skanker from Bob & Co. with a tra-la-la chorus, that actually has a harder message that 'Freedom Day will come'.
Go Tell It On The Mountain – Tosh again is on lead vocal duties with this gospel standard that label mate Nash covered during this period, as did soul crooner Brook Benton, who had a large Jamaican fan base.
Can't You See – Peter returns to this slight Studio One track in which he complains about poor treatment from his girlfriend.
Soon Come – see single.
Cheer Up – a tune of hope of the 'change to come'. 'We've been in captivity for so long,' sings Bob over a simple and light rhythm in a song that foreshadows one of Bob's favourite topics later in the decade. Bunny Wailer uses the line in his classic hit of 1981, 'Rise & Shine'.
Back Out is bright and breezy with a fine organ solo and is full of Jamaican patois. It's a message to 'back out' to someone who is interfering.
Do it Twice – Bob is in loving mood as he sings, 'Baby you're so nice, I'd like to do the same thing twice'. His ability to write and sing quality pop/reggae love songs is extraordinary, and tracks like these were the foundation of many of his international hits.

Left: Bunny Wailer, 1969. Above: Bob, Bunny & Peter on the stage of The Queen's Theatre, Kingston, 1969.

Bob Marley & The Wailers photographed in Byron Lee's Dynamics Studio yard in 1969, during a recording session. An unknown fourth person joins them in the last picture.

The Rise of Rasta

JAMAICA HAS A HISTORY OF MANY FAITHS, SOME OF WHICH managed to survive the passage from Africa, and also the mainstream Christian faiths that the missionaries of Europe and the UK brought to the island. The cult of the church leader also has a long tradition and various churches are known by the pastor's name, rather than as a branch of the Church of Jamaica. In the 1930s, the Rastafarian faith started to develop through the preaching of the first Rasta, Leonard Percival Howell, whose message earned him two years' hard labour.

Above left: The card that Leonard Howell handed out that led to his imprisonment.
Above right: A book published in Harlem, which reflects cultural influences that Marcus Garvey absorbed when he was in New York.

Howell's message was that the Jamaican poor should pay allegiance to the emperor of Ethiopia, Haile Selassie, and not to the British crown. The notion of a return to Africa for black people was first mooted by the Jamaican black nationalist leader Marcus Mosiah Garvey (1887-1940). His organisation, The Universal Negro Improvement Association, claimed five million members at its height and published its own newspaper, *Negro World*. He also established the Black Star shipping line (the White Star line owned the *Titanic*) to transport people back to Africa. Black nationalists in Harlem, whom Garvey visited, were telling fellow blacks to burn their US 'citizen ship' and buy 'Abyssinian ship'. Although Garvey's shipping line collapsed amid accusations of corruption, it remains a seminal element in the history of the growth of black nationalism in Jamaica.

When Howell (aka 'Gangunguru' or 'Gong') was released from prison in the early 1940s, he set up a Rastafarian compound, the Pinnacle Community, for 4,000 of his converts to the new way of life. It was here that the famous dreadlocks worn by Rastafarians first appeared. Members reportedly were shown photographs of African warriors: the locks were a 'back to Africa' statement. A decade later, in 1954, the police broke up the camp, sending its members into the ghetto. Many moved into the 'Back-a-wall' and 'Dungel' squatter camps (near Trenchtown) that

Above: The 'Holy Piby' is one of the so-called 'Black Bibles'.
Background: Typical 'robed' dress for a Rasta in the 1960s.

and history were highly appealing to Jamaicans. The main Ethiopian language, Amharic, was one of the original languages used to write the Bible; the others – Greek, Hebrew and, later, English – are considered cornerstones of culture, whereas Amharic is little-known. The sacred art of the Ethiopian Coptic Church has the same Bible stories that are known the world over but, unlike its Western equivalent circulated by missionaries, there were no white faces in the pictures.

Haile Selassie could trace his lineage back to the biblical union of Solomon and Sheba and was part of the Solomonic dynasty. At Lalibela, a small town in the middle of the Ethiopian highlands, there are 13 wonderful churches hewn out of solid rock, the ground forming the roofs. This collection of unique buildings is known as the eighth wonder of the world. It's an extraordinary country that few, even today, know much about. The *Lonely Planet* guide describes it as 'Africa's Petra' and says: 'Lalibela undoubtedly ranks among the greatest religio-historical sites, not only in Africa but in the Christian world.'

became key areas for the Rastafarians. The song, 'Back-a-wall' (Saturn label) was a warning, by Lord Creator (a much-loved Trinidadian performer), to 'keep clear of dem in Back-a-wall ... belly's swelling with hunger – money all around, but none of it touch dem – now they say that they must go.'

Ethiopia had an iconic appeal to the descendants of Africans who had been taken forcibly from their homelands: for a start, its ruler was a black African. Unlike many other African countries, Ethiopia had never been colonised by the West: Italy had invaded as a pre-Second World War manoeuvre, just as Germany got involved in Spain. Haile Selassie approached the then League of Nations in 1936 to ask for international help as his country was being invaded. He alluded to this speech when he spoke to the United Nations in 1963: it later inspired Bob to write the track 'War'.

From a spiritual and religious perspective, various disparate elements of Ethiopian culture

Top: A stained glass window inspired by Ethiopian Coptic Art.   Above: Rastas found familiar Bible stories illustrated in Ethiopian Coptic Art, populated by black characters.

Interestingly, Ethiopia's patron saint is St George, who also fought a dragon on a small island in northern Europe. Some historians believe that the Crusaders brought the tale back to Britain, where the story took root in English folklore. In fact, Ethiopia boasts several equestrian saints, all of whom seem able to kill all manner of man and beast, while seated on their steeds.

The appeal of such a country to a colony trying to find its own identity is easy to see. By the 1960s, Rastafarianism was continuing to grow in Jamaica, fed by the black consciousness movements, both intellectual and radical, in the US. Indeed Prince Buster, already a successful artist and Sound System owner, converted to Islam through the movement. Alliance with Rasta would at that time have been considered a rebellious act – Rastafarians were portrayed as dangerous cultists.

Bob developed his faith through a relationship with Mortimer Planner, a Rasta elder who had been an early convert and who also managed Bob & The Wailers for a while. However, it would be a decade before Rastafarianism became a dominant feature in Jamaican life.

Musically, only a few songs ever tackled Rastafarian subjects. 'Rasta Shook Them Up' – cut by The Wailers at Studio One – recounts the arrival of Haile Selassie in Kingston in 1966. A mento single by Lord Bravo ('Haile Selassie', Fire) tells the story of the same event. Mento, though frequently based around events in life and love, did offer up 'Ethiopia' by Lord Lebby as an early conscious song. Its flip, 'Dr Kinsey Report', comments on the groundbreaking sex researcher's work: this is typical of a duality that is found right across Jamaican music.

Above left: Mortimer Planner, Rasta elder and Bob's guide.
Above right: St George and the Dragon in the Ethiopian Coptic Church tradition.
Right: Emperor Haile Selassie.

'Trench Town Rock': Tuff Gong, 127 King Street

IN LATE 1970, AS THE RELATIONSHIP WITH LEE 'SCRATCH' PERRY BROKE DOWN, Bob set up the Tuff Gong record label at 127 King Street, on the corner of Kingston's Beeston Street. To make money on the Jamaican music scene, artists needed to control their own label and distribution, so despite the failure of Wail 'N Soul 'M, Bob Marley & The Wailers remained a presence in the industry as performers, retailers, distributors and label owners. King Street would be Marley's HQ for four years until he moved Uptown to 56 Hope Road, as his international career took off.

Bob's importance within the group is reflected in the fact that the Jamaican press of the time always focused on him. He was always to the fore in coverage and in the band's own publicity; for example, a poster for a Tuff Gong production headlines: 'Bob Marley & His Gang'. The number of press articles about, and advertisements for, the group reached a high during this period.

A distinctive brew of music, fashion, sport and politics was fermenting on the Kingston scene and the music put out on the new label would become hugely popular as a vital element in this broad cultural mix. Indeed, it was the football superstar Alan 'Skill' Cole who was to become Bob's manager and friend during this period.

The group began to win awards from *Swing* magazine and by 1973-1974, records on the Tuff Gong imprint were among the top-sellers.

Some of the earliest Tuff Gong productions appeared on the Tuff Gong imprint that quickly metamorphosed into the classic 'rugby ball' shaped design. Tuff Gong also produced various other artists and provided distribution for individual band members and their labels. (See 'Tuff Gong Productions' in the Discography).

An artist friend of Bob's, Guy Coombes, who designed the Tuff Gong label with the gong on it (see page 79), recalled when interviewed in 1981 that the idea for the label's name was his and was inspired by a memory of an African 'gong' that made the sound of a bell and was used for communication. As with most things Jamaican there are other stories: Lee Perry claims the name was his idea and others say that it was Bob's street nickname.

Certainly, more than 20 new singles were released carrying the 127 King Street address – which is more than were released on Island Records or on the now more famous 56 Hope Road address, again underlining the importance of this overlooked period of Bob's work.

Ever since Coxsone Dodd had first dressed The Wailers in satin suits, Bob had understood the importance of style and fashion. Images of the time show clearly the major influence that radical African-American fashions had on Bob and the Kingston music scene in general.

The next five years would see an extraordinary work rate from The Wailers, and from Bob in particular.

Top left: An advert from Swing *magazine for the Wailers Record Shack.*
Top right: Cover of Swing *featuring Alan 'Skill' Cole, football star and Wailers' manager.*
Below right: Bunny, Bob & Peter looking 'tuff' on the street.

Bob in the newly decorated Tuff Gong shop, 1971.

1970

BOB & RITA, LESTER STERLING'S ALL STARS
Hold On To This Feeling /
LESTER STERLING'S ALL STARS – Version
A terrific reworking of Junior Walker's Motown hit (number two in the R&B chart in 1969), that showcases just how well Bob and Rita's voices worked together. Again showing Bob's great interest in Black-American music and culture, **Hold On** has always been a great dancehall favourite, but largely ignored in the West because it doesn't fit Bob's perceived 'rebel' image. Its popularity at Sound Systems in the mid-1970s led to a remixed version on dub plate only. Lester Sterling, of The Skatalites, leads the exemplary musical backing.

1970

Several of the early Tuff Gong singles utilised rhythms from the Upsetter sessions and a few also appeared on Upsetter imprints but with Tuff Gong matrix numbers, showing that some sort of link still existed. Various reports say that Lee Perry 'helped' Bob with production duties on some singles, such as 'Trenchtown Rock' and 'Lick Samba'.

BOB MARLEY & THE WAILERS
Sun Is Shining / Run for Cover
Sun Is Shining has become known to a new generation of clubbers thanks to the dance remix in the 1990s. Although produced with Lee Perry at the controls, it only appeared on the Tuff Gong label as a single. A snail's pace skank, it blends mystical lyrics with praises to Jah and everyday experience, in true Bob style. He re-cut it for his Island album *Kaya*.
Run For Cover takes the Perry/Marley 'Soul Rebel' rhythm and develops a similar lyrical theme, of revolution and spiritual adventure. It was fitting that one of Black Uhuru's earliest singles was a steppers cut of 'Sun Is Shining' (Hit Bound, '77).

BOB MARLEY & THE WAILERS
Send Me That Love / Lovelight
Send Me That Love is a beautiful song of love that neatly ties together the spiritual and physical with the line, 'Send me that love I've been created for'. Its simple doo-wop style with a waltz-time rhythm track is the ideal backdrop to this glorious song.
Lovelight is a simple hymn to the joy of letting love, spiritual or earthly, into one's life. The chugging rhythm flows with a song whose verses are chorus-like.

THE WAILERS, Peter, Bunny and Bob.

'Skill' Cole now Wailers' manager

MANAGER, Allan 'Skill' Cole

It was 'Upsetter' Lee Perry, who steeered the Wailers in the past. It was he who guided them to fast-selling hits like 'Small-Axe' Duppy Conquerer, Love Light and a host of others. But now the group feels it is time for a manager change.

Skill and Bob describe the motivating force for the switch as 'heart'. "We have known each other for a long time now, Bob explains and somehow there always seemed to be this spiritual link. This we always wanted — someone who really understood our philosophy of life and someone capable and willing to live it with us. We knew it all along, Skill was the man for us".

Allan "Skill" Cole, one of Jamaica's leading footballers stepped into another field. He's now manager for three leading show business groups the Wailers, the Soulettes and the Pipers. The first two are among the most popular in show business today while the third is on their way up.

The Wailers are led by Bob Marley, whose wife, Rita leads the Soulettes, while the Pipers, originally the Wailing Souls, can be regarded as off-'spring' of the Wailers. (Their 'Row Fisherman Row' proves the close similarity).

Not surprisingly, the union started out with a real score cher, "Trench Town Rock" now No. 6 on the chart 'Skill' assures that their next recording — done by a combination of the Wailers and Soulettes will have just as much if not even more punch and relevance. "We always believe we can do better" all says.

While still holding the top spot in the football circles — he plays for Boys' Town — Skill is working towards a one the goal — a smashing success for his three musical teams.

BOB MARLEY & THE WAILERS
Pour Down the Sunshine /
JOHNNY LOVER
Like It Like This

 1971

Pour Down the Sunshine was an early attempt at fusing pop with reggae. Having covered pop songs in a reggae style at Studio One, Bob takes the process further in creating this new song that speaks of the sunshine that love brings. Johnny Lover was an early Jamaican DJ who went to live in New York.

Like It Like This is the DJ cut to The Wailers' self-produced cut of 'Don't Rock My Boat'. It had been recorded twice before, when it reappeared on the *Kaya* album as 'Satisfy My Soul'. DJ cuts had burst into the charts with the famed U-Roy and this was one of several that The Wailers produced of their own recordings.

BOB MARLEY & THE WAILERS
Rock My Boat /
JOHNNY LOVER
Like It Like This
A self-produced re-cut of 'Don't Rock My Boat' with the Johnny Lover DJ cut on the flip, which is miscredited to Bob on one of the pressings

1971

1971 was an extraordinary year for the group with the massive Jamaican hit, 'Trench Town Rock', a tour in the UK and a visit to Sweden for Bob.

JAD flew Bob, Bunny, Peter and the Barrett brothers to the UK for a tour that never really happened, though they supported Johnny Nash on some dates at schools and clubs. Bob worked with Johnny Nash, John 'Rabbit' Bundrick and others of the JAD team in Sweden on a film score for a Johnny Nash film. The film, *Vil Sa Garna Tro* (*Love Is Not A Game*) co-starring Christina Schollin, sank without a trace despite Warner Brothers buying it. The soundtrack remains in a vault somewhere.

Bob Marley & The Wailers also found time to release a dozen singles in Jamaica. Advertisements for the singles, old and new, that were being released on the King Street label are further evidence of Bob's commercial acumen. Posters for some of the releases were printed at the time but none have surfaced. A photograph of one for DJ-turned-recording artist U-Roy's 'Kingston 12 Shuffle' release can be seen in the 'Tuff Gong productions' section in the Discography.

Far left: Bob & Peter in a Tuff Gong promo picture, 1972.
Above left: Original poster for the group, circa 1971.

1971

BOB MARLEY & THE WAILERS
Trench Town Rock / Grooving Kgn 12
A joyous celebration of The Wailers' hometown area of Trenchtown, which has gone on to become a classic of the Marley canon. Although released in 1971, it sold over several years and won the group an award from Red Stripe in 1973 for the sale of 30,000 copies. There are two different pressings – one has an extra verse.

Grooving Kgn 12 is the version whose name reflects the soul vibe happening in Trenchtown, where the postcode is Kgn 12.
This track is virtually always referred to as a Lee Perry production, or there is a reference to him having helped out on engineering. Interviewed in 1975, Perry said of 'Trench Town Rock' (and 'Lively Up Yourself'): 'I had nothing to do with it, it's not mine. When me and Bob split, he do that for himself.'

BOB MARLEY & THE WAILERS
Concrete Jungle / Nice Time
Although pressed in the US, via JAD, this single was released in Jamaica. It's the same lyric that appears on the *Catch A Fire* album, but an earlier recording.
Concrete Jungle was a housing project in Kingston (Arnett Gardens) and Bob uses its bleakness to describe the quality of life of the majority of Kingston dwellers – a million miles away from the holiday image of happy, dancing natives. 'No chains around my feet but I'm not free,' sets the tone, but Bob always felt that, 'life, sweet life, must be somewhere to be found.'
A newspaper review of the time describes Concrete Jungle as The Wailers' latest single for Johnny Nash.
A Wailers' favourite, **Nice Time**, appears on the flip.

BOB MARLEY & THE WAILERS
Screw Face /
TOMMY McCOOK
Face Man
Full of Jamaican folk wisdom, **Screw Face** has a simple message: if you live a good life, you need not be afraid of anyone. A 'screwface' is a person of bad temper and/or bad attitude who, like a duppy (ghost), knows just who to pick on. Old Testament allusions also appear in a typical lyrical mix from Bob. A hit in Jamaica and highly regarded as a little-known classic. Tommy McCook, a former Studio One horn player, features strongly in the musical mix, particularly on **Face Man**.

BOB MARLEY & THE WAILERS
Lively Up Yourself /
TOMMY McCOOK
Live
A celebration of the joys of dancing and more. 'Keep on livelying up your woman,' sings Bob. Re-cut on *Natty Dread*, it's a great example of anthemic writing. Once again, Tommy McCook is on top form, especially on the version **Live** side. The photograph (right) of Bob playing in Downtown Kingston clearly shows that the jazz-style music stands are Tommy McCook's.

BOB MARLEY & THE WAILERS
Redder Than Red /
WAILERS ALL STARS
Red
'Red' is the JA slang for being under the influence of cannabis, as in red-eye. Following on from 'Kaya', it brings in the developing Rasta influence by way of the simple couplet 'Red – Dread'. 'Every night, every morning' appears to be Bob talking about his smoking habits.

BOB MARLEY & THE WAILERS
Craven Choke Puppy /
T McCOOK & WAILERS ALL STARS
Choke
Taking another traditional saying (Craven Choke) about not biting off more than you can chew or your eyes being bigger than your belly, Bob delivers another moral warning. When blues & soul journalist Chris Lane asked him about the single at the Live at the Lyceum press conference in London in 1975, he confirmed that the single was aimed at the previous Jamaican prime minister, Hugh Shearer.

BOB MARLEY & THE WAILERS
Lick Samba /
WAILERS ALL STAR BAND
Samba
A very Caribbean tune which reflects calypso or mento sensibilities. In such a seemingly slight song as this, Bob's lyrics show a vulnerability – 'And though I know you'll hurt me again, I'll go on, I'll feel the pain', as well as revealing the 'lover man' side to Bob.

BOB MARLEY & THE WAILERS
Guava Jelly /
WAILERS ALL STARS
Jelly or Guava (depending upon pressing)
Similar to 'Lick Samba' in both style and its risqué lyrics, this was covered both by Johnny Nash and, rather more surprisingly, Barbra Streisand. Guava jelly is actually a fruit jam. Green guava is, of course, the unripe fruit that is not yet ready to be enjoyed. It's used in calypso as a sexual metaphor. Guava jelly is just ready and waiting …

BOB MARLEY & THE WAILERS
Satisfy My Soul Jah Jah / Satisfy version
Still known as 'Power And More Power' from its first appearance as a sound dub plate,
Satisfy My Soul Jah Jah – a powerful roots gem – is a hymn to the Rastafarian faith. No relation to 'Satisfy My Soul'. It's a big tune in the reggae world and pretty much unknown to the crossover audience.

BOB MARLEY & THE WAILERS
Satisfy My Soul Babe /
WAILERS BAND
Version
Bob shows how effortlessly he can turn from the spiritual to the physical, as the song listed above becomes a hymn to a woman. Like the previous record, it's very scarce.

Top left: Bob receives an award from Red Stripe for sales of 30,000 copies of 'Trench Town Rock'.
Presented by Radio DJ and scene star, Maria Barnes, at the Swing Awards in 1973.
Above: Bob demonstrates an early example of one of his famous stage poses.

BOB MARLEY & THE WAILERS
Rock It Babe /
WAILERS ALL STARS
Rock It version
Taken from the *Catch A Fire* album, on which it
was called 'Baby Baby We've Got A Date',
Rock It Babe is a re-cut of a JAD original which
has now been lost. It's more American pop/soul
focused and harks back to an earlier Wailers
direction.

1972

While Bob continued playing guitar on the Johnny Nash UK schools tour, the other
Wailers returned to Jamaica. Late in the year, Bob Marley & The Wailers were signed to
Chris Blackwell's Island label. They would very quickly record enough material for an
album to be released the following year. However, their career in Jamaica continued to
flourish and they fed it with a few Jamaican-only singles.

BOB MARLEY & THE WAILERS
Midnight Ravers /
WAILERS ALL STARS
Ravers version
Full of powerful allusions to the Book of
Revelations (always a Rastafarian favourite),
Midnight Ravers is a deep roots tune.
Musically more Jamaica than London, it has fine
harmonies by Bunny and Peter. The version is top
class and shows The Wailers still very aware of
their Kingston audience and the developing
mixing on 'version' sides.

BOB MARLEY & THE WAILERS
Concrete Jungle /
Concrete Jungle (actually the Wail 'N Soul
'M cut 'Hurtin' Inside')
The Island cut of **Concrete Jungle** backed with
a Wailers rocksteady favourite.

Above: Bob gets some shut-eye, while eldest son Ziggy plays, 1971.

1973

The first album to emerge from Bob's deal with Island, *Catch A Fire*, received a limited release in Jamaica. The JA issue did have a unique label, but the sleeves were the 'Zippo' lighter design imported from the United States and the mix is exactly the same as the UK/US pressings. (See Discography for details.)

Bob Marley & The Wailers started what was to be the first of almost annual tours in support of their Island albums. The tour focused heavily on the UK and parts of the US. They returned to the UK later in the year for another tour which was cut short by bad weather. Bunny Wailer quit the tour in June. He was replaced by Joe Higgs on the US leg, never to return.

BOB MARLEY & THE WAILERS
Chant I / Curfew

Chant I appeared as 'Rasta Man Chant' on *Burnin'* and it captures the Wailers in full Rasta Grounation mode, but in the studio. The song is a spiritual led by Bob, with Bunny and Peter on harmonies. A large Rasta drum would appear on stage when it was played live.

Curfew also appeared on *Burnin'* (as Burnin' and Lootin') and features Bob in full militant style: 'We're gonna be burnin' and a lootin' tonight'. At the time, this overt call to direct action was played down.

Right: Catch A Fire *appeared on a rare design 'Tuff Gong' label. Only the* Burnin' *album would use the same design (see page 81).*

1974

The Island *Burnin'* album was released in Jamaica in 1974, on the short-lived Dread-hitting-a gong label. The sleeve used the Island artwork but was printed in Jamaica. Little touring took place during 1974 as the 'new' Bob Marley & The Wailers were recording the next album, *Natty Dread*. The group did open for Marvin Gaye's two Jamaican concerts in May: one at the Carib Theatre and one at the National Heroes Stadium.

The singles released in Jamaica gave Bob a series of popular tunes, with 'Belly Full' and 'Road Block' becoming two of the biggest hits of the year.

BOB MARLEY & THE I-THREES
Belly Full / (NO CREDIT) – version
Belly Full, which appeared on *Natty Dread* in slightly altered form (as 'Them Belly Full'), marks the arrival of their backing singers, the I-Threes – Judy Mowatt, Rita Marley and Marcia Griffiths – as a credited part of the group. 'Belly Full' speaks of the indifference to those who struggle in society and the ability of Jah music to lift the soul above sorrow, sickness and trouble. It also contains the classic line, 'A hungry man is an angry man,' which gave the song its street name of 'Angry Man'. A television documentary broadcast in 2005, about the refugee camps in Darfur, Sudan, ended with the reporter turning to the camera with the words: 'A hungry man is an angry man.'
The song was covered by Bob's long-time friend Noel 'King Sporty' Williams as 'Dance To The Music' (Konduko, 75). He also covered 'Concrete Jungle' (Konduko, 73). King Sporty appeared on a Studio One track ('Ska Jerk') and later created a special mix of 'Buffalo Soldier', when it became a posthumous hit.

BOB MARLEY, THE WAILERS & I-THREES
Knotty Dread /
WAILERS - version
Appearing as 'Natty Dread' on the eponymous album, the song is again slightly different here and has its version on the flip side. As Bob gives us a tour of Kingston and beyond, he finds the growing influence of Rastafarianism everywhere. Once again, a seemingly simple song takes on a life of its own and later in his career, 'Natty Dread' (aka Bob) would find himself in Zimbabwe.

BOB MARLEY & THE WAILERS
Road Block / Rebel Music
More from *Natty Dread* with Bob singing about a **Road Block** that has caused him trouble: 'Yes, I've got to throw away my little herb stalk'. Bob's conversation with the cop includes the classic line: 'Ain't got no birth certificate on me now'. The flip, **Rebel Music**, is a 'Road Block' version. This single was remixed by Aston Barrett with a strong bongo drums line, which transforms 'Rebel Music' into a tuff dub, that includes the herb line, above, from Bob. Dropping some of the vocal line into the dub was becoming popular in Jamaica. Currently unavailable on CD.

Left: Bob and Bunny at Lee Perry's newly opened Black Ark studio.
Above: Peter Tosh hangs out in front of the King Street Wailers' record shop, circa 1972.

Grooving Kgn 12

AS THE DECADES TURNED FROM THE 1960S TO THE 1970S, Kingston (postcode Kgn 12) was a vital and vibrant town. Its musical beat could be heard in the charts of the 'mother' country, owing to producers like Leslie Kong taking artists such as Desmond Dekker into the charts. He was one of several producers, including the up-and-coming Lee 'Scratch' Perry – aka The Upsetter – who were able to find a market for their music in the UK – where The Upsetters were one of the first reggae bands to tour.

This flourishing industry was bringing much-needed income into Jamaica and a cultural scene was developing in Kingston. Toots & The Maytals' hit, 'Funky Kingston', spoke of the influence of radical Afro-American culture in terms of style, fashion and music. James Brown and Curtis Mayfield were major stars and influenced many artists who drew heavily from their music and style; leading the pack were Bob Marley & The Wailers.

Contemporary newspapers were very much aimed at a small ruling elite and the entertainment columns were frequently reprinted from British papers. Jamaicans were more likely to be

Miss CHARIOT 1971 CROWNED

The scene is the SOMBRERO CLUB. The date: Saturday August 31. That's the night of the crowning of Miss Jamaica at the National Arena. Meanwhile over 500 people are seated in 'the Hat' awaiting another crowning.......Miss Musical Chariot. The MC is the dynamic Winston Barnes, he introduces the big man Bob Marley who will have the honour of crowning and kissing that pretty, curvaceous theng Sheila. Lotta cats wanna do that and more, but Marley gets the break.......The announcement is made, and everyone agrees.

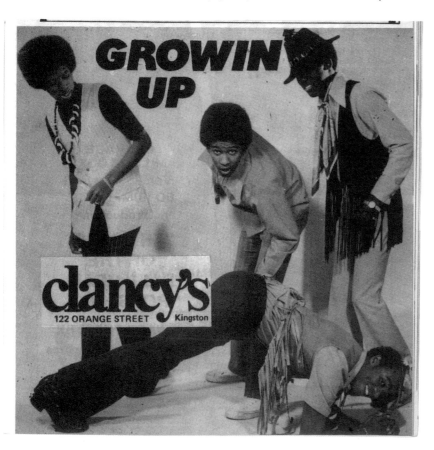

reading about Herman's Hermits or Lulu ('To Sir With Love' was a hit in Jamaica!) than local bands. But *Swing* magazine, originally a small giveaway photocopied gig listing, developed into a *Time Out*-style monthly. It featured music, fashion, sport (Jamaica has always performed well on the international stage in sprint track events), film, politics, theatre, cultural arts and beautiful women. Its 1973 coverline, 'Not just a magazine, but a way of life', reflected how it had changed and expanded as reggae's international appeal burgeoned.

Above: Fine and funky threads! Right: Swing: the music and culture magazine of Kingston. ('Seen' means 'Understood'.)

Right: US Soul artists like James Brown, Candy Staton, The Chi-Lites, Al Green and Marlena Shaw had their records pressed in Kingston – as did some UK pop artists like Gerry & The Pacemakers.

BLACK AND BEAUTIFUL

Above: A headline from Swing magazine echoes Afro-American Black Power slogans.

Swing also featured music from the ghetto, or 'Downtown' as well as 'Uptown' and more academic cultural events. The mix included middle-class Jamaicans who supported the likes of Count Ossie (who set up a Rasta camp) and the Mystic Revelation of Rastafari, Ras Michael or the poetry of Mutabaruka. These people were also looking for political change.

Danny Sims, an American living in Jamaica and the manager of singer Johnny Nash, brought Muhammad Ali and the African-American religious leader Elijah Muhammad *(see footnote on page 87) to Jamaica in 1969, but they were refused entry and declared *personae non grata*.

A year later, the same fate befell the civil rights activist Malcolm X when Sims tried to bring him to the island. Sims also brought many Afro-American musicians and DJs to Kingston, including producer Quincy Jones, guitarist Eric Gale, drummer Bernard Purdie and DJ Frankie Crocker.

It was a musical and social scene that the politically ambitious Michael Manley made good use of. The future prime minister announced his engagement to Beverly Anderson in *Swing*. Anderson was an actress, radio announcer, model and manager of the Red Stripe club, one of the favoured places on the scene. She became Manley's third wife.

Manley, with his socialist agenda, 'Power for the People' slogan and 'non aligned' international position, swept to power in 1972 partly as a result of courting the ghetto vote. He had borrowed heavily from biblical imagery and references, which he used liberally to pepper his speeches. He even took to using the name Joshua, promising to deliver his people from oppression – like his Old Testament namesake. When Manley had visited Haile Selassie in Ethiopia, in 1969, the emperor had given the politician a symbolic staff or walking stick. Manley called it his 'Rod of Correction' and wielded it in his election campaign: it was a powerful symbolic image that struck a chord with his target audience: the young, the unemployed and the dispossessed.

Manley held a Victory Bandwagon concert (named after the annual Bandwagon, part of the Song Festival). The poster (see page 109) shows that Bob Marley & The Wailers were one of many ghetto acts to play. Also appearing were Judy Mowatt and Clancy Eccles, who was to become Michael Manley's 'music' man. Long before Tony Blair's 'New Labour' party, Manley used music as a communication tool. Politics became a part of the music scene.

Jamaica's change of government caused concern in the US, especially as Manley was on good terms with Cuba. 'Non-aligned' meant 'against' in the world of cold-war politics – you were either

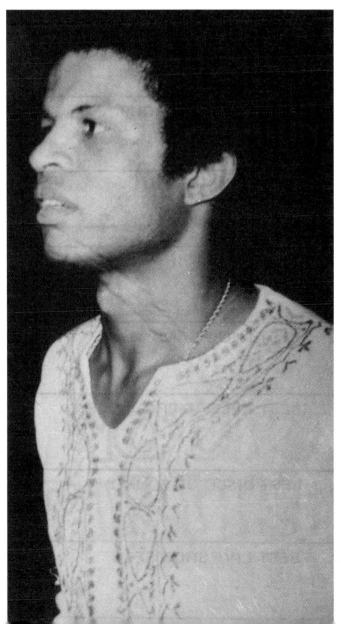

Top: 'Skill' Cole 'raps' with Jamaican Prime Minister Michael Manley.
Right: Don Taylor, Bob Marley's manager during most of his years with Island Records.

for the US or against. The US government began a policy that would shape Jamaica's future.

But on the streets and in the clubs, fashion-conscious musicians and Sound System fans enthusiastically adopted Afro-American street fashions, and Black Panther motifs. All the cool cats wore Afro hair and funky clothes, as the photographs of Bob on pages 72-73 show. Women, too, picked up on the African fashion vibe. The photograph of Rita & The Soulettes live on stage (left) shows them in their 'African-Dawta (Daughter)' glory.

The Black Panther poster (right) is the same as the one that hung by the counter in the Wailers' King Street shop. Peter carved his own Black Panther 'Fist' salute. The Jamaican bracelet below has an 'Afro' head with a Panther fist salute on both sides. Bob and Peter were big followers of fashion but it was Bunny who wore a red, gold and

POWER TO THE PEOPLE

FREE THE NEW YORK PANTHER 21

green jumper – an early showing of a trend for the Rasta colours that would become *de rigueur* in the last years of the decade.

Bob Marley & The Wailers were getting a great deal of local press coverage. It is clear that Bob was very much regarded as the front man and 'man about town': it was usually Bob who was interviewed, and Peter occasionally answered a few questions. Bunny, always the most reflective Wailer, made few press appearances. During this period, the group were signed to Island and, then, of course, began to attract mainstream media attention.

*Elijah Muhammad was the leader of the Nation of Islam ('Black Muslims') during the period of their greatest growth. The movement advocated black-operated businesses, institutions and religion. In 1974 Ali and Elijah Muhammad returned to Jamaica and this time were allowed in.

Far left: Rita Marley (centre) on stage with her group, The Soulettes, in full 'African Dawta' garb.

SIDE 2

THE INTERNATIONAL YEARS

1973 – 1981

The Wailers at Island, 1973-1974

SINGLES

BOB MARLEY & THE WAILERS
Baby Baby We've Got A Date /
Stop That Train (instrumental)

A JAD track re-cut for Island. Johnny Nash's version of it captures its lightweight feel much better. Appeared on the album as 'Rock It Baby' (as it did in Jamaica).

THE WAILERS

Concrete Jungle / Reincarnated Souls
This single was something like the one-hundredth single from Bob Marley & The Wailers (depending on how you count) and something like the one hundred and twentieth that Bob had performed on. Yet, for many, this was the first that they had heard of him. It was appropriately recycled from two years previously, but its message and impact was just as strong to its new audience. As the opener for the album **Concrete Jungle** jumps straight in with a mix of rock guitars and keyboards.
Reincarnated Souls is the Bunny Wailer song that would appear on his debut album three years later. It shows Bunny already following a more reflective and spiritual vibe. The track probably didn't appear on the album for that reason.

ALBUM

THE WAILERS

Catch A Fire
Concrete Jungle / Slave Driver / 400 years /
Stop That Train / Rock it Baby / Stir It Up /
Kinky Reggae / No More Trouble /
Midnight Ravers
Concrete Jungle – see single.
Slave Driver is the track from which the album took its name, with the lyric 'Slave driver the table is turned, Catch a fire so you can get burned' and the last couplet, 'Ev'ry time I hear the crack of the whip, My blood runs cold, I remember the slave ship, How they brutalized our very souls' is classic writing from Bob, going beyond the physical horrors of slavery to the deep psychological wound. Driven by a slow skank and choppy guitars it grips you from the start. Dennis Brown had a hit in the late 1970s with his version of it.

(continued on page 91, last column)

WHEN THE WAILERS WERE RECORDING AT STUDIO ONE, A FLEDGING ISLAND Records had released some of the Studio's output as singles in the UK. At the time they were releasing all kinds of material from various different Jamaican producers – they were not specifically developing and building Bob's band. Bob Marley & The Wailers were signed to Chris Blackwell's Island Records in the autumn of 1972, at which point they were given £10,000 upfront to deliver an album (about £80K at today's prices). Island had a growing reputation for releasing left-field and interesting rock and folk music. The plan was to market the group along with these other Jamaican bands, aiming at the student and trendy customer base that Island had identified.

1973: CATCH A FIRE
The album duly arrived at the Island HQ in late 1972 where, under the guidance of Chris Blackwell, it was made more listener-friendly for the targeted rock audience. With

Right: The famous 'Zippo' lighter sleeve for Catch A Fire.

400 years – Peter re-cuts a track from the Perry sessions, bringing some new life to it. The slower pace than the original and meandering keyboards don't really work.

Stop That Train again finds Tosh revisiting the past, playing on the Gospel roots of the song. The organ line sounds like it could have come out of a church service. The instrumental appears on the flip of 'Baby Baby, we've got a date' (see far left).

Rock it Baby – see single.

Stir It Up – Bob delivers an updated cut of the original rocksteady gem. (see Wail 'N Soul 'M). It became an audience favourite and despite never being selected for chart release, it's gone on to become a classic. The strength of the song shines through as it adapts so well to its new musical accompaniment.

Kinky Reggae – 'kinky' was a phrase of the time meaning 'sexy'. The chorus of 'Ride on' seems to have either a cowboy or other sexual link. It just rolls along beautifully and again became a live favourite.

No More Trouble is a simple paean for individual peace and the lyric, 'Make Love and not war! 'cause we don't need no trouble' are the nearest to the Hippie era that Bob wrote. Bounces along with the, now dated clavinet to the fore.

Midnight Ravers – see JA singles 'Trench Town Rock'.

additional production featuring guitar from Wayne Perkins and keyboards from John 'Rabbit' Bundrick (who had worked with Bob as a songwriter for JAD), the released version of *Catch A Fire* was created. The 'before' and 'after' albums are now available on the Deluxe edition of the remastered CD (see CD section in the Discography).

Bob Marley & The Wailers were re-christened 'The Wailers' again so as to be more rock-friendly, and the album was presented in a mock 'Zippo' lighter sleeve, together with publicity that attempted to position Reggae away from 'novelty/skinhead' music and towards serious music of poetry and rebellion.

1974: BURNIN'

Burnin' was a real mix of styles, as each of the group's key members developed their own voice. Bob and Peter mixed and created some classics, which spoke of radical responses, yet in a manner that was open and not polemic. Bunny was clearly going off on his own, slowly developing, spiritual path.

You can hear them going in different directions, with Bob clearly able to create the lyrics and style with the widest appeal. *Burnin'* was released in a full gatefold sleeve with the songs' lyrics and an inner sleeve with full band information. This was the first time that music from Jamaica had been treated with such respect. Both Bunny Wailer and Peter Tosh were featured as lead vocal on some tracks

Neither *Catch A Fire* nor *Burnin'* made a real sales impression in the UK or US and just a few tracks were released as singles. In fact, during this period, many of Bob Marley's original fans were less than impressed with the 'softening' of the rebel music that they had been used to listening to on Jamaican vinyl.

SINGLE

THE WAILERS

Get Up, Stand Up / Slave Driver

The single from the album was a rare Marley / Tosh writing collaboration on which the two sensibilities – of a catchy positive lyric and a defiant and radical lyric – blend together perfectly. Both are in fine voice and it puts down a marker of a more militant album.

ALBUM

THE WAILERS

Burnin'

Get Up, Stand Up / Hallelujah Time / I Shot The Sheriff / Burnin' and Lootin' / Put It On / Small Axe / Pass It On / Duppy Conqueror / One Foundation / Rasta Man Chant

Get Up, Stand Up – see single.

Hallelujah Time – After the forceful opening statement from Bob & Peter, Bunny drops his personal statement that's more akin to a church service as he talks of life and the legacy of slavery. Like 'Reincarnated Souls' it sounds like it's off his debut album and shows Bunny's musical path is

THE WAILERS

Above left: Island promotional photograph for 'The Wailers'; left to right: Bunny, Bob, Carlton 'Carly' Barrett, Peter and Aston 'Family Man' Barrett. Above right: Bob on stage in 1974.

going in a different direction from most of the album. **I Shot The Sheriff** Is the song that took Bob to an even wider audience, as Eric 'God' Clapton – a serious artist – covered it. This hit version took Bob's music to the mass audience. The song was apparently originally called 'I Shot The Cop' but Bob changed the song's setting to the Wild West to keep the powers-that-be off his back. It was actually banned in Jamaica from public performance in 1993! There's a fine funky instrumental cut of it by Isaac Redd Holt (JA Iron Mask) recorded a couple of years later.

Burnin' and Lootin' is another militant anthem, whose lyrics talk of the pressures of living in a country that's frequently under curfew.

Put It On – Bob goes back to an early Wailers' Studio One hit with a gentle spiritual-like song. Not bad for a second remake!

Small Axe – a slightly later classic from the

Upsetter sessions is revisited here with pretty good results. The writing credit has become solo – and began a subject of much debate: who wrote what when Bob Marley & The Wailers worked with Lee Perry.

Pass It On – back to Bunny's own path on this track that he would re-cut for his own Solomonic label. Almost a hymn delivered in a sweet soul-meets-gospel reggae style. The original cut of this, again with Bunny on lead, has recently surfaced and it's terrific.

Duppy Conqueror – another of their hits with Perry gets a makeover.

One Foundation finds Peter calling for unity on the 'one people vibe', which was usually Bob's preserve. Peter never returned to the song in his career.

Rasta Man Chant released as 'Chant I' in Jamaica. It ends the album on a high as the roots of Rasta music are used as a blueprint for this

THE WAILERS— LIVE AT THE SPEAKEASY

IT WAS at 1.50 a.m. that the lights of the stage at London's Speakeasy club shone on The Wailers, who had just walked on to the stage. They started off with a Count Ossie and the MRR-like Rastafarian chant entitled "Rasta Man". Bob Marley was singing the lead vocals, and playing bongos, and the other guitarist/singer, Peter Mackintosh was hitting a very large, home-made Rasta drum with his maraca.

Bunny Livinstone, the other singer, was also playing bongos, and the bass and drums of Aston and Carlton Barnett combined nicely, as always, with the organ of Earl Lindo.

After receiving a fair amount of applause for this first tune, Bob and Peter donned their guitars and the band strode into "Duppy Conqueror", one of their best records ever. "Slave Driver" from their latest album, "Catch-A-Fire" came next and then "Stop That Train".

Above: Bob in London in 1976.

ALBUM

BOB MARLEY & THE WAILERS
Natty Dread (Island)
Lively Up Yourself / No Woman, No Cry /
Them Belly Full (But We Hungry) /
Rebel Music (3 o'clock Road Block) /
So Jah Say / Natty Dread /
Bend Down Low / Talkin' Blues / Revolution

Natty Dread consisted of a mixture of new material and re-recordings of older tracks. The album was partly recorded in Jamaica, with mixing and even some backing tracks recorded in the UK. A former Studio One engineer, Sid Bucknor, handled those duties in the UK. The writing credits for some of these tracks were given to various friends of Bob's because of his dissatisfaction with his then current publishers, Cayman Music. See 'JAD' in the Discography.

Lively Up Yourself is a re-record of the 1971 Tuff Gong single and captures brilliantly the new international reggae sound Bob was creating. Al Anderson (an Island employee) makes his presence felt on lead guitar, and only the cognoscenti would know that this track wasn't new.

No Woman, No Cry has rightly gone on to become one of a handful of songs recognized around the world. Although the lyrics look back to Bob's hard times in Trenchtown, the music, delivery and style all point toward his future. Jamaican star Johnny Clarke covered it at the time, one of the huge number of singles that he released. At the more avant-garde end of reggae, the Light Of Saba did a version of 'No Woman, No Cry' (Total label) to great effect. Light Of Saba was a Rasta band which looked to jazz and the likes of Sun Ra, as well as reggae, and were led by the great Studio One saxophonist, Cedric 'Im' Brooks (see CD guide in the Discography).

Them Belly Full (But We Hungry) and **Rebel Music (3 o'clock Road Block)** were both Jamaican singles (see Side 1 of this book); the mix is slightly different here.

So Jah Say and **Natty Dread** – see single.

Bend Down Low is a re-record of this Wailers' favourite from 1966. Although light and poppy, a proposed single release was scrapped as it was reportedly deemed too lightweight for Bob's growing reputation as a 'serious' artist.

Talkin' Blues finds Bob as the self-sacrificing revolutionary with, 'Cold ground as my bed last night and rock was my pillow too'. The song contains the lyric, 'Cause I feel like bombing a church, now that I know the preacher is lying', which, as you might imagine, caused considerable comment at the time. Lee Jaffe delivers the strong harmonic line.

Finally, **Revolution** is full of typically Jamaican imagery culled from the Bible – 'Lightning, brimstone and fire' and 'Revelation'. Deeper and darker than much on the album – a perfect full stop.

Natty Dread, 1974

THE RELEASE OF *NATTY DREAD* IN LATE 1974 SAW THE MOST RADICAL CHANGE to date in The Wailers' camp. Original members Bunny Livingston and Peter Tosh left the group. Bunny had never liked touring, nor the necessary flying involved, and as a solo artist did neither very much. Peter actively hated touring and had always anyway been looking to develop his own career. He knew he was never going to replace Bob as front man.

The group reverted back to their pre-Island name of Bob Marley & The Wailers. The I-Threes – Rita, Marcia and Judy – would now provide harmonies. Both Marcia and Judy had been in the music business for the best part of a decade: Marcia had been half of the duo Bob (Andy) & Marcia, who scored a number one hit in Britain with 'Young Gifted and Black', now a classic. Judy had been leader of The Gaylettes and was successful in Jamaica. There were a further two key changes in what had evolved into a western-style rock band: Al Anderson and Bernard 'Touter' Harvey joined the group on guitar and keyboards respectively. There was no need for overdubs now that musicians with rock sensibilities were part of the band.

The year was marked by various firsts and lasts. In the early months, when the group were opening for The Jackson Five, The I-Threes appeared for the first time. Later in the year, the group made their first appearance on US television, when they performed 'Kinky Reggae' on the *Manhattan Transfer* show. In October, Bob, Bunny and Peter played together for the last time at the Kingston National Stadium at a benefit for the Jamaican

FROM THE ROOTS...

BOB MARLEY & THE WAILERS 'NATTY DREAD'

PRODUCED BY CHRIS BLACKWELL & THE WAILERS
ILPS 9281
ALSO AVAILABLE ON CASSETTE AND CARTRIDGE

THE WAILERS

Above: The last-ever appearance of The Wailers, Kingston 1975.   Inset bottom: The Wailers cardboard promotional window display for 'Burnin'.

Institute for the Blind, featuring Stevie Wonder – the Wailers/Wonder Dream Concert. Wonder called Bob on stage to join him and together they performed 'Superstition' and 'I Shot The Sheriff'. The Wailers' section of the gig is widely available as a bootleg, and reproduction posters for it are available.

It was also during this tour, which mainly took in the US and UK, that the *Live!* album was recorded. Meanwhile, *Natty Dread* joined Bob Dylan's *Blood On the Tracks* (his return to form) as one of the albums to be listening to in 1975. It even charted briefly – it only reached number 43, but Bob's critical credibility was rising sharply. The original album contained all the song lyrics on the inner sleeve, together with photographs of the band members taken by Adrian Boot. The cover shots were by Dennis Morris.

LIVE!

In May, 1975, Island released a promotional album that drew on of all three previous Island albums and the press reaction to Bob and the music. (See Promotional section in the Discography for details.)

Chris Blackwell's label had built Bob into the 'man most likely to', through three years of albums and gigs. The albums had brought the music to the attention of students and assorted rock fans across the country and the live gigs had built on Bob's existing reggae fanbase, who were desperate to hear the group that had only previously been available on crackly singles.

At the press conference for the gig at the Lyceum in London, attended by journalists from

mainstream newspapers as well as the music papers, Bob would not be drawn on why Bunny and Peter were not present, but Marcia Griffiths' absence was explained by her pregnancy.

In this pre-video music world, career-building was driven more by skill and belief and less by deep-pocketed global entertainment corporations. Bob's live performances were a terrific way to garner new fans – so what better move than to record one of these concerts to release on vinyl? Using the Rolling Stone Mobile Recording Studio, the concert at the Lyceum in London was recorded and released instantly. It became one of the very few classic live albums, and 'No Woman, No Cry' gave Bob his first hit single in the UK.

The concert was virtually a greatest hits show for Bob's long-term reggae fans, who had waited so long to see the group live. And there were plenty of new converts in the audience that night. By all reports, it was one of those rare and special gigs where all present realize that the artist on stage is 'arriving'. Unfortunately, as so often with reggae, there was a darker side to the occasion: there were major problems with pickpockets, for example. The sight of discarded wallets and purses on the floor after the gig caused music journalist Chris Lane to write that perhaps the DJ at the venue should have played 'Rasta No Pick Pocket' (a recent track by Junior Byles/Lee Perry). So it wasn't wholeheartedly a night of 'One Love', as painted by some. But it was a great gig: a terrific set, with the band cookin'. On 'Get Up, Stand Up' Bob quietly took over Peter's verses. The full set played that night also included: 'Slave Driver', '3 o'clock Road Block', 'Kinky Reggae', 'Natty Dread' and 'Stir It Up'.

The album remains in music magazine lists of the 'Best ever live gigs' albums, and rightly so. It was to give Bob a new, largely white and middle-class fanbase upon which to build his international career.

SINGLE 1974
BOB MARLEY & THE WAILERS
Natty Dread / So Jah Say
Natty Dread was released in Jamaica as 'Knotty Dread' – see Side 1 of this book.
So Jah Say is a drum machine-driven piece with Bob expounding Rasta consciousness in an almost sermon-like manner.

Another single, 'Talkin Blues'/ 'Bend Down Low', was given a catalogue number (WIP 6262) but never released.

ALBUM 1975
BOB MARLEY & THE WAILERS
Live!
Trenchtown Rock / Burnin' & Lootin' / Them Belly Full / Lively Up Yourself / No Woman, No Cry / I Shot The Sheriff / Get Up, Stand Up

SINGLE
BOB MARLEY & THE WAILERS
No Woman, No Cry / Kinky Reggae
The single released from the album, in a picture sleeve – then uncommon – took Bob to number 22 in the UK charts; it stayed in the chart for seven weeks.

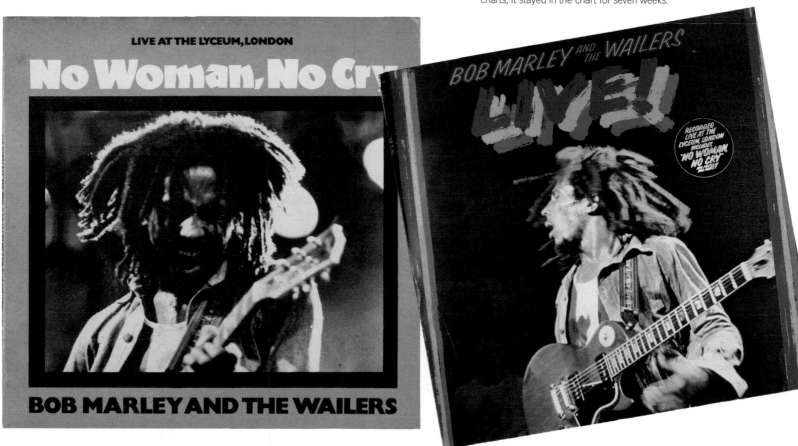

Left: The promotional sampler from Island included copies of all the press coverage the group had received and tracks from the Catch A Fire, Burnin' *and* Natty Dread *Island albums*

'Siddown pan my batty, fe five, six, seven hours'

THE WHOLE DEAL OF TOURING ABROAD WAS COMPLETELY different from playing live in Jamaica. It meant being away from home, long-haul flights, staying in cheap lodgings and driving between gigs in an old Transit or Commer van. It was often cold, lonely and very hard work. As with so many things to do with his music, Bob seemed able to accept that it had to be done.

It's very interesting to note that when Bunny and Peter were interviewed about their solo work, they were also asked about leaving The Wailers and both indicated that the trials of touring had contributed significantly to their decisions to go their own ways. Bunny actually left the group part way through a tour and returned to Jamaica. Bob's old friend and mentor, Joe Higgs, replaced him and finished the US leg. Bunny would never tour with the group again. He made it clear that he hated the cold and when asked about touring in support of his *Blackheart Man* album, he said he had no plans to leave the island. The dearth of live performances by Bunny has been a distinguishing feature of his career, as has a lack of inclination to work with the media.

When Peter was asked the same question, his reply began: 'I and I know why I and I refuse tour man!' He then launched into a story about getting up early, sitting in vans, where he, 'Siddown pan my batty, fe five, six, seven hours' ['was sitting down on my backside for five, six seven hours at a time']. The story goes on to complain about traffic jams, arriving late, not much food, too little time to sound check and no stage clothes. By the end of the tour he had lost nearly a stone in weight and had only £100 to show for it. Sucking his teeth, he said: 'We can't tour under dem circumstances deh.' He then likens the situation to slavery, as he sees The Wailers as 'no lickle amateur artist'.

When the question of the three original Wailers comes up, Peter is off again: 'We begin as The Wailers, as a three in one' and goes on, at length, to accuse Chris Blackwell of causing a divide. The 'Three in One' story and the link to the Wail 'N Soul 'M trademark of three hands locked together seems at variance with reality. Once they left the employ of Coxsone Dodd and became a group in their own right, they recorded and performed as 'Bob Marley & The Wailing Wailers'. Over the next five years Bob wrote

the vast majority of the songs and likewise took lead vocal duties on over 95 per cent of the tracks. It was Bob who appeared in the Jamaican press and Bob who accepted being in the same league as other Island bands who were trying to make it internationally. The 'Three in One' line also leaves Rita out of the story, and she was very much part of the group when it was first established, as photographs of the time show. JAD had also signed Rita as she was part of the group.

Chris Blackwell said at the time: 'Well, Peter and Bunny don't

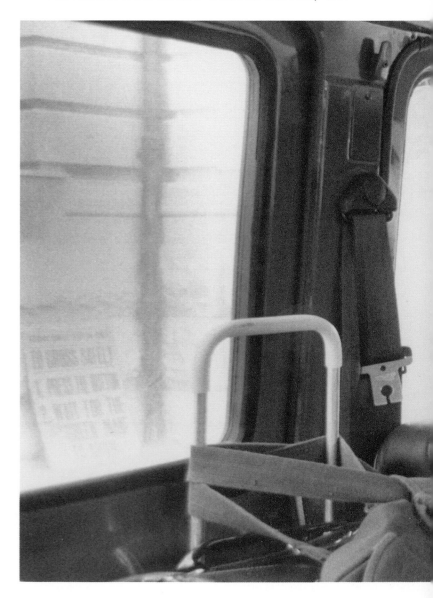

Right: Bob in the tour van, UK 1974.

like to tour ... we can only work with who we have who's touring.' Pressed about the group's name change, he said: 'Initially, the band always used to be called Bob Marley & The Wailers. The first two records we released, they were just called The Wailers. Island initially buried Bob Marley's image in The Wailers. And it was just after that time that they didn't make themselves available for promotion because they didn't want to tour, so the promotion naturally fell on Bob.'

Peter toured the States in 1978, as support for the Rolling Stones. The coaches were no doubt comfortable, but it wasn't a good career move. It seems a story oft-repeated in the music business: some artists simply don't like to tour, or to deal with the demands of the media.

Rastaman Vibration, 1976

ALBUM

1976

BOB MARLEY & THE WAILERS
Rastaman Vibration (Island)
Positive Vibration / Roots, Rock, Reggae /
Johnny Was / Cry To Me / Want More
Crazy Baldheads / Who The Cap Fit /
Night Shift / War / Rat Race

Positive Vibration – on this Moog-driven track, Bob's new style meets a traditional nyahbinghi Rasta track. It results in a rather downbeat start to the album.

Roots, Rock, Reggae – see single.

Johnny Was – see single.

Cry To Me – see single.

Want More is an attack on 'Back Biters' and the 'valley of decision' that awaits them. It was seen as adding to the negative vibe surrounding the album.

Crazy Baldheads kicks off Side 2 with a real killer. From the opening banshee-like wail, Bob & The Wailers deliver a *tour de force*. Lyrically, the song borrows from 'Freedom Time' (Wail 'N Soul 'M) but does seem a fully realized song, unlike some others on the set.

Who The Cap Fit – another track from the past, this time 'Man To Man' (Upsetter) is brought up to date. It's the most successful re-recording on *Rastaman Vibration*, as it utilizes the new band and harmony singers well, though the synth strings have aged rather.

Night Shift is a re-record of 'It's Alright' (Upsetter) that recounts Bob's job in a car factory in the US in 1966.

War was to become the second *bona fide* classic on the album. The lyrics are adapted from Haile Selassie's speech to the United Nations in 1968. 'War' has gone on to become a live favourite and various lines from it are often quoted. The lyrics remain relevant as wars driven by race hatred continue to rage.

In **Rat Race**, Bob rails against the arms race and separates Rasta from political violence (which was happening in Kingston). Not pretty but powerful. From the perspective of some 30 years later, it's an album of highs ('Crazy Baldhead' and 'War') and some lows ('Night Shift' and 'Cry to Me').

IN 1976, THERE WAS A NEW ALBUM FROM BOB MARLEY & THE WAILERS, AND both Peter Tosh and Bunny Wailer put out debut solo albums. It was a bit like Paul McCartney, John Lennon and George Harrison all releasing albums close together.

Bob was delivering his fifth album for Island while it was Peter and Bunny's first foray into the Western market. The albums, which actually featured similar musical line-ups, were all headed in different directions: but all were dressed to impress and were supported by the sort of marketing campaigns usually reserved only for rock bands. Surprisingly, it was Bunny Wailer who won this round hands-down, with one of the best reggae albums ever. But Bob would go away and come back stronger with a newer sound, and still find time to tour and promote.

RASTAMAN VIBRATION

Following on from the previous year's success this, in effect, became in rock parlance the 'difficult second album' for Bob. Recorded in Jamaica but finished in Miami, it featured a mix of re-records and originals. Island marketed the album to the max, with a full gatefold sleeve carrying the legendary tag line, 'This album jacket is great for cleaning herb,' and all the lyrics. The faux hessian sleeve of the album was reflected in the marketing with a

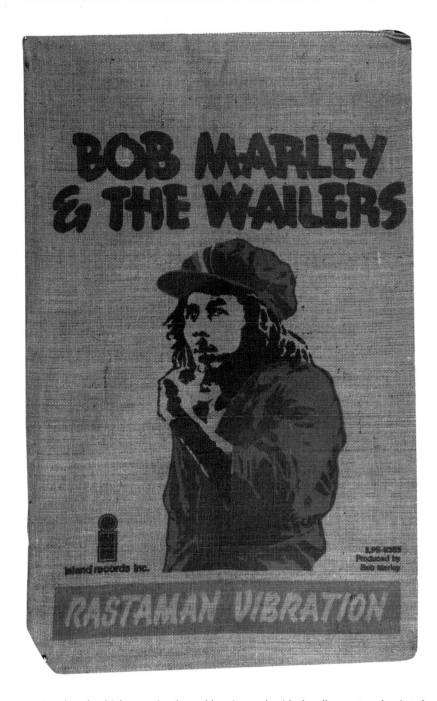

ALBUM LPS 9383 CASSETTE ZCI 9383 CARTRIDGE Y8I 9383

SINGLES

BOB MARLEY & THE WAILERS
Johnny Was
(Woman Hold Her Head & Cry) /
Cry To Me

1976

Johnny Was seems a dark track to release as a single. It's the story of a woman who holds her head and cries after her son is shot by a stray bullet. The woman protests that 'Johnny was a good man' but the line, 'Now she knows that the wages of sin are death, the gift of Jah is life' appears to be saying that, had Johnny been bought up a Rasta, things would have been different.
On **Cry To Me** Bob again recycles the past, this time bringing little new to the Studio One track. A weak spot on the album.

BOB MARLEY & THE WAILERS
Roots, Rock, Reggae /
Them Belly Full (But We Hungry Now)
Roots, Rock, Reggae has Bob recycling the 'Feel like dancing, dance cause we are free' lyric from 'Rainbow Country', in praise of reggae. A special plea to those who ran the formatted US radio stations with, 'Play I on the R&B, want all my people to see' shows that Bob was still after the elusive African-American audience. It's a great little skanker. The flip is from *Natty Dread*.

BOB MARLEY & THE WAILERS
Jah Live / Concrete
This is the UK release of the track recorded by Bob with Lee Perry when they heard of the death of Haile Selassie. Aimed at a Jamaican audience, it was quickly deleted in the UK. (See JA (Jamaican) vinyl.)

promotional pack which contained a real hessian sack with the album artwork printed on it – just right for bringing in the weed crop!

As with so many follow-up albums, critics found fault with *Rastaman Vibration*, but it charted at number 15 in the UK and number 8 in the US.

Bob & The Wailers toured for some three months in 1976 taking in the US, Canada, UK and Germany. Island Records had by now built an impressive roster of Jamaican reggae acts, including Burning Spear, Toots & The Maytals, The Heptones, Lee Perry, Max Romeo, Justin Hinds and Third World. These were promoted separately from the company's other rock acts, the themes of Rasta and Kingston being a crucial part of the marketing plans under the banner, 'Ghetto Rockers'.

The year would close with dramatic events in Kingston. Bob and Rita were shot, as was Bob's manager, when gunmen raided the Hope Road compound, prior to the Smile Jamaica concert (see page 109).

Above: One of the promotional items for Rastaman Vibration was this hessian sack.

ALBUM
BUNNY WAILER
Blackheart Man (Island)
Blackheart Man / Fighting Against Conviction / The Oppressed Song / Fig Tree / Dreamland / Rasta Man / Reincarnated Souls / Amagideon / Bide Up / This Train

1976

Presented in a full gatefold sleeve, printed with the lyrics, it clearly shows that, artistically, Bob's production hadn't received special treatment from Chris Blackwell. The album features the Barrett brothers, Peter Tosh (on guitar, melodica and backing vocals) and a long-time Wailers' associate, saxophonist and flute-player Tommy McCook. The artwork was by Neville Garrick, who was Tuff Gong's art director. The music shows the influence of US gospel artists such as The Soul Stirrers or the Highway Qs, both favourites of Bunny's.

The album was carefully marketed in the UK using the new disco 45 format to great effect on the 'Blackheart Man /Amagideon' release which showcased the full six-minute-plus original album version of the tracks. Released in a limited edition of 1,000 copies, it was aimed at DJs and kept the exclusive nature of limited Jamaican releases alive. Bunny's music would never again reach the heights of this album's critical and commercial success. He returned to Jamaican success, and interest in the UK, in the early 1980s with his *Rock 'n' Groove* album (Solomonic) which celebrated the joys of dancehall, much as 'Another Dance' (Studio One) had done. Bunny always ploughed his own furrow and continued to pay little heed to the need to promote his own career. A return to roots music in the 1990s with the *Liberation* album provided a brief glimpse of what might have been.

BUNNY WAILER

After Bunny's departure from the group, he signed to Chris Blackwell personally, as opposed to Island. Blackwell recalled, when interviewed in 1980, that Bunny was being very difficult and demanded that he sign a contract directly with Blackwell himself containing a clause that if Blackwell should die, he (Bunny) would be free of the contract. When Blackwell agreed, Bunny apparently hesitated for a few moments and then said, 'Good, that means I can get out of my contract at any time!'

In 1976, Island released albums by Burning Spear, The Heptones and Lee Perry, so the marketing of Jamaica was a priority for the company (see Kingston Red Hot). It was against this background that Bunny's debut solo album, *Blackheart Man*, was released. Bunny took the derogatory Jamaican name for Rastafarians and turned it around on his album, which is full of deep Rasta spirituality and pride. It captured the interest of the music press and received rave reviews: to this day it always appears in any list of all-time Top 10 reggae albums.

Blackheart Man was also perceived by many hard-core fans as the true voice of Jamaica, as opposed to the rock/reggae styling of Bob and his group. The purists would continue this argument for many years. For Island, the success of Bunny's work only served to add to the critical acclaim with which reggae was now being received.

September 11, 1976

Bunny leads "ghetto rockers" set

RELEASED on Island Records this week, "Blackheart Man", first solo album from ex-wailer, Bunny Livingston.

The focal point of the company's ~~right~~

The exception is "Reincarnated Souls", previously recorded by the Wailers group on the "Burnin'" album.

Session band on the LP includes Carlton "Family Man" Barrett and Robbie Shakespeare on bass; ~~Barrett~~, drums and ~~guitar~~; Tyrone ~~keyboards~~; Peter ~~rhythm~~ guitar; H. ~~keyboards~~; plus a ~~horn~~ consisting of ~~McCook~~, Dirty

Harry, Bobby Ellis and Herman Marcus.

Track listing is: Side One: "Blackheart Man", "Fighting Against Conviction" (previously titled "Battering Down Sentence"), "The Oppressed Song", "Victory" and "Dreamland"; Side Two: "Rasta Man", "Reincarnated Souls", "Armagideon (Armageddon)", "Bide Up" and "This Train". All selections were composed and written by Bunny Wailer.

BUNNY WAILER: first solo album

Bunny caught the attention of the UK's black music press.   Above left: Artwork inspired by the inside cover of Blackheart Man.

ALBUM

1976

PETER TOSH
Legalize It (Virgin)
Legalize It / Burial / Whatcha Gonna Do /
No Sympathy / Why Must I Cry /
Igziabeher (Let Jah Be Praised) /
Ketchy Shubby / Till Your Well Runs Dry /
Brand New Second Hand

The songs were a mix of old Wailers' material and newly written work. The album arrived in a lovely gatefold sleeve that included the lyrics and lots of back-a-yard Jamaican-type pictures. When it came to presentation, Richard Branson's Virgin very much followed the Chris Blackwell template. However, a tag line was added – 'From The Original Wailer' – which appeared in all the advertising. It was also echoed on the back of the cover, where a picture of Bob, Bunny and Peter was captioned 'The Original Wailers'. The photograph had been taken in Kingston in November 1975, when the trio played together for the last time.

Peter was presented as a 'herb' rebel. 'Legalize It' remains one of his best-known tunes.

PETER TOSH

Peter, who had always recorded as a solo artist as well as part of The Wailers, was able to realise his solo ambitions through a contract with Columbia in the US, and Virgin in the UK. The album was recorded in Jamaica and mixed in New York. It featured what was essentially The Wailers band but without the involvement of either Bob or Marcia. Bunny, Rita and Judy provided backing vocals while the Barrett brothers were on drum and bass, augmented by bass player Robbie Shakepeare. Sly 'n' Robbie would later tour with Peter as part of his Word, Sound & Power band. Also featured were new Bob Marley & The Wailers band members Al Anderson and Tyrone Downey.

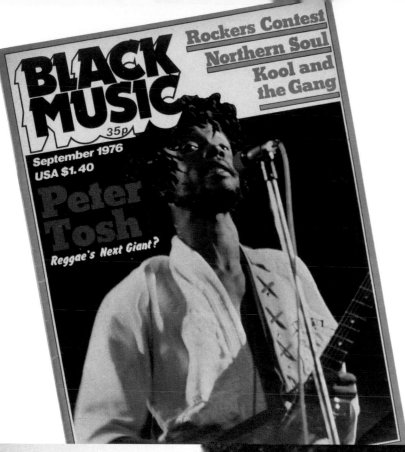

The album undoubtedly added to the growing interest in Rasta, especially tin he militant weed-smoker vibe. Tosh's 'Legalize It' has remained a herb anthem to this day. Overall, the album didn't attract the crossover market and it set a course for Tosh's career that never reached the mass market in the way he wanted it to. Despite some fabulous high points on future albums ('Equal Rights', 'Bush Doctor' and several re-cuts of old Wailers tracks) Tosh's music always fell between the markets of reggae, rock and pop. He found greater acceptance of his music in the US, and latterly in France. Crossover success almost came when he signed with the Rolling Stones and duetted with Mick Jagger on 'You Gotta Walk', but the subsequent albums were neither reggae nor rock.

WAS ISLAND BABYLON?

Notably, this period saw Island Records – and other record companies – viewed in a negative light, as some sort of evil Babylonian instrument. *Echoes* scribe Scotty Bennett (aka Penny Reel) was particularly outspoken on this issue, and reviewed Bunny's *Blackheart Man* as 'puerile slush'.

'Even down to the cover, this album has been designed for the spurious, emasculatory, impotent rock fan. Bunny Wailer has joined bro Bob as a purveyor of illegitimate product.'

The campaign continued through the decade with Bennett/Reel, now at the NME, even sporting an 'Island is Babylon' badge at various gigs to which the record company had given him tickets.

The accusations that Bob, Peter and Bunny were becoming over-commercialised were flawed. Even as far back as 1966, in Jamaica, the debut album by the then Wailers had been beautifully presented, with Bob, Peter and Bunny in a sub-Impressions-style pose on the front. The label was printed in silver ink, the cover had sleeve notes on the back and it had clearly been aimed at an international market.

The criticism of the recent output was especially harsh as the music on *Blackheart Man* is exactly the same as the Jamaica-pressed singles and the sleeve notes were written by Bunny. Jamaican music had actually been presented, pressed and packaged to a higher standard in the previous decade. It was owing to US-led sanctions and embargoes that the quality of albums and singles released in Jamaica – the vinyl and cardboard used to make and package them – had declined from the days of The Wailers' debut album. It was not some sort of anti-commercial statement.

Apparently, it had become a crime to market, support and package music from Jamaica as if it had originated in Liverpool or London. It seemed that unless you listened to impossible-to-obtain 'yard' pressings and hung about in the right places with the right people, the experience wasn't authentic. If Bob, Bunny or Peter wanted success and a larger audience, they were regarded as 'selling out'. This view, it seems to me, denies access to musicians from an impoverished Third World country the right to the fundamentals that create success in the Western world.

This entrenchment to some moral high ground has plagued the reggae business ever since. Anybody who has worked with Jamaican artists and in the Jamaican music business will tell you that its moral business standards differ little from those of the West.

The white label of Bunny's first Island Disco 45.

THE KINGSTON SCENE ON WHICH BOB MARLEY & THE Wailers became stars had strong political currents running through it. The astute Michael Manley had gone all out to woo the ghetto vote and used music as a key communication tool. As early as the late 1960s he released a single called 'It's In The Plan' by The Planners, which carried a simple campaigning message.

In the vibrant cultural Kingston of the early 1970s Manley mixed with musicians, sports celebrities, politicians and fashion models. As described in the 'Grooving Kingston 12' section, he used his fashionable, influential contacts to build support. Edward

Seaga, Jamaica's prime minister between 1980 and 1989, also targeted similar groups leading up to and during his term in office.

Bob Marley & The Wailers took part in the Victory Bandwagon concert for Manley (according to Bunny, it was because they were paid handsomely) – they were friendly with Clancy Eccles, who was Manley's right-hand man for organising and MC-ing music events. Yet Bob was very careful not to get sucked into giving any kind of official support. In 1976 he said: 'Politics no interest me. Dem Devil Business.'

Manley said of the Victory Bandwagon: 'We won a landslide in 1972. Unquestionably, Bandwagon and the protest music to be found in early reggae contributed much to that success.'

By the mid-1970s, Manley needed grass-roots support because the middle-class electorate were abandoning him. It was against this background that a major concert was announced – a free concert for the people, to be held in the grounds of Jamaica House on December 5, 1976. It was named 'Smile Jamaica', after Bob's current single. Bob had accepted the invitation to play on the understanding that no politics were to be involved but Manley was actually about to announce that elections would be held just ten days after the concert. Bob had spent much of the year touring in support of *Rastaman Vibration* and the effect of his return to Jamaica as a successful star cannot have escaped Manley.

While Bob and the group were rehearsing during the month before the concert, various threats were made that Bob should pull out, or else. Then, on December 3, 1976, two days before the event, seven gunmen broke into the Tuff Gong compound on Hope Street and shot Bob, Rita, manager Don Taylor and a friend of Bob's called Lewis Griffith. A bullet grazed Bob's chest and passed through his arm. Rita was shot in the head and Don, who had been standing in front of Bob, took five of the seven shots that were fired. Miraculously, no one was killed. Defiantly, Bob went on to play the concert in front of 85,000 people, his arm in a sling; a bandaged Rita sang backing vocals, despite her head injury.

Against the charged atmosphere of the time the attack was seen by many as political, but there were other explanations – for example, that various members of the Tuff Gong crew were involved in a horse-racing scam. So shaken was Bob by the shooting, however, that he left Jamaica for a period in exile. He also wrote a song inspired by the attack, 'Ambush'.

It was nearly 18 months before Bob would take the stage again in Jamaica.

By 1978 the violence in Kingston was a maelstrom but then three ghetto gunmen – Claudie Massop, Bucky Marshall and Tony Welch – approached Bob about organising a concert at which the two warring factions would declare a truce. Tony Welch had, in fact, been with Bob when he was shot before the 'Smile Jamaica' gig. Welch was known locally as the 'Socialist Gunman' and bought the 'Socialist Roots' Sound System and label. Men like Welch were – and still are – powerful people in the ghettoes where they controlled certain streets.

The 'One Love' peace concert went ahead in April with the help of the Twelve Tribes, a Rasta organisation, and climaxed with Bob bringing together Michael Manley and Edward Seaga on stage, in a highly symbolic three-way hand clasp. It has become an iconic image of Bob. Of course, the gunmen were on stage too – and there are those who claim that the event was used as a cover to smuggle guns: hidden inside equipment for the concert brought in from Miami. Peter Tosh also performed at the 'One Love' peace concert and his set, complete with his powerful speeches, can be found on a JAD CD.

That year, in June, Bob was awarded the United Nations peace medal. It was presented in New York by Mohmmadu Johnny Seka, the Senegalese youth ambassador to the UN, for Bob's devotion to: 'World unity and the struggle against oppression.'

'Never make a politician grant you a favour. They will always want to control you forever.' – Bob Marley.

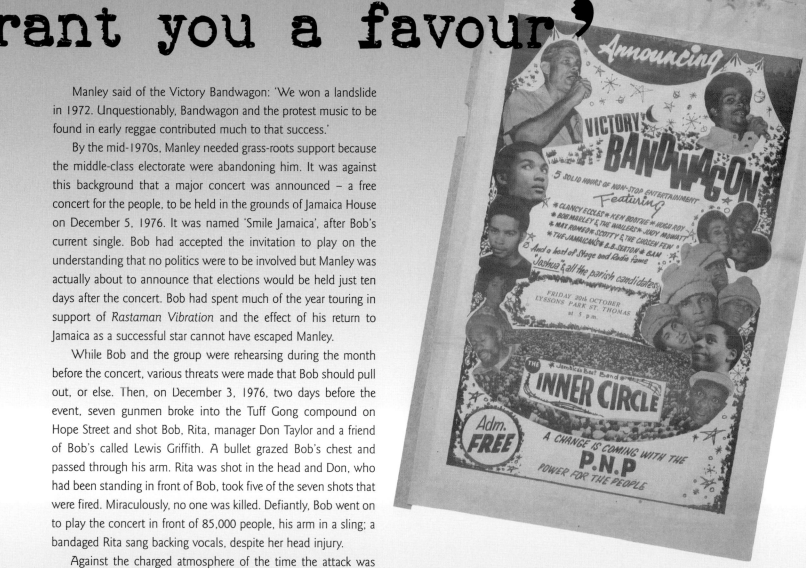

Left: Prime Minister Michael Manley used music and records to communicate with Jamaica's diverse population.
Top right: Promotional poster for the 'People's National Party Victory Bandwagon' series of concerts, which included Bob Marley & The Wailers.

Exodus, 1977

THIS ALBUM, RELEASED IN 1977, MARKED AN ENORMOUS CHANGE IN BOTH THE music Bob made and the scale of success he enjoyed. The recording of *Exodus* took place largely in the UK, using the latest studio equipment. Only a few tracks, originally intended for *Rastaman Vibration*, were recorded in Jamaica. Notably, *Exodus* included only one re-record of an old track, 'One Love.' It thus marked a renewed period of songwriting for Bob – although he included some themes and lyrics from the past, during the next five years he would produce some of the best material of his life.

The album crystallised a further development of Bob's international reggae sound, with dollops of funk and radio-friendly rock mixed in. The balance of the tracks was also far more typical of Bob's earlier Jamaican recordings, with light party and love songs as well as the message songs on which the Island albums had concentrated so far.

Again Island's marketing was top notch – it used the new, trendy 12-inch single (Maxi) format, with its longer playing time and better bass response, to take Bob's music to the burgeoning disco and club scene. This was the album that delivered British hits and built up his growing reputation in the US.

ALBUM

BOB MARLEY & THE WAILERS
Exodus (Island)
Natural Mystic / So Much Things To Say /
Guiltiness / The Heathen / Exodus /
Jamming / Waiting In Vain /
Turn Your Lights Down Low /
Three Little Birds / One Love /
People Get Ready

From the slow fade in **Natural Mystic**, a slow chugging beat blends in, with the feel of deep nyahbinghi music, but with powerful guitar pickings. The repetitive lyrics add to the chant feel: 'There's a natural mystic blowing through the air.' Bob originally recorded this track as a Dub plate special for Lee Perry, at the Black Ark in 1976, which explains its terrific reggae pop feel. The up-and-coming Black Uhuru (as Black Sounds Of Ultro) recorded a great cover version the same year. (Jammys 7/12-inch).

So Much Things To Say – 'So don't you forget, no youths, who you are – or where you stand in the struggle' sings Bob, as he remembers those who have been betrayed by people in high places, from Jesus Christ, to Jamaican national heroes Marcus Garvey and Paul Bogle. A gentle rocker, it carries a deep message about the spiritual battle that has always existed.

Guiltiness functions as a Part 2 to 'So Much Things To Say', with Bob condemning the 'downpressors': 'The big fish, that will always eat the small fish.'

The Heathen is a battle cry: 'Rise up freedom fighters, rise and take your stance' rages Bob. Musically, it's clearly influenced by Burning Spear but the guitar work of Junior Murvin provides the licks for rock heads. Its popularity on the dancehall scene of the 1990s is reflected in the extraordinary number of tunes that used the rhythm. 'Heathen Chant' (Runn.1996) showcased 24 cuts of the rhythm, by Digital B & X-Rated.

Exodus – see single.

Jamming – see single.

Waiting In Vain – see single.

Turn Your Lights Down Low – in a mellow mood Bob sings of love in a seductive manner, though Jah still makes an appearance. Sweet I-Threes harmonies enrich the vibe.

Three Little Birds – 'Don't worry about a thing, 'cause every little thing gonna be alright' is how this sweet, simple song of love and hope starts. The 'Three Little Birds' were apparently drawn to

Bob's doorstep to feed on the weed seeds discarded there! It was to be a hit some three years later. Musically, the use of synthesiser (strings) was the sort of affectation that was driving reggae fans screaming to the hills.

One Love/People Get Ready – Bob revisits a Studio One hit and delivers a version that perfectly illustrates his new sound. Simple, yet deep, with an almost anthemic feel, 'One Love' finds the band rocking and the I-Threes blending beautifully into the mix. A triumph. A posthumous hit in 1984.

ALBUM OF THE CENTURY

At the beginning of 2001, *Time* magazine named *Exodus* the best album of the 20th century. It said: 'Every song is a classic, from the message of love to the anthem of revolution.' And, 'But more than that, the album is a political and cultural nexus, drawing inspiration from the Third World and then giving voice to it the world over.'

Above: Promotional poster and advert for the Exodus *album.*

SINGLES

BOB MARLEY & THE WAILERS
Exodus / Exodus (instrumental version)
12" Disco

BOB MARLEY & THE WAILERS
Exodus / Exodus (instrumental version)
Released on what were to become the standard formats of 7-inch and 12-inch, **Exodus** firmly established Bob in the musical mainstream, especially in the UK. The song **Waiting In Vain**, was full of the powerful messages he had always delivered, but this was reggae laced with funk and pop radio sensibilities. The sound wasn't exactly Downtown Kingston but Bob was reaping the success he had worked so hard for. The instrumental was just that, a far cry from the explosive dubs starting to appear in Jamaica. Although driven by his still developing Rasta beliefs, the song, with lines like, 'Open your eyes and look within, are you satisfied with the life you're living?' spoke directly to young people in the West, many of whom at that time were feeling alienated from society.

BOB MARLEY & THE WAILERS
Waiting In Vain / Roots
Bob sparkles in **Waiting In Vain**– a beautiful song, which has its musical and lyrical roots in the Studio One tune, 'I'm Still Waiting'. His voice shows a softer side, while the music – a gentle, dipping, funky skank – would get anyone moving. There is even a little guitar solo for the rock fans.
Roots only ever appeared on this single. Using the imagery of trees, Bob proclaims himself 'the roots'. The line, 'Some are wolf in sheep's clothing' was an allusion to the Rasta look becoming a fashion statement and the fact that this style was often also a good cover for hustling of all kinds. It's a song full of Jamaican imagery, so perhaps that's why it surfaced only as a single.

BOB MARLEY & THE WAILERS
Jamming / Punky Reggae Party
12" Disco

BOB MARLEY & THE WAILERS
Jamming / Punky Reggae Party
a great invitation to get down and dance with Bob. The music is top-drawer funky reggae: he takes a slight song about dancing (and romancing) and finds a natural place in it for Rasta lyrics. Stevie Wonder's 'Masterblaster' carries the subtitle 'Jammin" in homage to this song (and to Bob).
Punky Reggae Party captures the spirit of punk London, where the cultures of alienation and do-it-yourself came together in the music. On the other hand, others (ex-punks) point out that it made a nice change to have a slow skank after all the pogo-ing – which, unlike skanking, was no good for romancing!
Lee Perry recorded this in London with members of Aswad. He took the tapes back to Jamaica and a different mix emerged on Tuff Gong / Black Ark disco 45s.

April 23, 1977   U.S. 95c/Canada 55c   15p

new MUSICAL EXPRESS

ROOTS
Trouble oop at
t'Plantation.
NME interviews
ALEX HALEY.

ROCK
RICK JAMES and
FRANKIE MILLER
wrestle with
hefty issues.

REGGAE
"Me no politica
man." Inside
BOB MARLEY'S
U.K. hideaway.

*The hip UK press devoted front pages to the
new stars from the Caribbean.*

BLACK ECHOES
TODAY'S MUSIC WEEKLY
May 1, 1976   12p

INSIDE

DONNA SUMMER POSTER

MARLEY GOES GOLD

BEFORE THE end of
their current US tour,
Bob Marley and the
Wailers will have a
gold album.

The new "Rastaman
Vibration" LP shipped
simultaneously in the States
and the UK had a total
advance order of more than
800,000. Already it is top of
BLACK ECHOES Reggae
album chart.

Meanwhile Marley and his band
have dates in America, Europe and
Britain to consolidate their growing
stature. They began an eighteen city
US trek last Friday and follow with
six dates in Europe before playing
the UK.

All but one of the group's London
dates (June 18, 18, 7 and 18 at
Hammersmith Odeon) are sold out.
In addition they play
Wolverhampton Civic
(22), Odeon Du Lune 20),
Bushton (23), Essex University (24),
Leeds University (26), and
Manchester Bell Vue (27).
Marley and the Wailers then
return to Jamaica.

● Album
review
Page 15

Photo:
ADRIAN BOOT

GLADYS AND HER PIPS
— Page 8

Mandrill monkey business
— Page 9

WIN 50 ROOTS REGGAE ALBUMS
— Page 10

Don Covay's see - saw career
— Page 11

PLUS: an interview with Oscar Peterson

Feel Them Spirit

BOB WAS A BRILLIANT LIVE PERFORMER AND CERTAINLY regarded stage appearances as essential, both to the music and his career. In the earliest pictures of the group, Bob is clearly the front man and in the photographs taken at the Queen's cinema in 1969, he can be seen using some powerful moves which he later used at stadium gigs.

To Bob, stagecraft was a vital element of the music and he worked hard to get it right. He would practise moves and get a reaction from anyone who was watching: should his hand drop this way or that? Should he hold his arm up this way or that? Like any great performer, he made it look easy but only because he put in the practice time.

In performance, Bob could transport his audiences. The opening lines from his early Studio One hit, 'I'm Gonna Put It On', are 'Feel them spirit, Feel them spirit, Feel them spirit'. The words are a calling card for the music of Bob Marley: that is exactly what he was able to communicate in concert.

Several songs in Bob's catalogue were in praise of dance and the Dub plate called 'Dancing From Within' (which became 'Jump Nyabinghi') starts: 'Love to see, when you groove with the rhythm, Cause I love to see, when you're dancing from within.' These lyrics talk about the freedom of the spirit, not just of the body.

Jamaica has a wide range of churches and beliefs that reflect African and European influences. A survey of religious groups on the island in 1942 found that of the population, 42 per cent were Anglican, 25.8 per cent were Baptist, 8.9 per cent were Methodist, 7.5 per cent were Presbyterian and 5.7 per cent were Roman Catholic. It also found a further 20 or so Christian sects with names such as Two-seed-in-the-Spirit, the Washfoot Brethren and the Two by Two.

The acknowledged power of certain individuals to interpret 'the message' was very strong in Jamaican religious life, and to this day the preacher is a key figure. There were also cult groups

with strong African traditions, including obeah men who practised white magic, and the Kumina tradition that looked to ancestors for guidance. And, of course, the growing number of Rastafari groups.

Another such religion, or 'native cult group' is Pocomania or Pukumina – meaning 'little mania' – which had a strong following in Kingston and other places on the island, though few would admit to membership. Pocomania used the Bible – especially the Old Testament – for services that were highly emotional and featured members 'speaking in tongues'. To let people know that a service was in the process of starting (which could take an hour or so), a drumming signal on handmade goatskin bongos began. At the service, people danced themselves into a trance-like state before speaking in tongues as the outward manifestation of their religious ecstasy. The high point, which might last several hours, was for congregants to 'feel the spirit'. Anyone who was there, whatever their

background, could be in touch with the spirit world. Services also drew the curious as it was, by all accounts, good theatre.

Bob's mother attended the United Church of the Lord Jesus Christ of the Apostolic Faith; these services also had strong elements of evangelistic worship. The congregation became 'possessed by de spirit' as part of their ritual. As a child, Lee Perry had attended a Zionist revival church that fused Pocomania and Baptist beliefs. He cites his experiences of Pocomania services as a musical influence. At the very least, Bob would have been aware of Pocomania: the noise from the drumming led to complaints to the police and the implementation of new local bylaws. It was another activity that Uptown Jamaicans didn't approve of.

The wider Jamaican religious experience of worship as a physical as well as a spiritual activity was clearly part of Bob's upbringing, as was the role of the individual as a messenger and interpreter of spiritual needs.

Bob feeling the spirit in Zurich, 1980.

Kaya, 1978

ALBUM

1978

BOB MARLEY & THE WAILERS
Kaya (Island)
Easy Skanking / Kaya / Is This Love /Sun Is
Shining / Satisfy My Soul /
She's Gone / Misty Morning / Crisis /
Running Away / Time Will Tell

Easy Skanking sets the tone of the album – laid back, mellow and cool.

Kaya updates the Perry track in a manner that adds little, while the synthesiser lines just don't work.

Is This Love – see single.

Sun Is Shining is an update of the Perry/Wailers hit of 1970 that is far more effective, with the I-Threes making their presence felt. The rock/reggae mix works much better. There is a Dub plate mix of this in circulation that is worth hunting down.

Satisfy My Soul – see single.

She's Gone is another insubstantial love song that doesn't quite make it.

Misty Morning, in contrast, moves along very gently and finds Bob showing just how much he can make out of something so lightweight.

(continued on page 117)

BY NOW BOB WAS FULLY INTO THE WESTERN MUSIC BUSINESS CYCLE OF ALBUM, singles and touring. He was basking in the glory of the globally successful *Exodus* and much was expected of the follow-up.

However, not everything was going well. Bob had been experiencing health problems caused by an old injury to his toe during a football game in France. Doctors recommended amputation of the toe but eventually another surgical route was found (grafting) that appeared to solve the problem …

Kaya, the 1978 follow-up to *Exodus* peaked at number 4 in the UK and number 50 in the US. It's dominated by the softer side of Bob's music and many reviews accused him of selling out. But love songs had always been a staple of his music and three tracks were Jamaican hits, from earlier in the decade, brought up to date. The Wailers – the Barrett brothers, Tyrone Downie, Alvin 'Seeco' Patterson and Junior Murvin – and the I-Threes are joined by Vin 'Don Drummond Jnr' Gordon's trombone and the horns of Glen Da Costa and David Madden. The album was supported with some 30 gigs in the US and six in Europe. There were two concerts in Jamaica that year.

Crisis tackles the theme of earthly disasters as well as praising Jah. But the music is the winner here, with the flip of the 'Is This Love' single featuring the terrific version.

Running Away marries Bob to the Barrett brothers' remarkable rhythm factory, to make a song that draws the listener in to this addictive track. It was written as Bob's answer to those who criticized him for running away from Jamaica after the attempt on his life. Often included in compilations.

Time Will Tell is a back-to-the-roots chant, as various drums (repeater, Kette and fundae) thunder and acoustic guitars twinkle. Reportedly written as a 'straight to the head' message to those who tried to shoot him, the lines, 'Think you're living in heaven but you're living in hell' take on a mantra-like feel.

SINGLES

BOB MARLEY & THE WAILERS
Is This Love / Crisis (version)
Is This Love was released as a taster for *Kaya*. This slight love song was a UK hit, purportedly written for Cindy Breakspeare his current muse and mother of one of his children, Damian. It's a great pop/reggae song with wide appeal. Meanwhile, Bob's social life was generating all kinds of excitement in the press and the infamous 'Wild man of pop' headline appeared around this time.

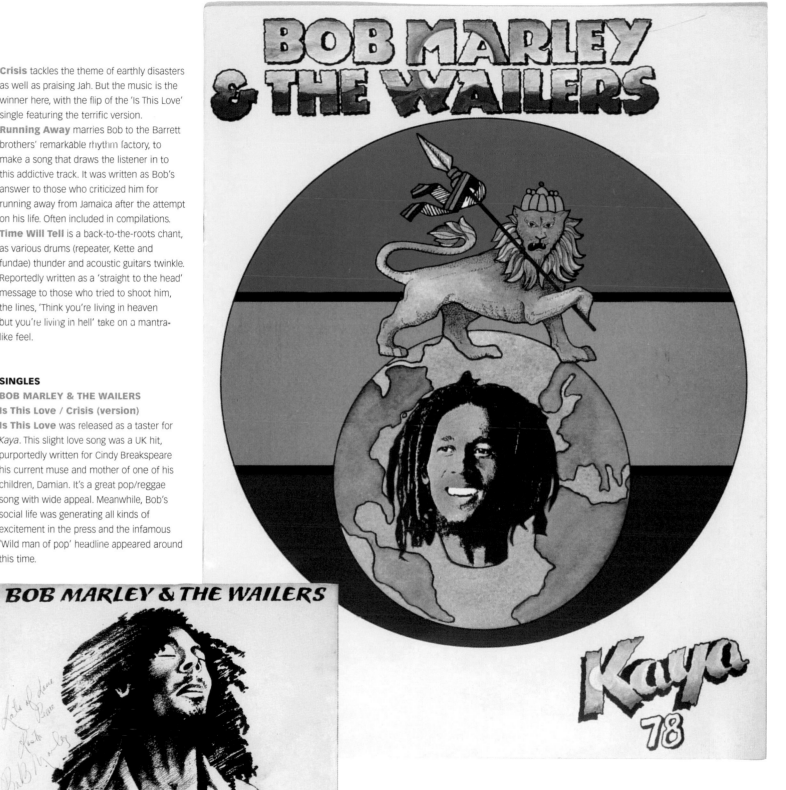

Tour programmes, promotional posters, singles in picture sleeves: Bob was now getting massive marketing support from his record company. The single (left) was signed on a record shop visit.

BOB MARLEY & THE WAILERS
Satisfy My Soul / Smile Jamaica
Satisfy My Soul is the fourth remake of an earlier track; this time the original dates back to the rocksteady era of 1968 when it was called 'Don't Rock My Boat'. Bob and The Wailers, with the I-Threes particularly evident, manage to breathe new life into this old number. It stands as a fine example of how Bob was always pushing to develop existing ideas and tracks. Here he succeeds, with some style, in making the track sound contemporary.

Smile Jamaica was the UK release of a track that Bob and Lee Perry had recorded in Jamaica some years earlier (see Discography).

BABYLON BY BUS

Taking its name from a line by journalist Penny Reel in the *NME* (the paper was the style leader and conscience for the music business of its day), *Babylon By Bus* was a live album that captured Bob and the band touring in support of *Kaya*. Chiefly recorded during their three-day residency in the Paris Pavilion in France, it was to many critics a very poor album. Unlike the power captured on *Live!*, *Babylon By Bus* was typical of the live albums put out by over-blown rock bands – just a double album of OK performances. It didn't have the elan to be a greatest hits live, instead it was a lightning rod for the 'Bob sells out' or 'He's out of ideas' accusations that were around at the time. The release was to mark a low point in Bob's Island career.

ALBUM
BOB MARLEY & THE WAILERS
Babylon By Bus (Island)
Positive Vibration / Punky Reggae Party / Exodus / Stir It Up / Rat Race / Concrete Jungle / Kinky Reggae / Lively Up Yourself / Rebel Music / War / No More Trouble / Is This Love / Heathen / Jammin'

There is little to be added to the above, except to note that the single, 'No Woman, No Cry' was taken from the *Live!* album, presumably because *Babylon* wasn't selling.

Singles taken from *Babylon By Bus*:
BOB MARLEY & THE WAILERS
Stir It Up / Rat Race

12-INCH SINGLE
BOB MARLEY & THE WAILERS
War / No More Trouble / Exodus
BOB MARLEY & THE WAILERS
No Woman, No Cry / Jamming

RECORD MIRROR
May 6, 1978 15p

Tubes special
plus colour
Johnny Rotten

BOB MARLEY
IN JAMAICA

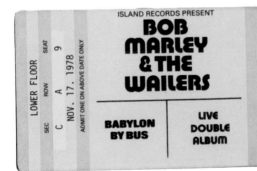

ISLAND RECORDS PRESENT
BOB MARLEY & THE WAILERS
LOWER FLOOR
SEC C ROW A SEAT 9
NOV. 17. 1978
ADMIT ONE ON ABOVE DATE ONLY
BABYLON BY BUS
LIVE DOUBLE ALBUM

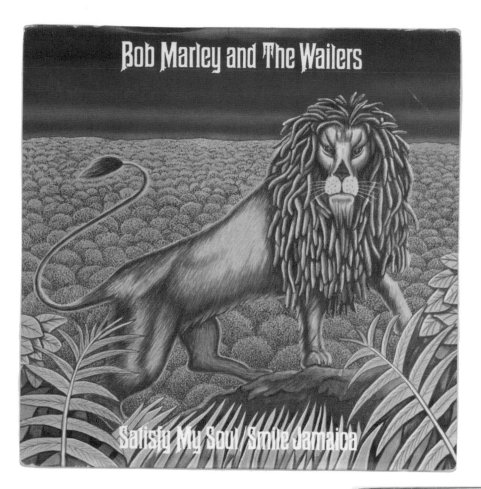

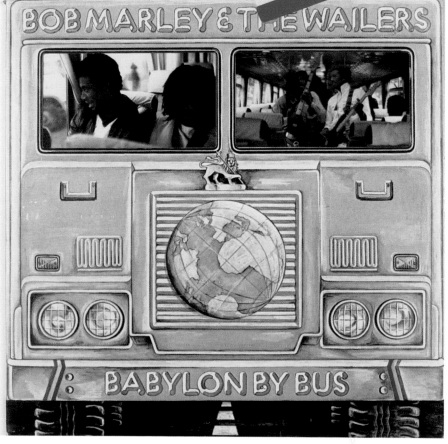

Following pages: Left and top: Bob enjoys the company of a Miss World contestant, at Regine's in Paris. Soon after, Bob was living in London with the winner of the 1976 title, Jamaican Cindy Breakspeare. Bottom: Chris Blackwell (centre) and the Head of Atlantic Records, Ahmet Ertegun (right), on the same evening.

Survival, 1979

THIS ALBUM, RELEASED IN OCTOBER 1979, WAS A MAJOR CHANGE IN direction and was the first to be recorded in Bob's new Tuff Gong studio at 56 Hope Road. Here football could be played during breaks in recording – plenty of photographs testify to this!

The songs are largely about Black history and the Africa/Jamaica link. The sleeve artwork, by Neville Garrick, is much more radical than previous album covers, showing the schematic for a slave ship surrounded by the flags of Africa. Apparently the original title was *Black Survival*. Lyrics for all the songs are once again printed on the inner sleeve. None of the tracks are re-records of previous songs. The album also credits some of Kingston's top musicians, such as Micky Bo and sax players Dean Fraser and Headley Bennett, as well as the obscure roots artist Sydney 'Left Hand' Guissine.

It's a mark of the ability and drive of the man that after years of album recording and touring (and unknowingly suffering from cancer) Bob could come back with such a strong set. The Bob Marley & The Wailers tour of 1979 saw him perform more than 50 concerts from Jamaica to Japan, from Hawaii to Harlem.

ALBUM
BOB MARLEY & THE WAILERS
Survival (Island)
So Much Trouble In The World / Zimbabwe /
Top Rankin' / Babylon System / Survival /
Africa Unite / One Drop / Ride Natty Ride /
Ambush In The Night / Wake Up and Live
So Much Trouble In The World – see single.
Zimbabwe – see single.
Top Rankin' is a plea to unite in the face of the fact that 'All they want to do is keep on killing one another'. The line is not poetic licence – the CIA's aim was to destabilise Jamaica, to which end it planned to arm the ghetto gangsters and encourage conflict along political divides.
Babylon System is another fine blend of Rasta music and international reggae. Babylon is cast as 'The Vampire, sucking the blood of the sufferers'. 'You can't educate I for no equal opportunity,' sings Bob, as there is history to be reconciled. 'Somebody got to pay for the work we've done, rebel.'
Survival – see single.
Africa Unite – see single.
One Drop has a lighter vibe and is another in a fine canon of tracks that celebrate music and passion. 'One Drop' is actually a drumming style, of which Carlton Barrett was a master.
Ride Natty Ride deals with fire as the great biblical cleanser. The I-Threes are very much in evidence, as is Lee Jaffe on harmonica. Bob recycles a few lines from 'Soul Rebel' about 'head corner stones', which only seem to confuse matters.
Ambush In The Night is drawn directly from the attempt on Bob's life. It points the finger at those fighting for power and 'bribing with their guns, spare parts and money'. The American economic policies against Jamaica meant that many spare parts (for cars especially) were hard to obtain. It's a tuff, One Drop, rhythm that sits well with the lyrics about courage and belief in the face of violence. 'Thru political strategy, They keep us hungry' was an accurate reflection of US policy at the time.
Wake Up and Live – see single.

Far right: Of Bob's passions, football came a close second to music, followed hot on the heels by women!

SINGLES

BOB MARLEY & THE WAILERS
So Much Trouble In The World /
So Much Trouble (Instrumental)
The lead-off track from the album straight away delivers a more Jamaican sound – there is much less of the rock styling and guitar solos of previous albums. Lyrically, the scope is wide with the theme –'You see men sailing on their ego trips, Blast off on their spaceship, Million miles from reality, No care for you, no care for me' – reminiscent of Gil Scott-Heron's classic song, 'Whitey's On The Moon'. Scott-Heron bemoaned the fact that 'I can't pay no doctor bill, but Whitey's on the moon.'

BOB MARLEY & THE WAILERS
Survival / Wake Up and Live
On **Survival,** the music is rather similar to 'Exodus' (probably why it was chosen as a single) in that Bob links contemporary tribulations with biblical travails: 'We're the survivors, Yes, the Black survival, We're the survivors like Shadrach, Meshach and Abednego, Thrown in the fire but never get burned.'
In a similar groove, **Wake Up and Live** is a perfect flip. Looping, funky base with tuff horns riffing away take the song into funkier territory than 'Survival'. This track features several of the Kingston musical session 'mafia'. The song's co-author is Anthony 'Sangie' Davis, originally of The Gatherers, with whom he cut the Lee Perry classic, 'Words', and again as a solo artist for Perry in 1977. Bob uses the Jamaican saying, 'One one cocoa full a basket' (little by little) as part of the lyric. This phrase is also the title of one of Gregory Isaacs' early (and best) tracks.

BOB MARLEY & THE WAILERS
Zimbabwe / Survival
BOB MARLEY & THE WAILERS
Zimbabwe and Africa Unite /
Wake Up and Live (12-inch disco 45)
Zimbabwe was one of the last bastions of white dominion over a native (black) population in Africa and in this track Bob hails the struggle of the Black liberators. Independence would soon come and Bob would be 'Natty Dread ina Zimbabwe' at the celebrations. Pop and politics mixed do not have a good track record, but this is how it should be done. The 12" disco 45 mixes also include **Africa Unite**, which follows on the sentiments of 'Zimbabwe', featuring the line 'Unite for Africans a yard' for all those in Kingston.

BOB MARLEY & THE WAILERS

ZIMBABWE

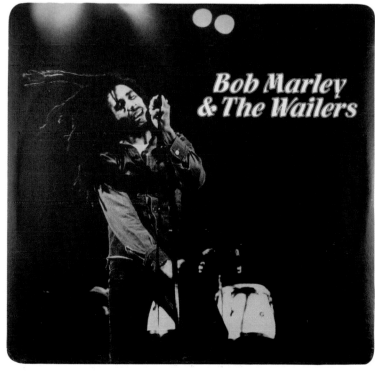

Bob Marley & The Wailers

Top: Judy Mowatt, one-third of the I-Threes, and a successful solo performer before and after her time with Bob.   Overleaf: Bob live in Jamaica, 1979, at Sunsplash II.

Kingston Red Hot

BY THE MID-1970s, POWERFUL ECONOMIC GLOBAL FORCES were putting pressure slowly, but with great strength and purpose, on the fragile, newly independent Jamaica. The US government's plan to bring Michael Manley to his knees meant that regular goods and supplies were becoming scarce. Shelves sat empty as guns were fired in the ghetto.

The rival gangs armed by the politicians (indirectly, of course) were fighting almost daily battles on the street. Max Romeo's 'War Ina Babylon' (released as 'Sipple Out Deh' in Jamaica) was one of several tunes that discussed murder on the streets. This was the beginning of a culture of violence from which Jamaica to this day struggles to recover. American policy led to the arming of what are now some of the most ruthless drugs gangs in the world. Jamaica's role, some years later, as a key link in the international cocaine supply chain further escalated the murder rate on this impoverished island.

But the British record industry was building on the success created by ska, rocksteady and reggae artists and getting involved in marketing Kingston and its ghetto artists. Island's 'Ghetto Rockers' and Virgin's 'Front Line' campaigns brought journalists, photographers and assorted camp followers to Kingston.

The companies had been signing up new and established artists, paying out advances sometimes, allegedly, from a suitcase full of readies: many artists just didn't have bank accounts. Some of these advances were worth the equivalent of £100,000 to £200,000 in today's money. However, some artists never generated enough royalties to pay off their advances.

There were many smaller labels doing business as well. The international success of Jamaican music meant that many entrepreneurs saw the island as a potential goldmine.

For visiting professionals who were joining the bandwagon, it was important to stay in smart hotels in safe parts of town. Kingston had more than its fair share of hustlers and there were people who used Rasta – with its connotations of justice and freedom – to run scams, 'befriending' visitors to take advantage.

Rasta also became a fashion statement across the ghetto and in smarter Jamaican circles. The red, black and gold colours and emblems became popular with retailers because they sold well to tourists, as they still do.

Away from the commercialism, there were deeply religious groups, such as The Twelve Tribes of Israel. They counted several top musicians as members, including Bob and I-Threes singer Judy Mowatt. She was an active member of the group and appears on the album illustrated. She also recorded, with the help of her partner and fellow Twelve Tribes member, Freddie McGregor, several artist members on her Ashandan imprint: Brigadier Jerry, Joy Tolluch, Anica Banks, The Light of Love, Ian Rock, Little Roy and Pablove Black. The Twelve Tribes ran a Sound System 'JahLoveMusik', which uniquely played only cultural (spiritual) music. Tribe members appeared for no fee and their label, Orthodox, was mainly aimed at members; several of the releases couldn't be bought generally. Bob recorded the 'Babylon Feel This One' Dub plate for them.

Bob's base at 56 Hope Road was a microcosm of cultural forces in play at the time. It was a magnet for American hippies who were attracted to the Rasta scene; there they found others who also enjoyed casual sex, smoking large amounts of weed and sitting around talking about peace. This didn't mean that the groups necessarily shared a wider belief system. A fun time was had but, like The Beatles' trip to India, things weren't quite as innocent as they seemed. It was from this period that many of the images that appear in books on Bob Marley, or on the subject of reggae generally, appear.

Above: Bob was a member of The Twelve Tribes, as was I-Three, Judy Mowatt (see photo on page 125).
Above right: (from left) Jacob Miller, Bob, I Jahman Levi and Junior Murvin in Kingston. All were Island artists and brought money, journalists and a new breed of tourists to Jamaica.

Jamaica – and Kingston in particular – was being marketed to first-world consumers as some sort of post-Woodstock hippie hangout. But it was never as simple as that: behind the idealism was a battle for power – economic and political – and the US sanctions and covert operations aimed at Michael Manley were biting hard.

These pressures were too much for some. The pioneering (and the best) writer on reggae, Carl Gayle, turned his back on music and dealt only with Rasta business. He now runs *Jahjug* magazine. He was one of several people who suddenly left the music industry. The pressure was also heavy on Jamaican producers, especially men like Lee Perry who had links to the UK. In 1977, Perry released a disco 45, 'City Too Hot', on which the anguish is audible as the rhythm beats on. The song alludes to divisive Rasta infighting, political violence, harassment from police and soldiers and the tit-for-tat mentality that ruled in Kingston. Perry burned down his own Black Ark Studio as a result of these pressures – it was to be a rebirth of fire for The Upsetter.

Right: A Jamaican magazine article from the late 1970s shows Rasta as part of the changing fashion scene.

Uprising, 1980

ALBUM

BOB MARLEY & THE WAILERS
Uprising (Island)
Coming In From The Cold / Real Situation / Bad Card / We & Dem / Work / Zion Train / Pimper's Paradise / Could You Be Loved / Forever Loving Jah / Redemption Song

Coming In From The Cold – driven by a simple, no-frills skank, the opening track finds Bob's voice sounding a bid reedy. The line, 'Why do you look so sad and forsaken, when one door is closed, Don't you know another is open' could almost be a prophetic message to those who would be left after his passing the following year. Life as a cycle is the theme, with 'The biggest man you ever did see, was once a baby'.

Real Situation has a light, loping beat with an equally light delivery of a lyric that posits Armageddon as inevitable: 'Well, it seems like total destruction the only solution'. Bob uses the neat Jamaican folk saying, 'Once a man and twice a child'.

On **Bad Card** – 'I want to disturb my neighbour, cause I'm feeling so right, I want to turn up my disco, Blow them to full watts tonight, In a rub-a-dub style, In a rub-a-dub style' – Bob sings defiantly, as he tells anyone who attempts to thwart him: 'You a go tired fe see me face, Can't get me out of the race'. Musically, the skank is a real 'dip' that worms its way into the consciousness and begs another listen.

We and Dem may be one of the tracks that Blackwell found depressing – musically, the simple skank never finds its rhythm above a slow plod. Lyrically it doesn't gel either, with lines such as, 'But we have no friends in high society' not really ringing true.

Work – over a chugging skank, Bob sings about just how much he believes in the work ethic. The reality of the man was far from the weed-smoking, womanising third-world hippie so frequently portrayed in the press. There are those who said that he worked himself to death, rather than seek proper treatment for his illness.

Zion Train finds Bob returning to the favourite spiritual imagery of a train carrying the people to freedom and redemption. The message is old but the telling of it is new and the whole band is on board.

Pimper's Paradise is a rare commentary on women and perhaps about the sort of behaviour Bob had witnessed in the music business and at

AS IT TURNED OUT, 1980 WAS TO BE THE LAST FULL YEAR OF BOB'S LIFE. HOWEVER, true to his hardworking form, he managed an extensive tour and an album. Not only did the tour take in much of central Europe, but for the first time the group went to Africa. It was on the last leg of the tour, in the US, that Bob collapsed.

The album, which was the second part of a proposed triptych of releases, again focused mainly on serious concerns. In fact, Chris Blackwell reportedly rejected many of the original tracks because they were too downbeat. Now firmly based in his own studio, Bob was able to rework various tracks and produced what were to become the hits – 'Could You Be Loved' and 'Redemption Song' – as late additions. The finished album is as strong a set of songs as on virtually any of his other albums.

The cover is full of contrasts: the front features a drawing of Bob rising up, seemingly out of the ground, his dreads almost like roots. A glorious sun is breaking over green hills in the background. The back cover has a black-and-white photograph of the band, in which Bob looks drawn and ill (which, of course, he was) and the rest of the band appear to be tired.

parties. It's not that he's saying anything derogatory – 'She loves to model, up in the latest fashion, She's in the scramble, and she moves with passion, She's getting high, trying to fly the sky' – it's more a warning about the dark side of the rock world. The I-Threes add to the light and darkness of the song with their sweet refrain.

Could You Be Loved – see single.

Forever Loving Jah – from the opening wails from Bob, this is an affirmation of faith and an acceptance of nature's cycle: 'Cause just like a tree planted by the river of water, That bringeth forth fruits in due season, Everything in life got its purpose.' The band provides a solid skank and once again the I-Threes bring depth and energy to the performance.

Redemption Song – see single.

Black ECHOES

25p

June 7, 1980

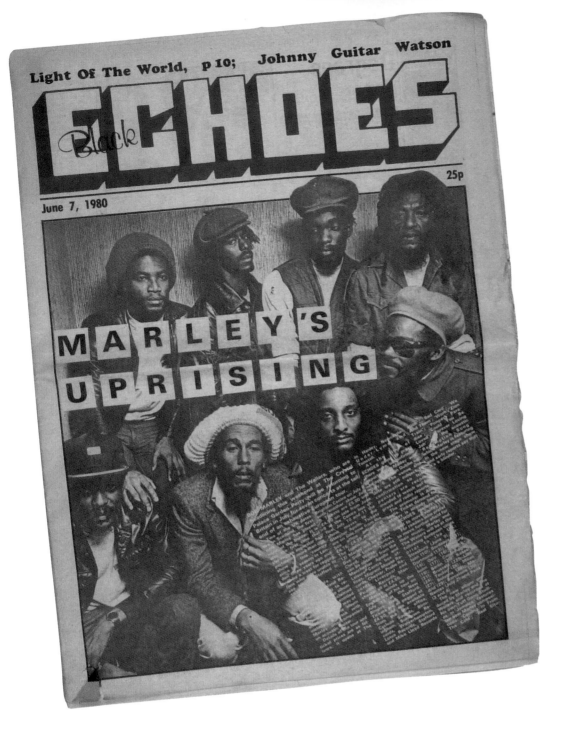

MARLEY'S UPRISING

BOB MARLEY & THE WAILERS
Three Little Birds /
Every Need Got An Ego To Feed
This track from *Exodus* was a chart hit after 'Could You Be Loved', whose popularity owed much to its use on a TV ad. The release of 'Redemption Song' after this must have made Bob's folk-reggae piece seem all the more strange. The flip is simply an instrumental of 'Pimpers Paradise'.

BOB MARLEY & THE WAILERS
Redemption Song / Redemption Song
(band version)
BOB MARLEY & THE WAILERS
Redemption Song / Redemption Song
(band version) and I Shot The Sheriff
(live) (12-inch disco 45)
On its first release, **Redemption Song** didn't even chart; not surprisingly, because although it would virtually become Bob's signature track, it was left-field compared to his other singles. It stands as an exemplary piece of songwriting and both his simple vocal delivery and strummed chords serve to highlight its simplicity and power. The whole style and feel of the work is far more Bob Dylan than reggae song, yet Bob pulls it off perfectly. From the opening lines of 'Old pirates, yes they rob I' to the last line of 'These songs of freedom, songs of freedom', he takes the listener on a journey through the depths of human history to the belief that powerful faith can overcome man's inhumanity to both man and the planet. 'Emancipate yourselves from mental slavery, None but ourselves can free our minds' is an example of how Bob was able to write about his beliefs in a manner that opened people's minds to a religion or beliefs that they were not familiar with. Like all great songs it's open to many interpretations. The opening line about pirates is also probably a reference to those who exploited his music, without paying him, and likening them to those who had exploited slave labour. No other artist has ever had to see so much of his work being sold in shops and not seeing any return from it.

The band version of the song is also an interesting listen.

SINGLES

BOB MARLEY & THE WAILERS
Could You Be Loved / One Drop
BOB MARLEY & THE WAILERS
Could You Be Loved /
One Drop & Ride Natty Ride
(12-inch disco 45)
Could You Be Loved was the obvious single from the album. It was clearly constructed to appeal to a broad range of music buyers, especially on the disco and club scene which was a powerful force at the time. It's the sort of track that got purist reggae fans mumbling about Island speeding up and remixing and ruining the song, but it actually brought Bob a bigger fan base. Lyrically, he still gets the message across: 'The road of life is rocky, And you may stumble too, So while you point your fingers, Someone else is judging you, Love your Brotherman.' The I-Threes add to the song, taking a verse with a driving beat and with the incessant 'Could you be, Could you be, Could you be loved' chorus.

The single was backed with **One Drop** from *Survival*, with the disco 45 having an extended mix of the track and also **Ride Natty Ride**, again from *Survival*.

BOB MARLEY & The WAILERS

Following pages: Bob commands the stage in a pose reminiscent of his early days of performing (see photo on page 77) as he sings 'Redemption Song' at the start of what was to be his last tour in 1980.

STARDOM

BOB MARLEY HAD BECOME ONE OF THE BEST-KNOWN musicians on the planet. His music spoke to people of many faiths, colours, creeds and classes, reaching right across the social divide.

By the mid-1970s, the concert tours included continental Europe as well as the usual UK and US dates. Island was releasing the music across Europe, the Far East, Australia, New Zealand, South America and Africa (where pirated cassette was the medium of choice). The band toured Australia, Japan and Hawaii in 1979, and in 1980 Bob performed in Africa twice: once in Libreville in Gabon and later in the year at the Zimbabwe independence concert in Salisbury.

Playing at the Zimbabwean celebrations was a great honour for Bob, who used large amounts of his own money to make the gig happen. It was only fitting that he was present to witness the country freed from white rule, having written the song 'Zimbabwe'. However, Bob noticed almost immediately that the concert was open only to a privileged minority and the event ended in a riot as the ordinary Zimbabweans outside the venue tried to get in. Bob didn't stay long.

His touring moved into the superstar league and to ease the quality of life on the road, Bob took on an ital cook. Ital food is natural and usually organic – pure, unprocessed and wholesome – the preferred Rasta diet. Gladstone Gilbert, aka Antonio 'Gilly' Gilbert, was typical of many of the people Bob employed as his career developed. Gilly had been a regular at Beeston Street (King Street) and his love of football meant he fitted right in with Bob & The Wailers. He recalled: 'Over the time we developed a daily routine. Get up in the mornin' and we would go and exercise, we go train ... Bob was a fitness fanatic, fit for the struggle physically and mentally.' Gilly made ital food for Bob on the road and at Hope Road. As he recalls 'The blender was always running. It was mostly for Bob's benefit.'

> ## 'Money is not my richness. My richness is to walk on the earth barefoot.'
> **BOB MARLEY**

Bob's love of music, football and women kept him going on the road or while he was recording. He was eating a healthy diet, getting lots of exercise, but also consuming a large amount of weed on a daily basis. Now the band was among rock's élite. *Black Music* journalists Chris May & Dennis Morris accompanied them on part of their 1977 'Exodus' tour, courtesy of Island. They found a performer at the peak of his powers. It was on this trip that Morris took the photographs of Bob dancing with a Miss World finalist. Also at the club were Raquel Welch and Bianca Jagger, who rushed up to Bob and gave him a kiss: Bob smiled, then turned to ask, 'Who was that?'

Bob had 11 children by eight different mothers. That is the known total at present. Clearly, he was a busy boy: recently it was claimed in an unauthorised biography of Anna Wintour, editor of American *Vogue*, that she spent a 'lost week' with Bob in New York in the late 1970s.

However, Bob wasn't the only womaniser in the band – Aston 'Family Man' Barrett's tally of flings makes Bob look like an amateur; Barrett's exploits were extreme, even in the 'baby-mother' culture of Jamaican society, where fractured family units were commonplace.

Bob was renowned for his phenomenal consumption of weed: In one interview, it was reported that Bob smoked a pound of it a day, which is an extraordinary quantity. But Bob didn't use the drug as an analgesic – he used it to make more of life: there was no sitting around and doing nothing for him. 'All the wickedness you do is revealed by the herb – it's your conscience and gives you an honest picture of yourself,' said Bob.

He also shared around his success, and in Jamaica supported hundreds of people, directly or indirectly. His stardom gave him the platform he wanted and he certainly enjoyed some of the trappings of success but he was not seduced by it, despite the long, hard road that he had travelled to reach it.

Posthumous Releases

THE FIRST ALBUM TO APPEAR FOLLOWING BOB'S DEATH WAS A MIX OF TRACKS culled from a variety of sources that certainly didn't deliver the album the artwork had been created for. The artwork by Neville Garrick, long-time Wailers collaborator and Tuff Gong art director, was reportedly conceived before Bob's death. The image of Bob as St George killing the dragon is especially relevant given that St George is patron saint of both Ethiopia and England. The artwork looks particularly fine on the picture disc release.

POSTHUMOUS COMPILATIONS

In sales terms, two compilations would dominate the posthumous releases. One, the simple greatest hits collection *Legend*, has gone on to sell more than 16 million and has become one of the bestselling catalogue albums of all time. The other was a four-CD box set covering Bob's full career, which went on to become the biggest selling box set ever: the limited edition of one million sold out.

SINGLE
BOB MARLEY & THE WAILERS *1982*
Buffalo Soldier / Buffalo (dub)
Comes in picture sleeve

BOB MARLEY & THE WAILERS
Buffalo Soldier
King Sporty Mix /
Buffalo (Dub) King Sporty Mix
Came free with above for limited time

12-INCH SINGLE
BOB MARLEY & THE WAILERS
Buffalo Soldier / Buffalo (dub)
Comes in picture sleeve
Buffalo Soldier was Bob's first posthumous hit and Island made a video to support its release. It was about the black-only units in the US army – they were known as buffalo soldiers by Native Americans. Once again Bob is highlighting lost black history and interlinking the Rasta struggle into the broader picture. The 'La-la-la, la-la-la-la' chorus which appears to have been borrowed from the popular *Banana Splits* television cartoon, certainly lightens the feel of the song. Before the change governing freebies in chart rules, Island was still able to give away a free bonus remix single, after the original had been out for a few weeks. The aim was to get fans to buy the record again, so they could get the special 'King Sporty Remix' single. King Sporty was an old associate of Bob's from Studio One, and husband of soul star Betty 'It Should Have Been Me' Wright.

Above: Rita in 1971 with (left to right): Sharon, Ziggy, Cedella and baby Stephen.

ISSN 0028 6362

NME
NEW MUSICAL EXPRESS

ROBERT NESTA MARLEY
6th April 1945 – 11th May 1981
"Soul Rebel – Natural Mystic"

Bob lives!
— Rita Marley

Joseph is a fruitful bough, even a fruitful bough by a well; whose branches run over the wall:
the archers have sorely grieved him, and shot at him, and hated him:
But his bow abode in strength, and the arms of his hands were made strong by the hands of the mighty
God of Jacob; the King of Israel. ✣ King of Kings, Lord of Lords, the Conquering Lion of the Tribe of Judah.
✣ Let the blessing come upon the head of Joseph, and upon the head of him that was separated from his brethren.
— Genesis 49:22-24, Revelation 19:16, Deuteronomy 33:16

The **TUFF GONG** family.
TUFF GONG INTERNATIONAL 50 Hope Road, Kingston 6, Jamaica. Telephone: 92-77919–92-77103

LEGEND
the best of
BOB MARLEY
and the WAILERS

ALBUM

1983

**BOB MARLEY & THE WAILERS
Confrontation (Island)**
**Chant Down Babylon / Buffalo Soldier /
Jump Nyabinghi / Mix Up, Mix Up /
Give Thanks and Praises / Blackman
Redemption / Trench Town / Stiff-Necked
Fools I Know / Rastaman Live Up**

Chant Down Babylon is a gentle
reggae/pop/One Drop-style take on the familiar
theme of earlier tracks like 'Chant I' (aka 'Rasta
Man Chant'). An out-take from the *Uprising* album,
it's pleasant enough but doesn't really add
anything to previous outings on similar themes.
An earlier cut called 'Burn Down Babylon'
circulates among collectors.

Buffalo Soldier – see single.

In **Jump Nyabinghi**, from the *Kaya* album
sessions, Bob returns to the theme of dancing as
a form of praise. It all flows along nicely enough
but a Dub plate cut called 'Dancing From Within'
is a much rougher mix, with no I-Threes vocals
and only partial lyrics from Bob   it sounds much
better than this 'finished' take.

Likewise on **Mix Up, Mix Up**, the heavy
synthesisers reveal an older track, probably from
the *Kaya* sessions and it's as the title suggests – a
real mix up and probably an unfinished track
made ready for release.

On **Give Thanks and Praises** another familiar
theme is revisited in a simple hymn to Jah. It
gently bubbles and sways along, and is probably
from the early 1980s.

(continued on page 140)

BOB MARLEY & THE WAILERS CONFRONTATION

Although some compilations emerged from Island, the upgrading of CD issues of vinyl albums has only taken place in recent years. Most other major artists have had their catalogues upgraded several times in the past two decades. The internal wrangling within the Estate in the wake of Bob's death meant it was difficult to get projects approved. This situation has changed and a new era for the legacy of Bob Marley & The Wailers is beginning.

But barely a week goes by without yet another shoddy compilation of early music being released. This section will focus only on official Island releases and round up any other issues that fill in gaps. Other posthumous releases of old Jamaican material are to be found in the Discography.

Blackman Redemption was a co-production with Lee Perry, though recorded at Dynamic and Aquarius Studios. The song is about the lineage of Haile Selassie: 'Coming through the root of King David, Through the line of Solomon, His Imperial Majesty is the power of authority'. Even on the original Jamaican single, it sounds as if Perry's contribution was minimal and this mix loses the horn line (probably Perry's work) at the beginning of the track.

Trench Town is the second homage to the ghetto of Kingston in which Bob lived and worked until his twenties. The gentle vibe says, 'We free the people with music' and is an answer to the people who asked, 'Did anything good come out of Trench Town.' It sounds like a finished track from the vaults.

Stiff-Necked Fools is the nearest Bob ever came to re-recording the fabulous 'Wisdom'. Musically it's sparse and there is virtually no harmony on the track. While there are some guitar licks that look backward, the slow beat, with no horns, looks forward to the dancehall era that would rule Jamaica in the early 1980s.

I Know seems to be an avenue that was explored and left behind as a bad idea during the late 1970s. Bob sounds uncomfortable with the song's keys and the synth strings have dated badly.

Rastaman Live Up retains its Perry co-authorship but this is not the cut that was released in Jamaica, co-produced by Perry. It's from another shelf marked 'Not good enough for the album we're working on'.

SINGLE
BOB MARLEY & THE WAILERS
Natural Mystic /
HUMAN CARGO – Carry Us Beyond
From the soundtrack to *Countryman*, comes in picture sleeve.
Countryman was a film made by Island records, which explored the concept of Rasta's deep connection to the natural world. The movie was a flop. The single, taken from the soundtrack, features the sounds of the Jamaican night over the intro. The full soundtrack album, with contributions by various artists, contained another seven Bob Marley & The Wailers tracks.

LEGEND: 1982

The release of *Legend* was supported by an extensive marketing campaign by Island, with 'One Love', the first hit single from the album, released on six different singles. Among them were a special poster bag and a 12-inch picture disc and a 12-inch white vinyl single. The single reached number 5 in the chart. The dance mixes that Blackwell commissioned from producer Eric Thorngren for the US only have resurfaced on the deluxe edition CD and are best avoided.

The massive success of this royal blue album, with its avuncular image of Bob and gold lettering, created an image that would become 'Bob' for millions.

The disco 45 saw the first release of a new cut of 'Keep On Moving' which was recorded in London with Lee Perry at the controls. Musicians include Drummie (from Aswad), Cat Core and Ibo Cooper (of Third World), and the vibe reflects cosmopolitan London, as opposed to young rebels in Kingston on the original cut.

COLLECTOR'S BOX SET
BOB MARLEY & THE WAILERS
The Box Set (Island)
The set contains the following albums housed in individual sleeves with a photograph of Bob on the front and the lyrics on the back:
Catch A Fire, Burnin', Natty Dread, Live!, Rastaman Vibration, Exodus, Kaya, Survival, Uprising. Comes with a certificate of authenticity, each set numbered in an edition of 10,000.

ALBUM
BOB MARLEY & THE WAILERS
Legend (Island)
Is This Love / No Woman, No Cry / Could You Be Loved / Three Little Birds / Buffalo Soldier / Get up, Stand Up / Stir It Up / One Love/People Get Ready / I Shot The Sheriff / Waiting In Vain / Redemption Song / Satisfy My Soul / Exodus / Jamming

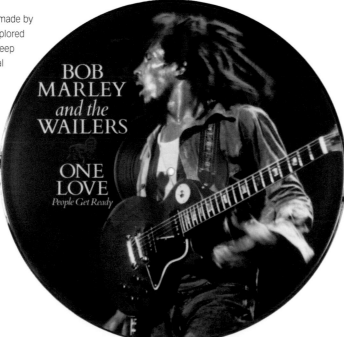

SINGLES
BOB MARLEY & THE WAILERS
One Love/People Get Ready / So Much Trouble In The World
Island IS 169 UK No 5, 11 weeks
released in picture sleeve & limited poster sleeve

12" Disco
BOB MARLEY & THE WAILERS
One Love/People Get Ready / So Much Trouble In The World
& Keep On Moving*
Island 12 IS 169 released in picture sleeve
Island 12 PIS 169 picture disc release
Island 12 PIS 169 white vinyl release
*produced by Lee Perry, recorded London 1977

BOB MARLEY & THE WAILERS
One Love/People Get Ready (Dub version) / One Love/People Get Ready & Keep On Moving*
Island 12 ISX 169 released in a picture sleeve
*produced by Lee Perry, recorded London 1977

SINGLE
BOB MARLEY & THE WAILERS
Waiting In Vain / Blackman Redemption
Island IS 180 released in picture sleeve
Island ISP 180 picture disc release UK No 31, 7 weeks

12" DISCO
BOB MARLEY & THE WAILERS
Waiting In Vain & Blackman Redemption / Marley Mix Up feat. Exodus & Positive Vibration & Pimpers Paradise & Punky Reggae Party
Island 12IS 180 released in picture sleeve

TALKIN' BLUES: 1991

Talkin' Blues was a low-profile release of the first new material since *Confrontation*. The project involved taking an interview between author, producer and journalist Dermot Hussey and Bob, and using it to punctuate the music. The majority of the tracks come from a live session recorded at the Record Plant studio in Sausalito, while the group were on tour in 1975. The group included Joe Higgs, as Bunny had returned to Jamaica after the UK dates. There also exists approximately seven hours of footage from around that time of The Wailers recording and practising in the 'Shelter' or 'Capital' sessions. This footage has never been released but excerpts from it are included in most documentaries about Bob.

Three of the tracks are from other recording sessions: 'Talkin' Blues' which has a laidback feel but no harmonica and the first verse differs from the version on *Natty Dread*. 'Am-A-Do' is a previously unreleased track which, the sleeve notes tell us, is a 'work in progress' and has been left as was (thankfully). 'I've got to do it with you again' and 'I need to feel rude' is the vibe of this funky piece, which is better than some of *Confrontation*. 'Bend Down Low' is yet another cut of the old rocksteady favourite, with the flute taking a lead role. From the *Natty Dread* sessions.

The live material is all good stuff, with the months of touring clearly paying off – the group sounds tight. 'Walk The Proud Land' makes its only appearance on an album here, as Bob revisits the Studio One 'Rude Boy' anthem. Likewise Peter Tosh takes lead vocal on his 'Can't Blame The Youth', which The Wailers never used on the early Island albums. Peter released his own version on the Intel-Diplo imprint. Finally, 'I Shot The Sheriff' is from the Live! at the Lyceum concert.

OTHER COLLECTIONS: 1992/2005

An avalanche of Bob Marley & The Wailers 'royalty free' tracks have been released and these are best avoided. Island released a *Legend* Part II, *Natural Mystic*, with even the artwork a copy of *Legend*. It failed to become a Part II in sales terms. Due to the internal issues within the Estate it has only been in the past few years that the whole CD range has been upgraded. These can be found in the Buyer's Guide section. Likewise, the whole of Bob's post-Studio One and pre-Island canon has been recently compiled on CD (by this writer) and is also in the Buyer's Guide section. Various rare and unreleased tracks emerged during this period but they can all now be found on the previously mentioned CDs.

SINGLE
BOB MARLEY & THE WAILERS
Three Little Birds / Three Little Birds Dub
Island IS 236 released in a picture sleeve

12" DISCO
BOB MARLEY & THE WAILERS
Three Little Birds*& Three Little Birds Dub*8* / Exodus*
Island 12IS 236 released in a picture sleeve
*remixed by J. Mendelson
**by Eric 'E.T.' Thorngren

ALBUMS
BOB MARLEY & THE WAILERS
1986
Rebel Music
Rebel Music (3 o'Clock Road Block) / So Much Trouble In The World / Them Belly Full (But We Hungry) / Rat Race / War / No More Trouble / Roots / Slave Driver / Ride Natty Ride / Crazy Baldheads / Get Up, Stand Up

BOB MARLEY & THE WAILERS
1991
Talkin' Blues
Talkin' / Talkin' Blues / talkin' / Burnin' & Lootin' / talkin' / Kinky Reggae /
Get Up, Stand Up / talkin' / Slave Driver / talkin' / Walk The Proud Land / talkin' / You Can't Blame The Youth / talkin' / Rastaman Chant / talkin' / Am-A-Do / talkin' / Bend Down Low / talkin' / I Shot The Sheriff

Songs Of Freedom
1992
In this groundbreaking four-CD box set, the story of Bob Marley & The Wailers was told in full. It was presented in the then new long box packaging with a fully illustrated colour booklet featuring words by Rita Marley, musician John 'Rabbit' Bundrick, Bob's biographers Timothy White, Chris Salewicz, Island publicist Rob Partridge and the pioneering ska artist Derek Morgan. The limited edition of one million copies, which sold out several years ago, is now available in a CD-size package. The selection of tracks is generally excellent, as are the sleeve notes. I will only highlight what had never been released before.

Previously unreleased tracks were:
'Iron Lion Zion' was released as a single, reaching number five in the charts. It stayed in the chart for nine weeks. 'Iron Lion Zion' takes an old Tuff Gong track on which Bob refers to Peter and Bunny – 'My brothers want to be stars, so they start tribal wars'. How much is original and how much is added remains unclear. Released as a single it was a hit not only in the UK and Europe but also in Jamaica, where it became a favourite of the number one Sound in Jamaica: Stone Love.
'Hammer' was a JAD track that hadn't been polished by the boys in New York. On a similar trip to 'Small Axe', but lyrically inferior. 'Acoustic Medley' was recorded in a hotel bedroom by Rabbit Bundrick, when he and Bob were working for JAD. Bob plays his guitar as he sings parts from 'Guava Jelly', 'This Train', 'Cornerstone', 'Comma Comma', 'Dew Drops', 'Stir It Up' and 'I'm Hurting Inside'. The final track on the tape, 'Cry To Me', was not issued at this point, but has been now. 'I'm Hurtin Inside' is another JAD track, this time a London re-cut of an earlier Wail 'N Soul 'M piece and, like much JAD material falls between the cracks. 'High Tide or Low Tide' is a previously unreleased track from the *Catch A Fire* session and is pretty lightweight. 'No Woman No Cry' is a live cut from the Roxy in Los Angeles from May 1976. On 'Why Should I' a horrible new rhythm has been given to a vocal from 1971. The I-Threes sing a complete new part, but fail to rescue this disaster. The original has recently been released and is typical of Tuff Gong productions of the time. Lyrically it's a fine work. 'Redemption Song' is a live recording from Bob's last concert, at Pittsburgh in September 1980. Bongo drums and the crowd join in with Bob, who by now knew that he had cancer.

Rita (above) relaxing at her farm in Jamaica in 1979
and (right) in London in 1978.

Remixing

NOTHING HAS RAISED THE HACKLES OF THE PURISTS more than remixing. From the release of *Catch A Fire* and the rumours that Island had remixed much of it, such actions were seen as the work of evil Babylonians who were despoiling sacred music. Of course, Trojan had been remixing, adding strings and tambourines, and speeding up various reggae tracks for years. When Lee Perry delivered his first 'proto-dub' album to Rhino in the UK, the company didn't know what to make of it, so it was speeded up and the few pure dub tracks were replaced.

JAD's plan for Bob Marley & The Wailers was to make their music appeal to Afro-Americans by getting top Afro-American session men to record with the group in Kingston and then polish the work in New York. This was not far removed from the strategy that had been so successful for Island.

After the additional production on *Catch A Fire*, it's interesting to note that Bob brought musicians into The Wailers who were able to play like the musicians used in the over-dubbing. Island's *Confrontation* album undoubtedly used post-production, over-dubs and the like to turn what were mainly work-in-progress tracks into finished songs. The million-selling *Songs Of Freedom* had two tracks on it that had been through post-production, and only the original vocal survived on 'Why Should I'.

Following Bob's death, the debate was immediately reignited by the release of *Chances Are* by Warners. It used tracks from the JAD catalogue and the skills of the then hot arranger and composer Larry Fallon to bring a contemporary sound and feel to the tracks. It sold well but did nothing amongst the die-hards to enhance the musical credibility of Danny Sims. For his part, he felt he was simply doing what Chris Blackwell had done but for a different audience. It's doubtful whether a single CD of this album would sell now as it was very much of its time.

It's interesting to note that all Coxsone Dodd's re-issues of Wailers' albums and the 'new' singles released from the 1970s have been overdubbed, particularly to give them a contemporary drum feel. The albums that Dodd licensed to the record company Calla and that have subsequently been re-packaged by CBS over the years, all contain overdubbed material.

(See 'Re-issues' section in the Discography.)

Above: Bob on the ferry to Munich in 1980.

Posthumous Recordings: An Overview

NEXT TO REVISIT BOB'S VAST CATALOGUE WAS BUNNY Wailer and his Solomonic label. On what was originally a joint project with JAD, new rhythms were laid down at Channel One studios by Sly & Robbie and Bunny. Old Studio One Wailers Junior Braithwaite and Constantine Walker helped in the development of full tracks. The voice of Peter Tosh's son, Andrew, was also somewhere in the mix. It became a Solomonic project and Bunny revoiced many of Bob's lead vocals. The first single, 'Music Lesson', appeared in the mid-1980s and got some serious London radio airplay. An album called *The Never Ending Wailers* eventually appeared several years later, in the early 1990s, but it's only for dedicated completists.

During the 1990s, as remixing gained critical acceptance with a new breed of producers and rappers, Bob's music became an obvious source for such projects. It was a popular European club hit of 'Sun Is Shining' that brought him back into the charts. The success of the Funkstar De Luxe mix opened the floodgates. JAD originally mixed a new version of 'What Goes Around Comes Around' that included the I-Threes and contributions from Stephen and Damian Marley. It failed to light up the charts but JAD did have a hit in parts of Europe with a house mix of 'What Goes Around Comes Around' by Alex Party; they then released several further remixes of old JAD material as dance singles. JAD also released the Soul Almighty album on which various old Marley JAD tracks were 'restored' with a contemporary feel by producer Joe Venneri and Marley historian Roger Steffens. Using the then new technology of ECDs (enhanced CDs) the listener could put the disc into their computer and hear the tracks before and after the work.

Island, meanwhile, looked to Jamaica and got some up-and-coming artists to revisit some of Bob's tracks. These can be found on a Sly & Robbie CD (*Hail Up The Taxi*, 1995), featuring Beenie Man and Luciano with 'Crazy Baldheads' and Beenie Man again on 'No Mama No Cry', a version of 'No Woman No Cry'. These are just a few of many such tracks that emerged from a period in Jamaica, when Bob's music could be heard at many Sound dances.

In 1997, Bill Laswell released a remix project called *Dreams of Freedom – Ambient Translations of Bob Marley In Dub*, and while the concept was worth a go, the choice of the ageing Laswell to twiddle the knobs reflected the fact that Island was continuing to lose touch with music's cutting edge. The 'Chill Out' movement might have provided a younger, more interesting vibe.

At these latest developmemts, purists were in bits and musos bored to tears.

Out of Island/Def Jam in the US came the next major project, *Chant Down Babylon*, in which Bob meets the new rap heroes on the block, led by the then queen of rap crossover, Lauryn Hill. Under the supervision of Stephen Marley, the involvement of the likes of Erykah Badu, Chuck D, Guru, Busta Rhymes, The Roots and old rockers Steven Tyler and Joe Perry meant that this high-profile project brought Bob's music to a whole new audience. There were no big hits but the novelty of Hill singing with the deceased father of her soon-to-be husband, Rohan Marley, on 'Turn The Lights Down Low' attracted radio play. However, it wasn't the commercial success they had hoped for.

Aside from the big budget and hype of the majors, the London-based indie label Fashion Records issued a brace of disco 45s that used the Island cut of *Natural Mystic* as a basis: Mykal Roze's 'I Love King Selassie' and Donna V's 'Prophecy Revealing' showed how you could recycle the past with respect and create something of interest, beyond the fact that it had a Bob Marley sample.

In the mid-1990s, 'Keep On Moving' and 'Pimpers Paradise' were given the remix treatment by I Kiano and T Wyatt and a one-off single emerged in the UK and Jamaica. It sank without trace.

These days there always seems to be some remix floating around – the technology for such projects is cheap and easy. The last single I bought had Elvis Presley singing 'Crying In The Chapel' over the Tuff Gong 'Satisfy My Soul Jah Jah' rhythm! It was a bootleg, complete with a Photoshopped sleeve picture of Elvis with dreads!

Bob Marley: His Musical Legacy

THE HISTORY OF BOB MARLEY, AS TOLD THROUGH THE years, has often been confused or ill-informed, and the roles of many key players in his story have been distorted, so that some figures acquire iconic and pivotal status and others are often overlooked or even vilified. The story of Bob Marley's *music* at least shows the full depth of his career and sheds some light on this talented, ambitious, passionate man.

Unlike some involved in the Caribbean music business, Bob readily accepted the importance of the whole commercial side of the venture – PR/marketing/touring. To quote from Joshie Jo Armstead, Bob was able to turn 'stumbling blocks into steppin' stones', whilst others saw the blocks as a series of traps laid by the Babylon West. Bob realized that as musicians like himself 'climbed the ladder' to the top rung in Jamaica, this gave access only to the bottom rung of the West's ladder. After years in the business and having been a celebrity in Kingston, he moved forward by travelling in the back of cold vans and playing in venues like the 'Cat's Whiskers' in Leeds. He did what all the rock bands at Island were doing – going out on the road, staying in cheap accommodation and sticking to punishing schedules – to build a fan base.

Like Ray Charles and Sam Cooke, Marley not only broke down barriers but took control of his publishing and worked from his own studio. And like these two giants of Soul, he took criticism from all sides, as he carved out for himself a place on the world's stage. Bob was part of the first generation of Jamaicans to whom Independence gave new hope. He was similar to one of his own heroes, Mr James Brown, in that he was certainly the hardest-working man in reggae. Like Charles, Cooke and Brown, he demanded commitment and the highest standards from those who worked with him.

If you look over his career, Bob Marley consistently wrote and recorded great songs year after year from 1964 onwards. Bob Marley's songwriting skills enabled him to speak to millions of people in an inclusive way. He learned from and developed with all the musicians, singers and producers he worked with. He knew that success was the result of hard graft, not just good luck. Bob often faced potential problems in his career, but he always chose to look to the future and believe in his power to move forward, while remaining true to himself. As a prophet his message must be that the future is yours to build, the past is for knowledge and power.

Bob Marley achieved his success largely without the help of the growing TV media; in fact he made very few television appearances. His career was all about records and concerts; his music spread by word of mouth and C90 tapes right across the globe and became the soundtrack to a generation of young people who backpacked around the world.

Bob Marley was not the best singer in Jamaica and he was an average guitar player, yet he managed to become the first worldwide music star from a 'Third World' ghetto. His story is that of determination to find success and to remain faithful to his own strong beliefs. He always found a way to respond to setbacks in a positive manner, and to deal with an imperfect world. He used his beliefs and passion to interact with the world, not just to attack or complain. He understood the transforming power of music and became a shaman-like figure in the global village. The vast appeal of his music endures to this day.

I leave the last words to Bob's brilliant and devoted
backing singers, The I-Threes:

RITA MARLEY:
'We recognise Bob as David. Just as how David had his harp, Bob had his guitar. The songs of Bob are Psalms now put to music.'

JUDY MOWATT:
'We should all try to live the life he sang about and I am hoping that entertainers like myself will maintain the standard that he has left, so that Bob in his spiritual realms will see that his work was not in vain.'

MARCIA GRIFFITHS:
'He came for a purpose and set a foundation for all of us and we can only use that to make ourselves better.'

All quotations May 1981, from a Bob Marley special in the
Jamaican Gleaner.

DISCOGRAPHY

Left: Bob with acoustic guitar in Kingston, 1971.

Users' guide

Each vinyl entry is taken from the record label:

Bob Marley & The Wailers – Jah Live /
Bob Marley & The Wailers – Concrete
Tuff Gong BM 2556 A/B

Each entry has the artist and the title of the 'A' side followed by the 'B' side. If the 'B' side is in brackets, it's a non-Wailers track. The third line indicates the imprint (label) name and is followed by the matrix number: so above it's Tuff Gong and BM 2556A/B. If the first matrix number is followed by an '&' and another number this means that there is an alternative set of stampers, but the music is the same. Any alternative mix of the same track will have a separate entry.

Matrix Numbers: The letters (e.g. BM) that start each matrix number signify who paid for the 'stamper' to be made. This was usually the person who was the 'producer' of the track or session, as in the film sense. Just as with film, there may be a 'director' who actually is responsible for the creative input into the record. These people may be one and the same person, or not. On the right is a guide to matrix numbers and the initials on them.
A further code such as 'DYNA' or 'DSR' may also appear in the matrix number: this indicates where the stamper was created (see right).
For UK entries the catalogue number is listed, not the matrix number.

Track Names: Occasionally, tracks will have more than one name by which they are known. This is because:

(i) The track may have become successful as a (pre-release) Dub plate on which no title was written: e.g. 'Satisfy My Soul Jah Jah' is still called 'Power & More Power' from its Dub plate days.
(ii) Its name may have changed between single and album release: e.g. 'Christmas Is Here' became 'Sound The Trumpet' when released on a various artists album.
(iii) Its name may have changed when it was released at a later date: e.g. 'Funeral' became 'Burial' when reissued some two years later (iv) The track was released under different names in JA & the UK: e.g. 'Burnin' and Lootin' from the 'Burnin'' album appeared as 'Curfew' in JA.
(v) The track may only ever have appeared as a blank single: e.g. 'Fire Fire' is also known as 'Babylon's Burnin''.
(vi) The name may have changed as second or third pressings were made, as a song became popular: e.g. 'Who Is Mr Brown?' became 'Who's Mr Brown?' then became 'Mr Brown'.
Just to add to the difficulty, Bob, Peter & Bunny frequently re-cut tunes. Thus 'Bend Down Low' appeared five times: Wail 'N Soul 'M, JAD, Upsetter, Black Ark ('Natty Dread' session), and Island ('Natty Dread' album). Lyrics from songs would also re-appear in later songs. Alternative names appear in the index.

When a name appears in brackets after a song title, it's the label on which that track originally appeared.

Matrix Numbers Codes:

DSR & DYNA = stampers created at Byron Lee's Dynamic Sounds Recording company, who took over from WIRL circa 1969
F & FRM = stampers created at Ken Khouri's Federal Records
RRS & RRM = stampers created at the Chin family's Randy's operation
WIRL = stampers created at Edward Seaga's West Indies Records Ltd.
Usually a record would be pressed by the same company that created the stamper

Producers' Codes (JA):

AB = Aston 'Family Man' Barrett, BL = Bunny Lee, BM = Bob Marley,
CB = Carlton Barrett, FM = Aston 'Familyman' Barrett,
GA = Glen Adams, KG = KG Records, believed to be Ken Garrison,
LK = Leslie Kong, LP = Lee Perry, NL = Neville Livingston aka
Bunny Wailer, PT = Peter Tosh, RM = Rita Marley,
SC = Alan 'Skill' Cole, TG = Tuff Gong, TP = Ted Powder,
Upsetter = Lee Perry, VR = Not known
Studio One (1) used many matrix codes, including;
C Dod, C Dodd, CN, CS, CS Dodd, FC, FCD, WC

Producers' Codes (UK):

BU = Bullet Records (Pama), ILPS = Island, GPW = Graham P Walker (Trojan),
TBL / TTL = Trojan (LP), TR / TMX = Trojan, WIP = Island
Some of these are to be found on JA pressed records as the stampers made their way there, usually with Mr Perry.

A note to collectors

The scope of this book

I have very deliberately focused on all Jamaican and UK releases, only including the US when on different labels from the UK and likewise Canadian. Barbados is included for its 'Tuff Gong' connection.

Island Records released Bob's material all around the globe and it is for another book to document those. It seems that, with the odd promotional release aside, that all Island releases were the same the world over – and that means the US, Canada, Brazil, France, Germany, Canada, Holland, Spain, Mexico etc.

I have not included the hundreds of albums that merely recycle all the same old tracks or even the CDs that have come out of Japan that do contain the odd rarity, as most are low-fi and certainly aren't official. I have also avoided the many CDs and albums of Bob Marley live as they are the subject of another book and are also all bootlegs – which deserve no publicity.

Collecting original vinyl

For those of you who collect original vinyl, please forgive me if I state the obvious.

Reggae records in Jamaica were pressed up in every number, from 20 to 20,000, and so it is with The Wailers. Some tunes, like 'Duppy Conqueror' or 'Mr Brown' or 'Trench Town Rock' were huge hits in Jamaica and sold 20,000 copies plus whilst others seem to have only been pressed up once in a run of 50 copies. Prices for quality JA singles start at around £10 (US$18) but go up to £1,000 (US$1,800) plus for the rarest tunes, such as 'Selassie Is The Chapel' or 'Diamond Baby' – but there are many in the £20 (US$36) to £50 (US$90) range.

Prices for UK-produced records are generally much better value, as the numbers pressed were higher. Top price goes for 'Judge Not' at something around £200 (US$365). Bob's chart tunes on Island can still be had for 50p (US$1)!

The basic rules for collecting are;

1. Decide what you want to collect. i.e. Jamaican, UK, US, World Wide, 7" /12" / Albums / Coloured vinyl. It is really best to avoid the endless compilations as they were sold in huge numbers and add nothing to the Bob Marley story.

2. Decide what condition you are willing to accept. Remember that grading for JA pressings is not like the UK or US and that many reggae records saw heavy active service on the decks and there was a tendency for owners to scrawl, scribble and otherwise adorn labels. Unsurprisingly 'mint' JA tunes – that is a good pressing, with clean labels – really do fetch a big premium, as they are rare.

3. Be sure of what you are buying. If you buy Studio One (1) the matrix numbers and label names are the same for the originals and some re-presses, with only label colourways differing, and for obvious reasons list writers may not make this clear. This also applies to Tuff Gong re-presses, where sometimes it's a matter of looking for the right address. *Caveat emptor.*

4. If buying from the web, eBay for instance, don't believe what's written. Check it out in this book – I'm sure people believe that they are selling 'originals' as they look 'old' and 'Jamaican' but could easily be re-presses from last week. The 'silkscreen' cover issue of *The Wailing Wailers* is frequently advertised as being the original pressing; it's actually a re-press from 1975 but still sells for £70-£120 (US$130-US$220). A real first pressing of *Wailing Wailers* will cost well over £1,500 (US$2,700).

5. Prices go DOWN, as well as up. Like everything else, tunes go in and out of favour and prices can vary enormously over a short period. Also a box of tunes turning up in a warehouse can deflate the price of a tune very quickly. The numbers of people buying worldwide is not that great – a 'thin market'– so if you are intending to buy as an investment – don't!

I hope the fever bites. Happy hunting…

DISCOGRAPHY

UK RELEASES OF JAMAICAN TRACKS, RECORDED 1962–1972

SINGLES

Chris Blackwell's fledgling Island Records released Jamaican music in the UK, which it licensed from the Island's major producers, such as Clement Coxsone Dodd, Leslie Kong and Bunny Lee, which meant that Island had nothing to do with the artists featured on the records that they released. This was also true for the other entrepreneurs who released Jamaican music, such as Rita & Benny and their 'Ska Beat' label.
Blackwell released music of all types from Jamaica, from gospel to comedy. His own early Jamaican-based recordings featured people like jazz guitarist Ernie Ranglin or more mainstream music by Jackie Edwards or The Caribs. Likewise, Trojan dealt with the producers and thus obtained Bob Marley and the Wailers through Lee Perry.

LESLIE KONG'S BEVERLEY'S PRODUCTIONS
1962
Robert Marley – Judge Not /
Robert Marley – Do You Still Love Me
Island WI 088A/B

Robert Marley – One Cup Of Coffee /
(Ernest Ranglin – Exodus)
Island WI 128B/A

COXSONE DODD'S STUDIO ONE (1) PRODUCTIONS
1965
The Wailers – It Hurts To Be Alone /
The Wailers – Mr Talkative
Island WI 188A/B

The Wailers – Play Boy /
The Wailers – Your Love
Island WI 206A/B

The Wailers* – Hoot Nanny Hoot /
Bob Marley** – Do You Remember
Island WI 211A/B
*act. Peter Tosh & The Wailers, **act. '& The Wailers'

The Wailers – Hooligan /
The Wailers* – Maga Dog
Island WI 212A/B
*act. Peter Tosh & The Wailers

Peter Touch & The Wailers – Shame & Scandal /
The Wailers – The Jerk
Island WI 215A/B

The Wailers – Donna /
The Wailers – Don't Ever Leave
Island WI 216A/B

The Wailers – What's New Pussycat /
The Wailers – Where Will I find
Island WI 254A/B

The Wailers – Simmer Down /
The Wailers – I Don't Need Your Love
Ska Beat JB 186

The Wailers – Lonesome Feelings /
The Wailers – There She Goes
Ska Beat JB 211

The Wailers – I Made a Mistake /
(Soul Brothers – Train To Skaville)
Ska Beat JB 226

1966
The Wailers – Love And Affection /
The Wailers – Teenager In Love
Ska Beat JB 228

The Wailers – And I Love Her /
The Wailers – Do It Right
Ska Beat JB 230

The Wailers – Lonesome Track /
The Wailers – Zimmerman*
Ska Beat JB 249 *act. 'Sinner Man'

The Wailers – Jumbie Jamboree /
(Skatalites – Independence Anniversary
Ska, aka 'I Should Have Known Better'
– Roland Alphonso)
Island WI 260

The Wailers – Put It On /
The Wailers – Love Won't Be Mine
Island WI 268

The Wailers – He Who Feels It Knows It /
The Wailers – Sunday Morning
Island WI 3001

The Wailers – Let Him Go (Rude Boy Get Bail) /
The Wailers – Sinner Man
Island WI 3009, B-side matrix WI 3009B+

The Wailers – Let Him Go (Rude Boy Get Bail) /
(The Wailers – The Masher*)
Island WI 3009, B-side matrix WI 3009B+2.
* act. By Soul Brothers

The Wailers – Dancing Shoes /
The Wailers – Don't Look Back
Rio R 116

The Wailers – Rude Boy /
(Roland Al & Soul Brothers –
Ringo's Theme (This Boy))
Doctor Bird DB 1013

The Wailers – Good Good Rudie* /
(City Slickers – Ocean's 11)
Doctor Bird DB 1021 *aka 'Jail House'

The Wailers – Rasta
Put In On /
(Roland Al & Soul
Brothers – Ska With
Ringo)
Doctor Bird DB 1039

1967
Ken Boothe* – Baby I
Need You /
(Ken Boothe – I Don't
Want To See You Cry)
Island WI 3035 *act.
The Wailers

Peter Touch & The Wailers – I
Am The Toughest /
(Marcia Griffiths – No Faith)
Island WI 3042

The Wailers – I Stand
Predominate /
(Norma Frazer – Come By
Here)
Studio 1 SO 2024

(Bop & The Beltones – Dancing Time) /
Bop & The Beltones* – Treat Me Good
Coxsone CS 7012
*act. 'Peter Touch & The Wailers'

The Wailers – Lemon Tree /
(Clarendonians – Money Love)
Blank DIR CS 2002 A 1H/ B 1H

1970
The Wailers – Jail House* /
(John Holt – A Stranger In Love)
Bamboo BAM 55
*aka 'Good Good Rudie'

WAIL 'N SOUL 'M PRODUCTIONS
1967
The Wailers – Bend Down Low /
The Wailers – Freedom Time
Island WI 3043

The Wailers – Nice Time /
The Wailers – Hypocrite
Doctor Bird DB 1091

1968
The Wailers – Pound Get A Blow /
The Wailers – Funeral
Fab FAB 34 white label only

The Wailers – Thank You Lord /
The Wailers – Mellow Mood
Fab FAB 36 white label only

The Wailers – Nice Time /
The Wailers – Hypocrites
Fab FAB 37 white label
only

The Wailers –
Stir It Up /
The Wailers – This
Train
Trojan TR 617

LESLIE KONG'S BEVERLEY'S AND BUNNY LEE'S PRODUCTIONS

1970

The Wailers – Soul Shakedown Party /
Beverley's Allstars – Version
Trojan TR 7759

The Interns* – Mr Chatterbox /
(Little Wonder – Walk Thru This World.)
Jackpot 730
*act. Bob Marley & The Wailers

The Wailers – Stop The Train /
The Wailers – Caution
Summit SUM 8526

1974

Bob Marley & The Wailers – Soul Shakedown Party /
Bob Marley & The Wailers - Caution
Trojan Records TR 7911

1983

Bob Marley & The Wailers – Soul Shakedown Party /
Bob Marley & The Wailers - Caution
Trojan Records TRO 9074 released in a picture sleeve

LEE PERRY'S UPSETTER PRODUCTIONS

1970

The Wailers – Duppy Conqueror /
Upsetters – Duppy Conqueror version
Unity UN 562

Bob Marley & The Wailers – My Cup /
(Lee Perry & The Upsetters – Son Of Thunder)
Upsetter US 340

Bob Marley & The Wailers – Duppy Conqueror /
(The Upsetters – Justice)
Upsetter US 348

1971

Bob Marley & The Wailers – Mr Brown /
The Upsetters – Dracula
Upsetter US 354

Bob Marley & The Wailers – Kaya /
Bob Marley & The Wailers – Version
Upsetter US 356

Bob Marley & The Wailers – Small Axe /
Bob Marley & The Wailers – All In One*
Upsetter US 357
*as the Jamaican release but without Lee Perry's
spoken intro.

Bob Marley – More Axe /
The Upsetters – Axe Man
Upsetter US 369

The Wailers – Dreamland /
The Upsetters – Dream Version
Upsetter US 371
There is a US 'Export' press of this single that has all the
same details as above but was manufactured with a US
style large centre. The label copy is the same as the UK
release but laid out differently.

The Wailers – Small Axe /
(Dave Barker – What A Confusion)
Punch PH 69

The Wailers – Down Pressor /
(Junior Byles – Got The Tip)
Punch PH 77

1972

Bob Marley & The Wailers – Keep On Moving /
Bob Marley & The Wailers – African Herbsman
Upsetter US 392

1973

Bob Marley – I Like It Like That* /
(Bunny Gale – Am Sorry)
Supreme SUP 216
*is an alternative cut of 'Don't Rock My Boat',
with slightly changed lyrics

1974

Bob Marley & The Wailers – Mr Brown /
Bob Marley & The Wailers – Mr Brown Version
Trojan Records TR 7926

WAILERS SELF-PRODUCTIONS

1970

Bob Marley & The Wailers – Run For Cover /
Bob Marley & The Wailers – To The Rescue*
Escort ERT 842. *aka 'The Sun Is Shining'

1971

Bob Marley – Soul Town* /
Bob Marley – Let The Sunshine On Me**
Bullet BU 464
*act. Johnny Lover – I Like It Like This
(Don't Rock My Boat - D.J. cut)
**aka 'Pour Down The Sun Shine'

Bob Marley & The Wailers – Lick Samba /
Bob Marley & The Wailers – Samba
Bullet BU 493

Bob Marley & The Wailers – Trench Town Rock /
Bob Marley & The Wailers – Grooving KGN. 12
Green Door GD 4005

1972

Bob Marley & The Wailers – Lively Up Yourself /
Tommy McCook – Live
Green Door GD 4022

Bob Marley & The Wailers – Guava Jelly /
Bob Marley & The Wailers – Redder Than Red
Green Door GD 4025

Bob Marley & The Wailers – Screwface /
Bob Marley & The Wailers – Face Man
Punch PH 101

Bob Marley & The Wailers – Lively Up Yourself /
Tommy McCook – Live
Punch PH 102

TED POWDER'S DYNAMIC PRODUCTIONS

1981

Bob Marley – Thank You Lord /
Bob Marley & The Wailers – Wisdom
Trojan Records TRO 9065
released in an art
sleeve

JAD PRODUCTIONS

26 May 1972

Never actually released in Jamaica, this UK-recorded tune
was CBS's only attempt to break Bob Marley in the UK.
Bob Marley – Reggae On Broadway /
Bob Marley – Oh Lord, Got To Get There
CBS 8114

ALBUMS

No Coxsone Dodd Studio 1 material was ever released in
the UK as a complete 'Wailers' album, although tracks did
appear on various artists' collections.
Perry exploited his existing links with Trojan and the first
album of Bob Marley & The Wailers material released was
housed in the famous sleeve that has a young woman in
combat fatigues, with her battle dress open, standing in
front of a poster of the Dunns River Falls – top quality! –
every expense spared.
The album, on Upsetter, did little and soon disappeared.
Trojan passed on the offer of Soul Revolution II from Perry.
Of course once Island started to promote and get interest
in The Wailers, Trojan re-issued Soul Rebels (on Trojan) and
released Soul Revolution II as African Herbsman and
included two Tuff Gong productions: 'Trench Town Rock'
and 'Lively Up Yourself'. A year later Soul Rebels was
re-issued plus 'Duppy Conqueror' and 'Mr Brown' and
minus 'My Sympathy', as Rasta Revolution. Ah, the joys of
creative marketing!

1971

Soul Rebels
Upsetter TBL 126
Soul Rebel, Try Me, It's Alright, No Sympathy, My Cup,
Soul Almighty, / Rebels Hop, Corner Stone, 400 Years,
No Water, Reaction, My Sympathy.

Soul Rebels
Trojan TBL 126
Soul Rebel, Try Me, It's Alright, No Sympathy, My Cup,
Soul Almighty, / Rebel's Hop, Corner Stone, 400 Years,
No Water, Reaction, My Sympathy.

Although Soul Revolution Part II never appeared, a test
pressing emerged with TTL66A coupled with TTL 66B.
It contained five vocal tracks: Keep On Moving, Don't Rock
My Boat, Put In On, Fussing & Fighting, Duppy Conqueror
and Memphis plus their versions on Side 2.

1973

African Herbsman
Trojan TRLS 62
Lively Up Yourself, Small Axe, Duppy Conqueror,
Trench Town Rock, African Herbsman, Keep On Moving,
Fussing And Fighting, Stand Alone, / All In One,
Don't Rock The Boat, Put It On, Sun Is Shining, Kaya,
Riding High, Brain Washing, 400 years.

This is the Jamaican release of Soul Revolution plus two
Wailers self-produced tracks 'Lively Up Yourself' &
'Trench Town Rock'.
The first pressing has rough orange & white
labels with '12, Neasden Lane' address; later
copies have blue label.

1974

Rasta Revolution
Trojan TRLS 89
Soul Rebels album plus 'Duppy
Conqueror' & 'Mr Brown' and
'My Sympathy' dropped.
Original issue has '12, Neasden
Lane' address.

DISCOGRAPHY

JAMAICAN RELEASED VINYL 1975 – 1985

Although Bob continued to release vinyl out of 56, Hope Road during these years, increasingly it was the same as released globally. The musical trends happening in Jamaica weren't specially catered for. This was particularly true in terms of the lack of dub mixes on the flip of singles. Sound Systems were supplied with mixes, though, and these now circulate on the collectors' market. Most mixes are of well-known tracks, but there are a few unreleased songs. Bob recorded 'Babylon Feel This One' for the Twelve Tribes sound 'JahLoveMusik', a track that remains unreleased.

Bob Marley produced all tracks, unless noted otherwise.

1975
Bob Marley & The Wailers – Bend Down Low /
Bob Marley & The Wailers – Talkin Blues
Black Art. A 4861 / 4861 B
A very funky version of this Wailers standard, featuring the I-Threes and probably from the same session as Talkin Blues – which is the same cut as on Natty Dread and on the single below. It's my favourite cut of the track. Perry attended the album sessions and it seems this release was connected to him. The single could be bought in shops at the time.

Bob Marley & The Wailers – Jah Live /
Bob Marley & The Wailers – Concrete
Tuff Gong BM 2556 A/B & BM 2381 / 2382 RRS
Recorded in response to the death of Haile Selassie and produced by Bob Marley & Lee Perry. Selassie's death caused much debate and discussion in Jamaica, with some people thinking that the news was false to those who wanted to kill themselves. Typically Bob's response was positive. 'Concrete' is the version to 'Jah Live' and is one of the best dubs that Marley ever released. Comes in a yard-style picture bag with Haile Selassie on one side, and a photo of Bob on the other.

Bob Marley – Talking Blues /
The Wailers – Talking Blues (Version)
Tuff Gong Micron 6088 / Micron 1675.

The track from the Island Natty Dread album was released as a single in Jamaica with a DJ cut by I Roy on the flip, which was uncredited. It shows that Bob was still making music strictly for his home audience, though this would be the last time he recorded a DJ cut to one of his tracks.
UK reggae group the Cimarons recorded a cover version of 'Talking Blues' (Talent. 1975) and scored a Jamaican number 1 with it.

No credit – No Woman, No Cry / No Credit – Kinky Reggae
Tuff Gong TS 7830 / IS 037 B produced by Steve Smith & Chris Blackwell, live at The Lyceum. As UK release.

1976
Bob Marley & The Wailers – Smile Jamaica, Part One /
Bob Marley & The Wailers – Smile Jamaica Part Two.
Tuff Gong, 'Sun' label in red & yellow
There are five issues of this record that all look the same:
SMILE 1976 A/B – One side is the Lee Perry, Black Ark, recorded vocal of 'Smile Jamaica' whilst the other is the Harry J recorded vocal cut.
BM 3436A / BFM 1977A – as above. Neither track has been remixed, contrary to various lists.
BM 3400A/B – Both sides are Harry J recorded, one vocal, and one dub.
BFM 1977A/B – Both sides are Lee Perry, Black Ark, recorded, one vocal, and one dub.
SMILE 1976B / BFM 1977B – as above.
For the concert of the same name Marley cut the same song twice. One for Lee Perry, at the Black Ark, and once for Harry J. The lyrics actually vary between the two songs. The Perry cut is much more typical of the sound that his Black Ark studio was producing than any other track he cut with Marley.
Marley said of this single: 'I said 'Smile you're in Jamaica.' I didn't say 'Smile Jamaicans, be a Jamaican.'
For some reason 7 stampers have made the above 5 singles, which actually feature only 4 different tracks: Perry recorded vocal & dub and Harry J recorded vocal & dub.

Bob Marley & The Wailers – Rat Race /
The Wailers – Part II
Tuff Gong BM 2812 A / BM 2817
Bob Marley & The Wailers – Rat Race /
The Wailers – Race Version
Blank (Tuff Gong) AB 2951/2
The common single has the track, as released on the Rastaman Vibration album, but is a short edit and misses the last verse. The label design of a Rasta and lightning is unique to this release (see over). 'Part II' is a minimal dub, very much aimed at JA audiences.
The second single listed has the full cut on the topside and the version is a 'Family Man' dub mix with horns to the fore.
Unreleased elsewhere.

1977
Bob Marley & The Wailers – Exodus /
The Wailers – Exodus Instrumental
Tuff Gong TS 3880 A/B
Bob Marley & The Wailers – War /
Bob Marley & The Wailers – Roots, Rock, Reggae
Tuff Gong DSR 2376A / 2377B
Both are straight issues of the UK releases. No attempt was made to mix them for the 'Steppers' & 'Rockers' markets, or the growing Dub market.

DISCO 45
Bob Marley – Punky Reggae Party /
Bob Marley – Punky Reggae Version
Tuff Gong Lee Perry 2060A/B
Released in colour picture sleeve.
L. Perry & B. Marley – Punky Reggae Part of Park 1 /
L. Perry & B. Marley – Punky Party Part 2
Black Art LP 4050A/B
These are as the UK release but Perry returned to Jamaica where he remixed the track at Joe Gibbs Studio, using many of his Black Ark regulars. He managed to get Bob to re-voice his part (in Miami). The version finds Perry in full flow. The release on his own label neatly credits himself first!

1978
Bob Marley – Blackman Redemption /
Uncredited – Version
Tuff Gong FRM 6051 A /52B

Bob Marley & The Wailers –
Rastaman Live Up /
The Wailers – Don't Give Up
Tuff Gong FRM 6923A/24B &
Tuff Gong International FRM 6923A/24B

Both these tracks were recorded just prior to the 'One Love Peace Conference' and both had Lee Perry at the controls, though in Dynamic and Aquarius Studios, not his own. They both hit the Jamaican Top 5 and they were a pair of songs aimed at the nation that was, by now, in turmoil to keep the Rasta faith. The Mediations provided harmonies for the session. 'Blackman Redemption' appeared on 'Confrontation' but it was a different cut of 'Rastaman Live It Up!' that appeared on the same album. Rumour has it that far more typically sounding Perry mixes exist on Dub plate. Such reports have been known to be down to a chalice full of top grade Lambs Bread (ganja).

DISCO 45
Bob Marley & The Wailers & Ranking Toyan –
Mr Chatter Box /
(Tyronne Evans – With You Girl)
Lee's GGR 2806A/B
The ever-sharp Bunny Lee updated his 'Mr Chatter Box' by adding a then fashionable toast; typical 'Striker' business.

1979
Bob Marley & The Wailers – Ambush /
Bob Marley & The Wailers – Ambush In Dub
Tuff Gong DSR 8679A/80B
Bob Marley & The Wailers – One Drop /
Bob Marley & The Wailers – One Dub
Tuff Gong DSR 9356A/57B
Two singles as found on the *Survival* album, though the dubs never surfaced in the UK.

Bob Marley & The Wailers – Nice Time /
Bob Marley & The Wailers - Hypocrites
Tuff Gong DSR 8346A/47B
Though actually a repressing of the old Wail 'N Soul 'M rocksteady classics, this release actually charted in the UK reggae Top 5 singles!

DISCO 45
Bob Marley & The Wailers – Could You Be Loved /
Bob Marley and The Wailers – One Drop / Ride Natty Ride
Island Label 12 WIP 6610. WIP 12 6610A/B
A bit of an oddity, as it uses the Island label, but with no logo. It has a different label layout from the UK issue and uses a different stamper.

1980
Bob Marley & The Wailers – Comin' In From The Cold /
Bob Marley & Wailers – Dubbin' In
Tuff Gong DSR 1528A/29B
Bob Marley & The Wailers – Bad Card /
Bob Marley & The Wailers – Rub-a-Dub Style
Tuff Gong Bad Card A / Dubb card B
Two singles as found on *Uprising*, though the dubs never surfaced in the UK.

1980: DISCO 45
Bob Marley & The Wailers – Redemption Song* /
Bob Marley & The Wailers – Zion Express
Tuff Gong TG 086A/B
*This is the full band cut of 'Redemption Song' backed by 'Zion Train' ('Uprising').
Bob Marley & The Wailers – Ride Natty Ride /
Bob Marley & The Wailers – Ride Dis Yah Dub
Tuff Gong TGD 091A/B
Ride Natty Ride is as on the *Survival* album and the dub was JA only.

1981
Bob Marley – I Know /
Bob Marley – I Know Dub
Tuff Gong TG 1987A / DSR 2917B

DISCO 45
Bob Marley – I Know / Bob Marley – I Know Dub
Tuff Gong DSR 3161A/62B – released in full art sleeve
Appeared on the *Confrontation* album.

JAMAICAN ONLY INTERVIEW ALBUMS
1980
The Bob Marley Interviews V&N S21
Bob Marley being interviewed by Neville Willoughby, a fellow Jamaican musician (signed to JAD) journalist and broadcaster. This album has an interview from 1973 on one side and an interview from 1978 on the other. Few copies survive, as Bob made Neville destroy them all. Willoughby had sent out promo copies to DJs and a few made it to the US. They are the same interviews that Tuff Gong used on the album below.

1982
Interviews Tuff Gong RM007A/B
Bob Marley being interviewed by Neville Willoughby, with excerpts of the following tracks: Natural Mystic, Trenchtown Rock, Redemption Song, Babylon System, Time Will Tell, / Natural Mystic, Revolution, Survival, One Drop, Roots Rock Reggae, Guava Jelly, Rat Race

DISCOGRAPHY

JA Vinyl 1962–1985
The trainspotters' guide

The following listing of Jamaican releases of Bob Marley & The Wailers music is aimed directly at collectors as it is a guide to the range of label designs, and coloured vinyl, thatwere released originally.

It lists: A Side, B Side, label and matrix number and then the colour of the ink used for titles / logo and what colour the actual label is. Finally any coloured vinyl pressings are noted – this mainly applies to the Studio 1 section.

If an artist title appears in brackets it is not a Wailers track.

NPT&C = No Printed Titles & Credits

LESLIE KONG – BEVERLEY'S: 1962
Robert Marley – Judge Not /
Robert Marley – Do You Still Love Me?
Beverley's Records FLK 2338/2339
black on yellow

Bobby Martell – One Cup Of Coffee /
(Don Drummond – Snow Boy)
Beverley's Records FLK 2476/2475
black on yellow

COXSONE DODD – STUDIO 1: 1963 – 1966
Original pressings are generally those with coloured labels and logo and credits printed in silver ink. Some releases only appeared as coloured ink on white. Re-presses all used the original stampers and are mainly black print on white labels, but not always. See Reissue section for full details. Blank pressings can be found with the 'Muzik City' stamp or a 'Downbeat' stamp.

The Wailers - Climb Up The Ladder /
The Wailers - Straight & Narrow Way
Coxsone FC 6159-1 / FC 6157-1
silver on black. red, yellow & blue vinyl

The Wailers - Simmer Down /
The Wailers - I Don't Need Your Love
Coxsone C DODD II 13 / C DODD II 12
silver on black or red. blue, green & yellow vinyl

The Wailers - Tell Them Lord /
The Wailers - Christmas Is Here
Muzik City FC 6423 / FC 6407
red on white

Bob Marley and The Wailers - Do You Remember? /
Peter Touch & The Wailers – Hoot Nanny Hoot
Muzik City FC 6406 / FC 6425
red on white

The Wailers – Habits /
Peter Touch & The Wailers – Amen
Muzik City FC 6477 / FC 6478
blue on white

Bob Marley & The Wailers - I Left My Sins /
Bob Marley & The Spiritual Sisters – Just In Time
Tabernacle WIRL CS 1069-1 / WIRL CS 1066-2
silver on blue

The Wailers - It Hurts To Be Alone /
The Wailers - Mr Talkative
Coxsone CN4 / CN3
silver on red. blue & yellow vinyl

The Wailers - Love & Affection /
The Wailers - Teenager In Love
Coxsone FC 6649 /FCD 51
black on red
The Wailers & The Mighty Vikings - There She Goes /
The Wailers & The Mighty Vikings - Lonesome Feelings
Wincox WC 5 / WC6
green on white

The Wailers - Dana /
The Wailers - Don't Ever Leave Me
Coxsone C DOD-17 / C DOD-16
black on yellow

The Wailers – I Made A Mistake /
Bonny & Rita – The Vow
Studio 1 FC 6535 / FC 6538
black on yellow

The Wailers - And I Love Her /
The Wailers - Do It Right
Coxsone FC 6677 / FC 6680
silver on red

The Wailers - Another Dance /
The Wailers - Somewhere To Lay My Head
Coxsone FC 6950 II / FC 6951
silver on red

Bob Marley & The Wailers - Cry To Me /
Bob Marley & The Wailers - Wages Of Love
Coxsone WIRL CS 1175 / FC 7042
silver on red

The Wailers - Diamond Baby /
The Wailers - Where's The Girl For Me
Coxsone FC 6570 / FC 6573
silver on black

Bob Marley & The Wailers - Good Good Rudie /
(City Slickers - Ocean 11)
Coxsone WIRL CS 1176-1 / WIRL 1122-1
silver on blue or red

The Wailers - Hooligans /
Peter Touch – Maga Dog
Studio 1 FC 6574 / CSD 46
red & black on white

Bob Marley & The Wailers - I'm Gonna Put It On /
Bob Marley & The Wailers - Love Won't Be Mine This Way
Coxsone WIRL 1118-1 / WIRL 1119-1
silver on black or red & black on yellow

The Wailers - I Am Still Waiting /
The Skatalites – Ska Jam
Coxsone 1 FC 6924-1 / FC 6909
silver on blue

The Wailers - Jumbie Jamboree /
(R. Alphonso Studio 1 Orch – I Should Have Known Better)
Studio 1 CS 76 / CS 0007 ((arched Studio, with a fat '1' beneath)
silver on blue & black on red

The Wailers - One Love /
The Wailers - Do You Feel The Same Way Too
Coxsone CS 0027 / CS 0022
silver on blue

The Wailers - Playboy /
The Wailers - Your Love
Blank (Studio 1) FC 6589 / CSD 41
red on white. No early type Coxsone label has surfaced. The Studio 1 label is the later 'Flag' or 'Trumpet' label

The Wailers - Rude Boy /
(Soul Bros Orch.- Ringo's Theme)
Coxsone WIRL CS 1026-4 / WIRL CS 1007
silver on red

The Wailers - Shame & Scandal /
(Rolando Al. & His Soul Brothers - Sca-Balena)
Studio 1 CS 0028 / CS 0002 (arched Studio, with a fat '1' beneath)
silver on blue & black on red

Bob Marley & The Wailers - What's New Pussy Cat /
Bob Marley & The Wailers - Where Will I Find
Supreme FC 6767 / FC 6768
black on white

Bob Marley & The Wailers - White Christmas /
Bob Marley & The Spiritual Sisters – Let The Lord Be Seen In You
Supreme FC 6935-II / FC 6936
silver on blue

The Wailers - Dancing Shoes /
Peter Touch & The Chorus – Don't Look Back
Coxsone CS DODD 101 / WIRL CS 1535-1
red on white

The Wailers - I Stand Predominate /
(Norma Fraser – Come By Here.)
Blank DIR CS 2005B IH / WIRL CS 3145-1

The Wailers - Lemon Tree /
(Marcia Griffiths - Feel Like Jumping) or (Soul Brothers – Hot Rod)
Blank DIR CS 2002 B 1H / FCD 7340 or CS 0600

The Wailers – Lonesome Track /
The Wailers – Sinner Man
Coxsone WIRL CS 1221-2 / WIRL CS 1208-2
black on red

The Wailers - Let Him Go /
The Wailers - Sinner Man
Coxsone WIRL CS 1499-1 / WIRL CS 1208-2
black on red

The Wailers - Rasta Shook Them Up /
(Soul Brother's – Ringo's Ska)
Coxsone WIRL CS 1317-2 / WIRL CS 1264-1
black on red

Peter Tosh – The Toughest /
(Marcia Griffiths – No Faith)
Blank WIRL 1793-1 / CSD 149

The Wailers - Rock Sweet Rock /
The Wailers - Jerking Time
Coxsone WIRL CS 1534-1 / WIRL CS 1533-1
orange on white

The Wailers - Sunday Morning /
The Wailers - He Who Feels It Knows It
Coxsone WIRL CS 1438-1 / WIRL CS 1423-2
black on red

The Wailers - What Am I Supposed To Do /
(Jackie Mittoo & The Soul Brothers – Do The Bogaloo)
Coxsone WIRL CS 1748-1 / WIRL CS 1596-1
red on white

The Wailers - I Need You /
(Ken Boothe – Don't Want To See You Cry)
Blank (Studio 1*) CS DODD 122 / CS DODD 146
red on white *as 'Playboy'

Bop & The Beltones* – Treat Me Good /
(Bop & The Beltones - Dancing Time)
(Coxsone) Studio 1 DIR CS 2005 A 1H / CS 900
green on white *actually Peter Tosh & The Wailers

Peter Touch & The Chorus – Making Love /
(Soul Bros. – Voo Doo Moon)
Coxsone WIRL CS 1591-1 / WIRL CS 1532-1
black on white

Peter Touch & The Chorus – Can't You See /
Rita Marley – Time To Turn
Supreme CC DODD 64/ WIRL CS 1477-1
red on white

ALBUM
The Wailing Wailers accompanied by The Soul Brothers
Studio 1 – WIRL LP CS 1266A/66B
silver on red.
This album, and all Wailers Studio One material, has been re-pressed many times. See Reissue section for details.

WAIL 'N SOUL 'M: 1967–1969

Blanks may be stamped with the 14, Crescent Road address, some carry a printed label with the 18A, Greenwich Park Road address or with a Wail 'N Soul 'M stamp. As can be seen from the number of pressings, their first three releases were extremely popular at the time. I have credited all blanks as 'Bob Marley &', though some have Peter or Bunny lead vocals. 'Type 2' labels have the 'Wail 'N Soul 'M' printed vertically. See page 34.

Bob Marley & The Wailers with the Soul Brothers
Bend Down Low / Freedom time
Wail 'N Soul 'M C S Dodd 127/128
red/silver, black/green.

Bob Marley & The Wailing Wailers
Stir It Up / This Train
Wail 'N Soul 'M RM 45 628B / WIRL RM 3274-2
classic black/red&green&gold label – 'Stir It Up' side only
& silver/red, black/yellow, red/black, all type 2 labels

Bob Marley & The Wailing Wailers
Nice Time / Hypocrite
Wail 'N Soul 'M WIRL BM 3023-1 / WIRL BM 3084
classic black/red&green&gold label
& red/white, silver/ black, black/ red all type 2 label

Bob Marley & The Wailing Wailers
Mellow Mood / Thank You Lord
Wail 'N Soul 'M WIRL BM 3085-1 / WIRL BM 3086-1
classic black/red&green&gold label
red/white, silver/ black, both type 2 label

Bob Marley & The Wailing Wailers
Bus Dem Shut / Lyrical Satirical I
Wail 'N Soul 'M RM 45 628A / WIRL BM 3273-1
classic black/red&green&gold label

Bob Marley & The Wailing Wailers
Funeral / Pound get a Blow
Wail 'N Soul 'M WIRL 3672-1 BM / WIRL BM 3673-1
classic black/red&green&gold label - Funeral side only

Bob Marley & The Wailing Wailers
Steppin Razor / Hurtin Inside
Blank WIRL BM 3707-1 / WIRL BM 3708-1

Bob Marley & The Wailing Wailers
Play Play / Bend Down Low
Blank WIRL BM 3709-2 / CS Dodd 127

Bob Marley & The Wailing Wailers
Them Have Fi Get a Beatin' / Fire Fire
Blank WIRL Wailers 4229 -1 / WIRL BM 4230-2
Bob Marley & The Wailing Wailers
Don't Rock My Boat / Fire Fire
Blank WIRL BM 4238-3 / WIRL BM 4230-2

Bob Marley & The Wailing Wailers
Chances Are / The Lord Will Make A Way Somehow
Blank WIRL BM 4236-1 / WIRL BM 4237-1

Bob Marley & The Wailing Wailers
Trod On aka Tread Along / Version
Blank DYNA NL 524 / 526

Bob Marley & The Wailing Wailers
Feel Alright / 'Rhythm'
Wail 'N Soul 'M DYNA NL 823-1 / DYNA NL 825-1
red/white (t2), one side only. (my dream? An NL 824/NL826 Wailers blank!)
A Tuff Gong repress has a matrix 'NL 824' - it's a different (& better) mix.

Bob Marley & The Wailing Wailers
Trouble Is On The Road Again / Comma Comma
Blank DYNA Wailers 833-1 / 834-1

Bob Marley & The Wailing Wailers
Freedom Time / This Train (repress)
Wail 'N Soul 'M WIRL BM 3408-2 / WIRL BM 3274-2
classic black/red&green&gold label

VARIOUS PRODUCTIONS: 1968–1971

Bob Marley plus Two
Mellow Mood / Bend Down Low
WIRL WIRL 4443/42
red & black on pink

Bob Marley – Selassie Is The Chapel /
Mortimer Planner – A Little Prayer
Blank DYNA VR 238 / 249
Legend has it that only 26 copies were pressed!

The Whalers – Adam & Eve
The Whalers – Wisdom
Tiger DYNA DS TP 1627-1 / 1628
It's the standard dynamics 'Tiger' label

Bob Marley – Mr Chatterbox /
(The Corsairs – Good Night My Love)
Blank* DYNA BL 1991-1/1992-1
*stamped: 'Lees Records and ' Agro Sound, 101 Orange Street, Phone 26027'

Bob Marley & The Wailers – Sugar Sugar /
Peter Tosh & The Wailers – Green Duck
Blank DYNA Randys 1056-1 / DYNA Randy 415-1

Glen Adams – Rebel version /
Bob Marley & The Wailers – Nice Time version
Giant G 810B / G 813B
green&red&blue&black/yellow.c/w.green&red&blue&black/pink

Bob Marley & The Wailers – Black Progress / Version
Blank* BM 1006 /1007
*some copies stamped 'Power Label'

Rita Marley & The Mad Dogs – Give Me A Ticket
Peter Tosh & The Mad Dogs – Give Me A Ticket
Tempa DYNA RM 1478-1 / 1480-1
red/white: NPT&C
label design credits: 'music by the Mad Dogs and 'Arr. Bob Marley'

Rita Marley and The Mad Dogs – Give Her Love / Version
Blank DYNA RM Rita 1503-1 / 1479-1

BEVERLEY'S: 1970

All carry the standard Beverley's label. I have a 'blank' of 'Soul Shake Down Party' that's stamped 'Complimentary' and is the only Jamaican record with such a stamp that I have.

Bob Marley & The Wailers – Soul Shake Down Party /
Beverly's All-Stars – Shake Down Version
Beverley's Records DYNA LK 1776-1 / 1777-1
some labels credit 'The Wailers', on both sides (typed)

The Wailers – Stop The Train /
The Wailers – Caution
Beverley's Records DYNA LK 1780-1 / FLK 3104

The Wailers – Soon Come /
Beverly's All Stars – Version
Beverley's Records DYNA LK 2264-1 / 2265-1

ALBUM

The Wailers – The Best Of The Wailers
Beverley's FLK 3397A/B (BLP 001 on label)
Some pressings (bootleg?) have the photography on the back cover printed 'reversed', so black is white and white is black. (BLP 001 matrix)

LEE PERRY PRODUCTIONS: 1970–1972

There were several pressings of many of these singles, often with different label colourways or shortened titles. From the number of different pressings it can be seen that the following were all very popular singles:
'Duppy Conqueror', 'Who Is Mr Brown', 'Small Axe', 'More Axe' and 'Dreamland'.
All 'Upsetter' labels have the imprint name printed vertically.

Bob Marley & The Wailers – Duppy Conqueror /
Upsetters – Zig Zag
Upsetter & Upset DYNA 2010/09
black/white: NPT&C, & Upset - red&black/white: NPT&C
Upsetter FLP 3345/46
red/white, orange&black/white, silver/black

Bob Marley & The Wailers – Duppy Conqueror /
(Upsetters – Boss)
Upsetter DYNA 2110 / DYNA 1445
silver/black: NPT&C

Bob Marley & The Wailers – Man to Man /
Upsetters – Necoteen
Upsetter DYNA KG 2269/70
red/white & green/white

Bob Marley & The Wailers – Who Is Mr Brown /
Upsetters – Dracular
Upsetter NVM / GWP+6
brown&red/white, blue&black/white, red&black/white,
with 'Who's Mr Brown' credit: brown&black/white.
with 'Mr Brown' credit: blue&black/white &
green&black/white

Bob Marley & The Wailers – Mr Brown /
Upsetters – Dracular
Upsetter DYNA SEP LP 3014/15
red/white: NPT&C
a brown coloured vinyl press is reported, but not seen!

Bob Marley & The Wailers – My Cup /
Upsetters – My Dub
Blank Upsetter 574/73
stamped 'Power Label' or 'Produced & Distributed by Lee Perry'

Bob Marley & The Wailers – All in One /
Part Two
Upsetter & Upsetter Records DYNA LP 3332/33
red/white: NPT&C & black/green

The Wailers – Dreamland /
(Upsetters – Good Luck)
Upsetter & Upsetter Records DYNA L Perry 3770/68
red&black/white & black/orange

The Wailers – Dreamland /
Upsetters – Dreamland version 2
Blank DYNA L Perry 3770/71
some miss-labelled as 'The Hurricanes:
'Got To Be Mine' (Spinning Wheel)

Bob Marley & The Wailers – Small Axe /
(Upsetters – Down The Road)
Upsetter & Upsetter Records DYNA LP 3921/81
blue/green/white & blue/orange, black/pink,
& Upsetter Records US 357A / GPW10
black/green: NPT&C, miss-labelled as
'The Hurricanes: 'Got To Be Mine' (Spinning Wheel)

Bob Marley & The Wailers – More Axe /
Bob Marley & The Wailers - Axe Man
Upsetter & Upsetter Records DYNA L. Perry 3949/50
black/yellow&red: NPT&C & black/blue, black/green:
NPT&C

Wailers – Downpressor /
Righteous Upsetters – Downpressor version
Upsetter Records DYNA LP 4157/59
black/yellow

Bob Marley & The Wailers – Kaya /
Upsetters – Version
Upsetter & Upsetter Records GPW 7/8
red/white: NPT&C & black/green: NPT&C

Peter Tosh & The Wailers – Second Hand /
Upsetters – Part 2
Justice League DSR LP 5972/ GWP 46B
black&blue/green&white & black/yellow&white

Bob Marley & The Wailers – African Herbsman /
Bob Marley & The Wailers - Keep On Moving
Justice League DSR LP 6951 / 6933
black/orange&white, black/red&white
*some copies have the version to The 'Stingers' Preacher
Man instead of 'African Herbsman'

Bob Marley & The Wailers - Send Me That Love /
Bob Marley & The Wailers - Love Light
Upsetter DYNA Bob Marley 3176/77
red/white: NPT&C, brown/white: NPT&C

ALBUMS
Bob Marley & The Wailers – Soul Rebels
Upsetter TBL 126
black/yellow/red, red&black/white, blue/white

Bob Marley & The Wailers – Soul Revolution Part II
Upsetter TTL65A/66A
black/white, blue&red/white & Upsetter (Horizontal)
red/green/white

Bob Marley & The Wailers – Soul Revolution
Maroon LOPTTL65B / T165A
black/red

Bob Marley & The Wailers – Upsetter Revolution Rhythm
Upsetter TTL65B/66B
brown&black/white
Most copies have 'Soul Revolution Part II' labels. Later
issues are housed in SR II sleeves that are black/green and
have a horizontal Upsetter logo, and Micron as distributor,
on the label.

TUFF GONG 127, KING STREET: 1970–1974
Blanks and labelled copies, from this period, sometimes
carried a 'Tuff Gong 127 King St.', a 'Wail 'N Soul 'M
Records' or a 'Wailers Records' stamp. All labels are the
classic Tuff Gong logo unless indicated. The credits on later
pressings got shortened. As can be seen from the number
of pressings several singles were very popular: 'Sun Is
Shining', 'Hold On To This Feeling', 'Trench Town Rock',
'Screwface', 'Craven Choke Puppy', 'Belly Full', 'Knotty
Dread', 'Lively Up Yourself' and 'Roadblock'. Bob takes lead
vocal, or co-lead on the first release, on all these singles,
of which 95% were written by Bob. Bunny's composition,
and lead vocal 'Pass It On', was never released at the time.
The picture cover with Bob & Big Youth, on one side and
Selassie on the other, is from a Big Youth release in the
late 1970s – (check Bob's locks!), not one of the releases
below.

Bob & Rita, Lester Sterling's All Stars –
Hold On To This Feeling /
Lester Sterling's All Stars – Version
Tuff Gong DYNA WLRS 2148 / 2117-1
black/red, green&black/yellow, green/white. See page

Bob Marley & The Wailers – Sun Is Shining / Run for Cover
Bob Marley & The Wailers - Run for Cover
Tuff Gong DYNA Bob Marley 2208 / 2209
red/green/white, green/white, brown/white. See page
Tuff Gong DYNA Bob Marley 3174/ 3175
blue&orange/white, and on orange vinyl -
blue&orange/white.

Bob Marley & The Wailers – Send Me That Love /
Bob Marley & The Wailers – Lovelight
Tuff Gong DYNA Bob Marley 3176-1 / 3177-1
brown/white: NPT&C, black/white - on one side,
brown&black/white other

Bob Marley & The Wailers – Pour Down The Sunshine /
Johnny Lover – Like It like This
Tuff Gong DYNA Bob Marley 3361 / 3358-1
green/white - on one side, brown/white: NPT&C. on the
other

Bob Marley & The Wailers – Rock My Boat /
Johnny Lover – Like It Like This
Tuff Gong DYNA Bob Marley 3516-1 / 3358-1
red/white: 'I Like It Like This' credited to BMWs,
green&black/white, brown&black/white.

Bob Marley & The Wailers – Trench Town Rock /
Bob Marley & The Wailers - Grooving Kgn. 12
Tuff Gong DSR BM 4410 / 4411-1 (short cut)
brown&green/whitec/wgreen/white, blue/white, red/white
Tuff Gong NVM / NVM (long cut)
red/white, black/white. (long cut has extra verse)

Bob Marley & The Wailers – Concrete Jungle /
Bob Marley & The Wailers – Nice Time
Tuff Gong 5003
black/yellow, silver/blue

Bob Marley & The Wailers – Screw Face /
Tommy McCook - Face Man
Tuff Gong DSR TG 4915-1 / 4916-1
blue&green/white, mauve/white, red&black/white
& miss-labelled as 'Lovelight'

Bob Marley & The Wailers – Lively Up Yourself /
Tommy McCook – Live
Tuff Gong DSR TG 4917-1 / 4918-1
red&black/white*, blue/white
*there are two of these, one has edited credits

Bob Marley & The Wailers – Redder Than Red /
Wailers All Stars – Red
Tuff Gong DSR TG 4946-11 / 4914-1
black/white, red/white

Bob Marley & The Wailers – Craven Choke Puppy /
T. McCook & Wailers All Stars – Choke
Tuff Gong FBM 7730-B / 7762-A
blue/white, red&black/white*, green&black/white*
*has edited credits

Bob Marley & The Wailers – Lick Samba /
Wailers All Star Band – Samba
Tuff Gong FBM 7731-A / 7731-B
red&black/white*, yellow/white
*there are two of these, one has edited credits

Bob Marley & The Wailers – Guava Jelly /
Wailers All Stars – Jelly or Guava*
Tuff Gong NVM / FBM 7732-B
red&black/white, red/yellow-orange

Bob Marley & The Wailers – Satisfy My Soul Jah Jah /
Bob Marley – Satisfy version
Tuff Gong FRM 8107-A / 8107-B
red&black/yellow-orange, red&black/white

Bob Marley & The Wailers – Satisfy My Soul Babe /
Wailers Band - Version
Tuff Gong DSR RM 7163-1 / FRM 8107-B
red&black/white

Bob Marley & The Wailers – Rock It Babe /
Wailers All Stars – Rock It version
Tuff Gong DSR RM 7683-1 / 7685-1
Tuff Gong FM 7500-A / DSR RM 7685-1
red&black/white

Bob Marley & The Wailers – Midnight Ravers /
Wailers All Star - Ravers version
Tuff Gong DSR RM 7682-1 / 7684-1
red&black/white, red&black/yellow.

Bob Marley & The Wailers – Concrete Jungle* /
Bob Marley & The Wailers – Concrete Jungle**
Tuff Gong DSR RM 8601-A / WIRL BM 3708-2
blue/blue, red/white. *is the Island cut.
**is actually 'Hurtin' Inside'

Bob Marley & The Wailers – Chant I /
Bob Marley & The Wailers – Curfew
Tuff Gong RM 2266-B RRS / SCR M #12 3205-A RRS
blue/black

Bob Marley & The I-Threes – Belly Full /
(no credit) – version
Tuff Gong AB 4704 RRS / AC # 4696B
Tuff Gong AB 4944 / 4945
black/green, red/green, black/blue

Bob Marley, Wailers & The I-Threes – Knotty Dread /
Wailers – Version
Tuff Gong FCT-45-A / 45-B
rust/green, red/pink, red/yellow, black/pink, red/white

Bob Marley & The Wailers – Road Block /
Bob Marley & The Wailers – Rebel Music
Tuff Gong TG 1469/ TG 1468, & DSR BM 9602-A/B,
 & TG 1649 / DSR BM 9602-B
rust/green, red/white, black/white: NPT&C.

Bob Marley & The Wailers – Road Block /
Bob Marley & The Wailers – Rebel Music
Tuff Gong AB 4709A / 4710B
black/yellow: NPT&C, rust/green.

ALBUMS
The Wailers – Catch A Fire
Tuff Gong - 1-9329-F-3 / 2-9329-F-7
black/red. 'Dread hitting Gong' label.

The Wailers – Natty Dread
Tuff Gong – FT-TG-002A/02B
black/red. 'Dread hitting Gong' label.

TUFF GONG, 56, HOPE ROAD: 1976–1981
From this point on many of the releases reflected the
Island releases. Only the dub versions were not released in
the UK. Some of Bob Marley and the Wailers output from
this period also surfaced at Sound Systems on Dub plates,
offering different 'less commercial' mixes. All labels are the
red/green/gold classic Tuff Gong label (see page 157).
Some labels have an image of Bob's head on (BH) and
later ones have the star/clasped hands logo (star/c) – as
on page 157. Variants are indicated.

Bob Marley & The Wailers – Bend Down Low /
Bob Marley & The Wailers – Talkin Blues
Black Art. A 4861 / 4861 B
from Natty Dread sessions - 'photocopied' Black Ark label
(page156)

Bob Marley & The Wailers - Jah Live /
Bob Marley & The Wailers - Concrete
Tuff Gong BM 2556 A/B & BM 2381 / 2382 RRS (BH)
comes in picture sleeve of Bob & Selassie

Bob Marley - Talking Blues /
The Wailers - Talking Blues (Version)
Tuff Gong Micron 6088 / Micron 1675 (BH)
Version is a DJ cut by I-Roy

No credit - No Woman, No Cry /
No Credit - Kinky Reggae
Tuff Gong TS 7830 / IS 037 B (BH)

Bob Marley & The Wailers – Smile Jamaica, Part One /
Bob Marley & The Wailers – Smile Jamaica Part Two
Tuff Gong SMILE 1976A/B & BM 3436A/BFM 1977A &
BM 3400A/B & BFM 1977A/B & SMILE 1976B/BFM 1977B
All have the same label. See page 156.

Bob Marley & The Wailers – Rat Race /
The Wailers – Part II
Tuff Gong BM 2812 A / BM 2817
black/white. Unique label with a dread and a lightning logo

Bob Marley & The Wailers – Rat Race /
Bob Marley & The Wailers – Race Version
Blank (Tuff Gong) AB 2951/2

Bob Marley & The Wailers – Exodus /
The Wailers – Exodus Instrumental
Tuff Gong TS 3880 A/B

Bob Marley & The Wailers – War /
Bob Marley & The Wailers – Roots, Rock, Reggae
Tuff Gong DSR 2376A / 2377B

Bob Marley – Blackman Redemption /
Uncredited – Version
Tuff Gong FRM 6051A / 6052B (BH)

Bob Marley & The Wailers – Rastaman Live Up /
The Wailers – Don't Give Up
Tuff Gong FRM 6923A/24B (BH)
Tuff Gong International FRM 6923A/24B
Black/white - New style logo including star/clasped hands

Bob Marley & The Wailers – Ambush /
Bob Marley & The Wailers – Ambush In Dub
Tuff Gong DSR 8679A/80B

Bob Marley & The Wailers – Nice Time /
Bob Marley & The Wailers - Hypocrite
Tuff Gong DSR 8346A/47B

Bob Marley & The Wailers – Comin' In From The Cold /
Bob Marley & Wailers – Dubbin' In
Tuff Gong DSR 1528A/29B (Star/c)
red/white – New style logo including star/clasped hands

Bob Marley & The Wailers – Bad Card /
Bob Marley & The Wailers – Rub-a-Dub Style
Tuff Gong Bad Card A / Dubb card B

Bob Marley & The Wailers – One Drop /
Bob Marley & The Wailers – One Dub
Tuff Gong DSR 9356A/57B
black/white - New style logo including star/clasped hands

Bob Marley – I Know /
Bob Marley – I Know Dub
Tuff Gong TG 1987A / DSR 2917B
red&black/yellow. New 'boxed' logo

Bob Marley & The Wailers – Buffalo Soldier /
Bob Marley & The Wailers – Buffalo Dub
Rita Marley Music BMW 9762A /B
black/brown

Bob Marley & The Wailers – Buffalo Soldier /
Bob Marley & The Wailers – Buffalo Dub
Rita Marley Music RM 2-3-83 A/B
black/brown. Red, Green and Gold vinyl. Picture sleeve.

Bob Marley & The Wailers – One Love/People Get Ready /
BMW / – So Much Trouble In The World
Tuff Gong IS 169 TGX 1 A-1U-1- / TGX 1 B-1U-1-
& Tuff Gong XW0042A/B (Star/c)

DISCO 45

Bob Marley – Punky Reggae Party /
Bob Marley – Punky Reggae Version
Tuff Gong Lee Perry 2060A/B
comes in full colour picture sleeve

L. Perry & B. Marley – Punky Reggae Part of Park 1 /
L. Perry & B. Marley – Punky Party Part 2
Black Art LP 4050A/B
Black/red&green&gold Black Art label, see page 157.

Bob Marley & The Wailers with Ranking Toyan –
Mr Chatter Box /
(Tyronne Evans – With You Girl)
Lee's GGR 2806A/B
green&red/white - Lee's imprint

Bob Marley & The Wailers – Could You Be Loved /
B.M.W's - One Drop / Ride Natty Ride
Island Label WIP 12 6610A/B
has UK island label and hand written matrix

Bob Marley & The Wailers – Redemption Song /
Bob Marley & The Wailers – Zion Express
Tuff Gong TG 086A/B
comes in Tuff Gong Disco 45 sleeve, see page 157

Bob Marley & The Wailers – Ride Natty Ride /
Bob Marley & The Wailers – Ride Dis Yah Dub
Tuff Gong TGD 091A/B
comes in Tuff Gong Disco 45 sleeve, see page 157

Bob Marley – I Know /
Bob Marley – I Know Dub
Tuff Gong DSR 3161A/62B
red&green/yellow, 'boxed' Tuff Gong logo & clasped
hands/star logo
red/green/yellow art sleeve

Bob Marley & The Wailers – Buffalo Soldier /
Bob Marley & The Wailers - Buffalo Dub
Rita Marley Music BMW 9761A/ B
comes in picture sleeve

Bob Marley & The Wailers – Trenchtown /
Bob Marley & The Wailers – Dub In Trenchtown
56 Hope Road TG 12-11-83 A/B
black/white&blue, 56 Hope Road label
comes in a full picture cover of Bob, Rita and children circa
1971

No Credit – One Love /People Get Ready /
/ No Credit – So Much Trouble In The World / Keep On
Moving
Tuff Gong 12 IS 169 A/B
in JA printed, UK picture sleeve

ALBUMS

All albums are as UK and have the 56, Hope Road address.
Later pressing carry the 220, Marcus Drive address.

Bob Marley & The Wailers - Catch A Fire
Tuff Gong 1-9329-F-3 / 2-9329-F-7
black/red – Dread banging Gong label. page 79
Tuff Gong ILPS 9241A/B
some copies on clear vinyl

The Wailers – Burnin
Tuff Gong FT TG 002 A/B
black/red – Dread banging Gong label (page 81)
Tuff Gong - ILPS 9256A/B

Bob Marley & The Wailers – Natty Dread
Tuff Gong - ILPS 9281

Bob Marley & The Wailers – Live!
Tuff Gong - ILPS 9376

Bob Marley & The Wailers – Rastaman Vibration
Tuff Gong - ILPS 9383

Bob Marley & The Wailers – Babylon By Bus
Tuff Gong & Tuff Gong International - ISLD 11

Bob Marley & The Wailers – Exodus
Tuff Gong - ILPS 9498
some copies on clear vinyl

Bob Marley & The Wailers   Survival
Tuff Gong - ILPS 9542
New International style logo
some copies on green vinyl, red vinyl and gold vinyl.

Bob Marley & The Wailers – Uprising
Tuff Gong - ILPS 9596 (Star/c)

Bob Marley & The Wailers – Confrontation
Rita Marley Music - BMW 9760A/B

DISCOGRAPHY

US, BARBADIAN & CANADIAN RELEASES

There was little Bob Marley & The Wailers material released in the US before they were signed to Island and what there was received very limited distribution. Coxsone Dodd relocated his operations to New York in the early 1980s but all Studio One releases are listed in the Jamaican or UK sections, with only material licensed to third parties being listed below.

SINGLES
JAD PRODUCTIONS

This was the first attempt by anyone to market Bob Marley, as an artist, to the Western world, and was aimed at the Soul market in the US. Credited to Bob, Rita & Peter (Bunny was in jail on a cannabis charge), the single was also released in Jamaica on WIRL and in France, on JAD, with an art cover.

The tracks chosen were two Wailers rocksteady hits from the previous year: 'Bend Down Low' and 'Mellow Mood' cut in a Reggae/Soul/Pop style. 'Bend Down Low' was to be re-cut at least three more times.

1968 (OCTOBER)
Bob, Rita & Peter – Bend Down Low /
Bob, Rita & Peter – Mellow Mood
JAD J211

1981
Bob Marley – Reggae On Broadway /
Bob Marley – Reggae On Broadway
Cotillion 46023
1972 material remixed, taken from the 'Chances Are' album.

12" Singles
1981
Bob Marley – Reggae On Broadway /
Bob Marley – Gonna Get You
WEA K 79250T   features material recorded 1972, remixed.

LEE PERRY UPSETTER PRODUCTIONS
1971
Bob Marley & The Wailers – Doppy Conquer* /
Bob Marley & The Wailers – Doppy Conquer**
Shelter SPRO 6286   Promotional release.
*Mono cut, **Stereo cut

Bob Marley & The Wailers – Doppy Conquer /
(Upsetters – Justice)
Shelter P 7309

Peter Tosh & The Wailers – Secondhand /
The Upsetters – Secondhand Part Two
Upsetter UP 9001

1972
Bob Marley & The Wailers – Small Axe /
Upsetters – Version.
Upsetter LP 009
some copies credit 'Small Axe' to 'The Upsetters'

Bob Marley & The Wailers – More Axe /
Upsetters – Axe Man
Upsetter LP 3950/49

1973
Bob Marley & The Wailers – African Herbsman /
Bob Marley And The Wailers – Stand Alone
Black Heart 45-8042

Bob Marley & The Wailers – All In One /
Bob Marley & The Wailers – Kaya *
Black Heart 45-8043
*different vocal mix from JA release

1975
Bob Marley & The Wailers – Duppy Conqueror /
Upsetters – Duppy Version
Clock Tower CT 505

NB There is a single on Upsetter, 'Cross The Nation', credited to Bob Marley & The Wailers that is actually by Little Roy

12" SINGLES

Two tracks that were originally cut for Dub plate only surfaced via the short-lived 'Disco' label. Both tracks were cut at the Black Ark, with Lee Perry at the controls and feature his early work with drum machines, from 1975/6.

1983
Bob Marley & The Wailers – Rainbow Country /
Bob Marley & The Wailers – Rhythm Track
Disco 101

Bob Marley & The Wailers – Natural Mystic /
Bob Marley & The Wailers – Rhythm Track
Disco 102
These are mastered from tape and not at the same speed as the original Dub plates. The 'rhythm' track is just that and not the mixed dubs that appeared on the original Dub plates.

TUFF GONG PRODUCTIONS

The Wailers and their Tuff Gong label & shop were able to release a few titles in the US in the early 1970s. These are of particular interest as they feature versions not released elsewhere.

1971/2
Bob Marley & The Wailers – Trench Town Rock /
Bob Marley & The Wailers Grooving Kingston
G&C records C&G 5000

Bob Marley & Hugh Roy – Kingston 12 Shuffle* /
Wailers All Star Band – Ammunition
Tuff Gong (Records**) 5002
*act. a dub cut of U-Roy's 'Kingston 12 Shuffle', (the DJ version to 'Trench Town Rock')
**there are at least two pressings, one on 'Tuff Gong Records',
one on 'Tuff Gong'.

Bob Marley & The Wailers – Concrete Jungle* /
Bob Marley & The Wailers – Nice Time**
Tuff Gong 5003
*the original version, not as released on Island in the UK.
 **the Wail 'N Soul 'M production.

Bob Marley & The Wailers – Lick Samba /
Bob Marley & The Wailers – Screw Face
Tuff Gong Records TG 5004

Bob Marley & The Wailers – Lively Up Yourself* /
Bob Marley & The Wailers – Guava Jelly**
Tuff Gong (Records***) TG 5005
*Bob calls out 'People Get Ready' at the end of the track – not on any other release
**has an extra verse to JA issue. This cut is on the 'Songs Of Freedom' box set.
***There are at least two pressings of this: one with a black/yellow 'Tuff Gong' and the other with the brighter silver on purple 'Tuff Gong Records' design,

Bob Marley & The Wailers – Mellow Mood* /
Bob Marley & The Wailers – Thank You Lord*
Tuff Gong Records TG 5006.
*both Wail 'N Soul 'M productions

Bob Marley & The Wailers – Craven Choke Puppy /
Wailers All Star Band – Choke
Tuff Gong Records TG 5007

Bob Marley & The Wailers – Steppin' Razor* /
Bob Marley & The Wailers – The Letter**
Tuff Gong TG 5009.
*a Wail 'N Soul 'M production. ** Rita lead vocal cut

Bob Marley & The Wailers – Midnight Ravers* /
B. Marley – Ravers Version
Tuff Gong TG 5014.
*features an extra verse to the JA issue

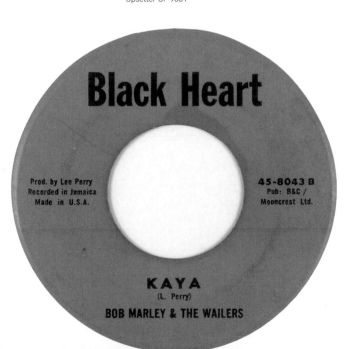

NON-WAILERS, TUFF GONG PRODUCTIONS

Pipe & The Pipers* – Harbour Shark /
Wailers All Stars Band – Shark
Tuff Gong Records TG 5001.
*aka The Wailing Souls

Pipe & The Pipers* - Back Biter /
Wailers All Star Band – Biter
Tuff Gong Records TG 5008
*aka The Wailing Souls

Rita Marley – I've Been Lonely /
Rita Marley – Version
Tuff Gong TG 5011

Tuff Gong TG 5010/12/13 have yet to surface, or maybe they don't exist.

Judy Mowatt – Pour Some Sugar /
Judy Mowatt – What An Experience
SIRE SAA –729, also as Sire promotional 7" in 1976,
Mono/Stereo versions of 'Pour Some Sugar'
An Ashandan JA release (1974), but label states
Produced by Alan Cole and Bob Marley for Tuff Gong

COXSONE DODD STUDIO 1 PRODUCTIONS
1966

The Wailers – I Need You /
(Ken Boothe & The Soul Brothers
– I Don't Want To See You Cry)
BRA A2011A/B

1972/3

The Wailers – Going Home /
The Wailers – It Hurts To Be Alone
Musik City MC 004A/B

1973

The Wailers – It Hurts To Be Alone /
The Wailers – I'm Going Home
Tranquility T 002

CANADIAN RELEASES

Just one oddity has appeared and whether it's a bootleg of some sort or if Jamaican WIRL did a one-off deal with Columbia in Canada, who knows?

Bob Marley & The Wailers – Nice Time* /
Bob Marley & The Wailers - It Hurts To Be Alone**
Wirl Records WLS 1045 & M-9376/7.
*Wail 'N Soul 'M production. ** Studio 1 production

BARBADIAN RELEASES

A series of seven-inch singles were released on either a 'Total Sounds' label or on 'Tuff Gong' out of Barbados from the middle to late 1970s. They are interesting as they feature pairings found nowhere else and are much higher quality pressings than Jamaican-pressed Tuff Gong singles.

1976

Bob Marley – No Woman No Cry /
Bob Marley – Kinky Reggae
Total Sounds TS WIRL 100
both 'Live At The Lyceum'

Bob Marley & The Wailers – Rat Race /
The Wailers Rat Race Part 2
Total Sounds TS WIRL 105

Bob Marley & The Wailers – Roots Rock Reggae /
Bob Marley & The Wailers – Cry To Me
Total Sounds TS WIRL 106

Bob Marley & The Wailers – War /
Bob Marley & The Wailers – Who the Cap Fit
Total Sounds TS WIRL 108

1977

Bob Marley & The Wailers – Exodus /
Bob Marley & The Wailers
 – One Love / People Get Ready
Tuff Gong B556

Bob Marley & The Wailers – Waiting In Vain /
Bob Marley & The Wailers – Turn Your Lights Down low
Tuff Gong B598

1978

Bob Marley & The Wailers – Is This Love /
Bob Marley & The Wailers – Crisis version
Tuff Gong B636

ALBUMS - US

COXSONE DODD STUDIO 1 PRODUCTIONS
1976

The Birth Of A Legend Calla 2 CAS 1240
I Made A Mistake, One Love, Let Him Go, Love & Affection,
Simmer Down, / Maga Dog, I Am Going Home, Donna,
Nobody Knows, Lonesome Feeling, / Wings Of A Dove,
It Hurts To Be Alone, I'm Still Waiting, Who Feels It, Do You
Remember, / Dancing Shoes, I Don't Need Your Love,
Lonesome Track, Do You Feel The Same Way Too,
The Ten Commandments of Love.
This release featured simulated Stereo remixes from the
original Mono master tapes. It was re-issued in the
US & UK as two singles albums 'Birth Of A Legend'
and 'Early Music'. Twelve tracks were licensed to
Pickwick International who issued them as
'Bob Marley & The Wailers With Peter Tosh'

LEE PERRY PRODUCTIONS

circa 1971/2
Bob Marley & The Wailers – Soul Revolution
Black Heart TTL65A/66A
Keep On Moving / Don't Rock My Boat / Put It On /
Fussing & Fighting / Duppy Conqueror V/4 / Memphis
c/w Riding High / Kaya / African Herbsman /
Stand Alone / Sun Is Shining / Brain Washing

Bob Marley & The Wailers – Soul Revolution II
Black Heart LP 001A/B*
Keep On Moving / Don't Rock The Boat / Put It On /
Fussing & Fighting / Duppy Conqueror V-4 / Memphis
/ Riding High / Kaya / African Herbsman /
Stand Alone / Sun Is Shining / Brain Washing.
Both come in a light green sleeve with pictures in black & white
* Silver & black label with the numbers 001A/001B on
Matrix numbers are hand written and this release appears
to be a bootleg

JAD PRODUCTIONS
1981

Chances Are Cotillion SD 5228
Reggae On Broadway, Gonna Get You, Chances Are,
Soul Rebel, Dance Do The Reggae, / Mellow Mood,
Stay With Me, I'm Hurting Inside, Soul Rebel
Material recorded 1968/71 and remixed for this release.

1982

Jamaican Storm Accord SN 7211
There She Goes, Mellow Mood, Treat You Right,
Chances Are, Soul Rebel, / Hammer, You Can't Do
That To Me, Touch Me, Put It On, How Many Times.
Material recorded 1968/71. No added production on this
release
Released as 'Soul Rebel' (New Cross, UK) & Bellaphon
(GR)

BARBADIAN RELEASES

The following albums were released and have all the same
details as the standard UK releases:
'Rastaman Vibration' (Total Sounds), 'Exodus' (Tuff Gong),
and 'Kaya' (Tuff Gong).

DISCOGRAPHY

RE-PRESSES: JAMAICAN SINGLES

STUDIO 1
This first batch are all from the years when The Wailers
were active at Studio One and have early-style silver ink
on coloured labels or Studio 1 'flag' design labels.

The Wailers – One Love /
(Blues Busters – Donna)
Coxsone FCD 743-A / FC 135 Silver ink, on blue.

Bob And The Wailers* – Simmer Down /
I Don't Need (Your Love)
Coxsone C Dodd II – 13 / C Dodd II – 12
Silver ink on red – not dinked! i.e. as a UK single.
*credit shows who was becoming the leader of the group!

The Wailers – Cry To Me /
(The Skatalites – Ska La Parisien)
Coxsone CS 1175-3 / CN 9 blue on white

The Wailers – It Hurts To Be Alone /
The Wailers – I'm Going Home
Coxsone CN 4 / CN1
green on yellow c/w black on white

The Wailers – Jail House /
(The Boss – Great Muga Ruga)
Studio 1 WIRL CS 1176-1 / CS DOD 225
black Studio 1 trumpet, yellow label

The Wailers – Rudie Rudie /
(The Boss – Great Muga Ruga)
Studio 1 WIRL CS 1176-1 / CS DOD 225
red Studio 1 trumpet, white label

The following re-presses feature previously unheard tracks
or new mixes and the addition of 'Versions':

STUDIO 1 – Red trumpet
Bob Marley – One Love /
Marley & The Skatalites – One Love Version
CD 1036A / CD 1036B
gives JA address but from US

Bob Marley – One Love /
Sound Dimension – One Love Version
CD 1036A / CD 1036B
label states 'Made in Jamaica'

Bob Marley & The Wailers – Rocking Steady /
Bob Marley & The Wailers Studio One All Stars
 – Rocking Steady PT. 2
SO 0084A 84B
label states 'Made in Jamaica'. Also with Blue Trumpet

STUDIO 1 – Green trumpet
Peter Tosh – I Am The Toughest /
Sound Dimensions – Toughest version
CD 1033A/B

STUDIO 1 – Rosette, black on white
Bob Marley & The Wailers – Rudie /
Wailers & The S. O. Band – Rudie Version
CN 3207 – A / CN 3207 – B

STUDIO 1 – Microphone inside a figure '1', black on white
3135, Fulton St., Brooklyn, N.Y. distribution address
Bob Marley & The Wailers – One Love /
Bob Marley & The Wailers – One Love Version
CS 9016A / CS 9016B

STUDIO 1 – Red '1' design, on yellow background
Bob Marley – Just In Time /
Brentford All Stars – Part Two
SOL 78A / SOL 78B

From the earliest days Clement Coxsone Dodd has re-
pressed singles on a very ad-hoc basis, usually using the
original stampers, but not necessarily in the same
pairings as they were first released. Most date from the
1970s.

Coxson
The Wailers – I'm Going Home /
The Wailers – It Hurts To Be Alone
CN 1 / CN 4   green on white

The Wailers – Ska Jerk /
The Wailers - I'm Still Waiting
FC 6909 / FC 6924 – 11 green, or red, on white

The Wailers – What Am I Supposed To Do /
(Jackie Mittoo – Do The Boogaloo)
WIRL CS 1748-1 / WIRL CS 1596-1 red on
white

COXSONE
This is the most popular re-press label,
all with a black design on to a white or
cream background, unless otherwise
noted. Released in the mid-1970s as
Bob Marley's international profile
grew.

The Wailers – Climb The Ladder /
(Bob Andy – I've Got To Go Back Home)
FC 6159 – 1 / CN 3602

The Wailers – Cry To Me /
(Hugh Godfrey – My Time)
WIRL CS 1175 - 3 / CS DODD 139 black on orange

The Wailers – Dancing Shoes /
The Wailers – Shame & Scandal
FCD 7448 A / CS 0028

The Wailers – Dancing Shoes /
Peter Touch – Don't Look Back
CS DODD 101 / WIRL CS 1535 – 1   black on red

The Wailers – It Hurts To Be Alone /
The Wailers – I'm Going Home
CN 4 / CN1   black on red

The Wailers – I'm Gonna Put It On /
No Credit – Version
DSR 9095 A / DSR 9096 B

The Wailers – Jerk In Time /
(The Skatalites – Killer Diller)
WIRL CS 1533 – 1 / CS 71 black on orange

The Wailers – Lonesome Feelings /
(Bunny & Skitter – I Need You)
FCD 7430 B / CR 127

Bob Marley & The Wailers – Playboy /
(Slim Smith – Born To Love You)
FC 6589 / FED 7373

The Wailers – Rude Boy /
(Sir Coxsone's All Stars – Pine Juice)
WIRL CS 1026-6 / FDR 561   black on yellow

Bob Marley & The Wailers – Rudie /
Wailers & Studio One Band – Rudie Part Two
CN3207 – A / CN 3207 – B

The Wailers – Simmer Down /
Bob Marley & The Wailers – Sunday Morning
C&N XX – X2 / WIRL CS 1423 – 2

The Wailers – What Am I Supposed To Do /
(Jackie Mittoo – Do The Boogaloo)
WIRL CS 1748-1 / WIRL CS 1596-1

STUDIO 1 – Red trumpet
The Wailers – Another Dance /
(Theophelus Beckford – Jack And Jill Shuffle)
FC 6950 II / CR 132

STUDIO 1 – Black trumpet
The Wailers – Another Dance /
(Theophelus Beckford – Jack And Jill)
FC 6950 II / CR 132

The Wailers – Hooligan /
(Jackie Mittoo – Jerico Skank)
CSD 53 / FCD 7355-A

The Wailers – I Need You /
(Ken Boothe – Don't Want To See You Cry)
WIRL CS 2025 – 1 / WIRL CS 2074 – 1

The Wailers – Let Him Go /
(Bob Andy – Unchained)
WIRL CS 1499 – 1 / NVM

STUDIO 1 – Hanging Mic
The Wailers – I Need You /
(Ken Boothe – Don't Want To See You Cry)
WIRL CS 2025-1 / WIRL CS 2074-1   black on white

The Wailers – Another Dance /
(Theophilus Beckford – Jack & Jill Shuffle)
FC 6950 II / CR 132   blue on white

TABERNACLE

Soul Harmoniers* – Just In Time /
(The Pentecostal Singers – Sing Like The Apostles)
WIRL CS 1069-1 / FCD 7202 black on red
*actually Bob Marley & The Wailers

Soul Harmoniers* – Just In Time /
(The Trying Brothers – Satan)
WIRL CS 1069-1 / DSR CN 5447-1 black on white
*actually Bob Marley & The Wailers

Freedom Singers* - Let The Lord Been Seen In You /
(Marvetts – Marvetts Arms)
FC 6936-11 / C + N2 – 11 green on white
*actually Bob Marley & The Wailers

LATER RE-PRESSES
COXSONE
3135 Fulton St Brooklyn, N.Y. address
The Wailers – Climb The Ladder /
(Bob Andy – I've Got To Go Back Home)
FC 6159 – 1 / CN 3608 – 1

The Wailers – Habits /
(Joe Higgs – Dinah)
FC 6477 / CS DODD 80

The Wailers – Made A Mistake /
(Jackie & Doreen - The Vow)
FC 6535 / C DODD II – 3

STUDIO 1 - Black trumpet
3135, Fulton St., Brooklyn, N.Y. distribution address
The Wailers – Another Dance /
The Wailers – Hooligan Ska
FC 6950 II / CSD 53

The Wailers – Don't Ever Leave Me /
(Lee Perry – Pussy Galore)
C-DODD 16 / FC 6869

The Wailers – Do You Feel The Same Way /
The Wailers – Destiny
C. S. Dodd – Do You Feel The Same Way A /
C. S. Dodd - Destiny B

ALBUMS: RE-PRESSES AND
LATER COMPILATIONS

From the 1970s onwards Coxsone Dodd pressed various Wailers albums, always with some additional production, usually drums. The 'silkscreen' cover issue is often listed as being 'original', probably as it looks old and 'roots' but is in fact from circa 1975; it was issued with at least two colour variations of the cover. Later compilations added two Lee Perry productions. All of these carry the cover with an image of Bob, Bunny & Peter standing. Listed below are the pressings from different stampers, and/or record label, that have surfaced so far. Some listings state that the titles of the tracks vary in the 'tears' but I can only find that on the silkscreen, the top tear that has 'Rude Boy' in it has vanished.

The Wailing Wailers
Studio 1 (Black trumpet), circa 1970, FCD 8081 A / B Put It On, I Need You, Lonesome Feeling, What's New Pussycat, One Love, When The Well Runs Dry, / Ten Commandments Of Love, Rude Boy, It Hurts To Be Alone, Love & Affection, I'm Still Waiting, Simmer Down As original issue, but with added overdubs throughout, especially the drums. The sleeve carries a 'Manufactured & Distributed by West Indies Records Ltd' and a 'UniPrint' credit.

The Wailing Wailers
Studio 1 (Black trumpet), silkscreen cover
circa 1975, FCD 8081 A / B
Put It On, I Need You, Lonesome Feeling, What's New Pussycat, One Love, When The Well Runs Dry, / Ten Commandments Of Love, Rude Boy, It Hurts To Be Alone, Love & Affection, I'm Still Waiting, Simmer Down As original issue, but with added overdubs throughout, especially the drums. There are at least two variations of the cover: black&red/ochre and black&yellow/white. Sleeves now credit 'Jamaica Recording & Publishing Studio' as manufacturer and 'Stephensons' as lithographers.

The Wailing Wailers
Studio 1 (Rosette), circa 1978, WW I A/B,
Put It On, I Need You, Lonesome Feeling, What's New Pussycat, One Love, When The Well Runs Dry*, / Ten Commandments Of Love, Rude Boy, It Hurts To Be Alone, Love & Affection, I'm Still Waiting, Simmer Down. (*act. 'Ska Jerk'. As original issue but with added overdubs throughout, especially the drums.

The Wailing Wailers
Studio 1(Red '1' on yellow, Brooklyn address),
circa 1982, SOLP 1001 A/B
Put It On, I Need You, Lonesome Feeling, What's New Pussycat, One Love, When The Well Runs Dry*, / Ten Commandments Of Love, Rude Boy, It Hurts To Be Alone, Love & Affection, I'm Still Waiting, Simmer Down. (*act. 'Ska Jerk) As original issue but with added overdubs throughout, especially the drums.

All the following albums have added overdubs
The Best Of
Coxsone, (Black on white), silkscreen cover, circa 1975, FCD 127 A/B
I Am Going Home, Bend Down Low*, Mr Talkative, Ruddie, Cry To Me, Wings Of A Dove, / Small Axe**, Love Won't Be Mine, Dancing Shoes, Sunday Morning, He Who Feels It Knows It, Straight And Narrow Way.
*produced by The Wailers, **produced by Lee Perry. The cover is
black&red&green/yellow and is textured 'crocodile-skin' cardboard.

The Best Of
Studio 1 (Rosette), silkscreen cover,
circa 1975, SOL 127 A/B (plus album title)
I Am Going Home, Bend Down Low*, Mr Talkative, Ruddie, Cry To Me, Wings Of A Dove, / Small Axe**, Love Won't Be Mine, Dancing Shoes, Sunday Morning, He Who Feels It Knows It, Straight And Narrow Way.
*produced by The Wailers, **produced by Lee Perry
The cover is yellow&blue/black

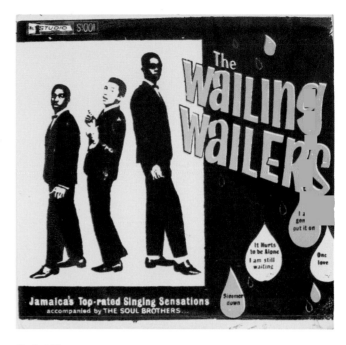

The Best Of
Studio 1(Rosette, Brooklyn address), silkscreen cover,
circa 1975, SOL 127 A/B (plus album title)
I Am Going Home, Bend Down Low*, Mr Talkative, Ruddie, Cry To Me, Wings Of A Dove, / Small Axe**, Love Won't Be Mine, Dancing Shoes, Sunday Morning, He Who Feels It Knows It, Straight And Narrow Way.
*produced by The Wailers, **produced by Lee Perry.
The cover is black/yellow

The Best Of
Studio 1 (Trumpet, blue).
Different design to above, circa 1975, SOL 127 A/B
I Am Going Home, Bend Down Low*, Mr Talkative, Ruddie, Cry To Me, Wings Of A Dove, / Small Axe**, Love Won't Be Mine, Dancing Shoes, Sunday Morning, He Who Feels It Knows It, Straight And Narrow Way.
*produced by The Wailers, **produced by Lee Perry

The Best Of
Studio 1 (Trumpet, black), circa 1976, SO 1106 A/B
Destiny, Ruddie Boy, Cry To Me, Love Won't Be Mine, Play Boy, Sunday Morning, / Put It On, I Need You, What's New Pussycat, Where Is My Mother, Wages Of Love, Jailhouse*. Distributed by Buddah. *act. Ruddie Boy, repeated

Marley, Tosh, Livingston & Associates Studio 1(Rosette),
circa 1981, FCD 4041 A/B
Another Dance, Lonesome Track, Rolling Stone, Can't You See, Let Him Go, / Dance With Me, Maga Dog, I Want Somewhere, Hoot Nanny Hoot, Dreamland*
*produced by Lee Perry

Bob Marley & The Wailers – Soul Rebels – Rough Gang CD LP 001
Soul Rebel, Try Me, It's Alright, No Sympathy, My Cup, Soul Almighty / Rebels Hop, Corner Stone, 400 Years, No Water, Reaction, My Sympathy*
*act has Duppy Conqueror on album Looks like it was when Perry linked up with Dodd. Produced by 'C. S. Dodd'! Distributed by New York Studio 1 2005

DISCOGRAPHY

WAIL 'N SOUL 'M RE-PRESSES

Following the example of their previous employer, Bob Marley & The Wailers frequently kept re-pressing older material that was still in demand. The following combinations have also surfaced, and all used the original stampers. All carry blank labels. There are more re-presses of these sides to be found in the 'Wailers at 127, King Street' re-press section.

Bob Marley & The Wailing Wailers
Steppin Razor / Hypocrites

Bob Marley & The Wailing Wailers
Steppin Razor / Nice Time

Bob Marley & The Wailing Wailers
Hurtin Inside / Lyrical Satirical I

Bob Marley & The Wailing Wailers
Play Play / Nice Time

Bob Marley & The Wailing Wailers
Fire Fire / Pound Get a Blow

Bob Marley & The Wailing Wailers
Fire Fire / Bus Dem Shut

Bob Marley & The Wailing Wailers
Them Fi Get A Beatin' / Chances Are

One release carried proper labels and had new stampers made:
Bob Marley & The Wailing Wailers
Freedom Time / This Train
Wail 'N Soul 'M
WIRL BM 3408-1 / WIRL RM 3274-2

UPSETTER RE-PRESSES

Only one reissue of non-Perry-produced Wailers material has surfaced, on a Perry label:

Bob Marley & The Wailers – Freedom Time /
Bob Marley & The Wailers – Hurtin' Inside
Upsetter WIRL BM 3408-2 / WIRL BM 3708-2
yellow / red one side, blank other, NPT&C

Reissued in Jamaica probably circa 1974/5, were the following two singles:

Bob Marley & The Wailers – All In One /
Wailers Part Two
Upsetter RRS Studio 17 005/06

Marley & The Wailers – Man To Man /
Upsetters - Nicoteen
Upsetter RRS Studio 17 002/01

Studio 17 003/004 is Dave Barkers 'Groove Me'

TUFF GONG, 127, KING STREET RE-PRESSES

Bob Marley kept his hits available and adverts of the period featured catalogue titles, as well as the current releases. In keeping with the money-making goal of these releases, surplus current labels were used up and most releases don't carry (correct) song titles and credits, thus the listing below is by song title only.

WAIL 'N SOUL 'M TRACKS BOTH SIDES:

Bob Marley & The Wailers – Feel Alright /
Bob Marley & The Wailers - Hurtin Inside
Blank DYNA NL 824-1 / WIRL BM 3708-1
The mix on 'Feel Alright' is different from the Wail 'N Soul 'M release, with the strange percussion (that sounds like cutlery being dropped!) thankfully absent. The matrix shows it to be an original stamper.

With fully printed labels:

This Train / Hurtin' Inside

Play Play* / Nice Time
*'Play Play 'is credited to The 'Soulettes'

Funeral* / Pound Get A Blow
*Funeral is credited as 'Burial'

The following have assorted blank and titled labels that bear no relationship to what's on the records:
Funeral / Pound Get A Blow
Bus Dem Shut / Funeral*
*carrying at least two differently titled labels
Fire Fire / Bus Dem Shut
Freedom Time / Play Play
Steppin' Razor / The Letter

TUFF GONG / WAIL 'N SOUL 'M TRACKS:

Concrete Jungle / Rock it Baby
Hold on to this Feeling / Hurtin Inside
Nice Time / Rock It Baby version
Satisfy My Soul Jah Jah / Fire Fire
Send Me That Love / Hurtin' Inside
Send Me That Love / Play Play
Sun Is Shining / Nice Time
I suspect that this re-press listing is far from complete.

TUFF GONG, 56, HOPE ROAD RE-PRESSES

The only re-press of this time was 'Nice Time' backed with 'Hypocrites'. It was given a full release and is listed in the Jamaican vinyl section (page159).

TUFF GONG, 220, MARCUS DRIVE RE-PRESSES: SINGLES

Bob Marley & The Wailers – Bad Card /
Bob Marley & The Wailers – Rub-A-Dub Style
Tuff Gong Bad Card A / Dubb Card B,

Bob Marley – I Know/
Bob Marley – I Know Dub
Tuff Gong TG 1987A / DSR 2917B
one release has 'Tuff Gong with star' logo and the other the 'star' with the triple hand clasp

Bob Marley & The Wailers – Ride Natty Ride /
Bob Marley & The Wailers – Smile Jamaica*
Tuff Gong145- 9843A / WIPX 1823,
*the Lee Perry-produced cut

Bob Marley & The Wailers – Smile Jamaica* /
Bob Marley & The Wailers – Jah Live
Tuff Gong DSR 5300 A / DSR 5301 B,
*the Lee Perry produced cut

Bob Marley And The Wailers – Keep On Moving* /
Bob Marley & The Wailers – Pimpers Paradise
Tuff Gong MML 1769 / MML 1770.
*produced by Bob Marley & Lee Perry with additional production by I. Kiano & T. Wyatt

12" SINGLES

Bob Marley & Lee Perry – Punky Reggae Party /
Bob Marley & Lee Perry – Punky Reggae Version
Tuff Gong DSR 4774/75 released in original picture sleeve but with a 'Ziggy's Record Manufacturing' credit

A series of three 12" singles were issues circa 1995
Bob Marley & The Wailers – Buffalo Soldier /
Bob Marely & The Wailers - Buffalo Dub
Tuff Gong BMW 9761A/ B
released in a black/silver Tuff Gong sleeve.

Bob Marley & The Wailers – One Love /
People Get Ready /
Bob Marley & The Wailers – So Much Trouble In The World
IS 169 12 TGX 1A-1U-1-/ 12 TGX 1 B-1U-1-
released in a black/silver Tuff Gong sleeve.
the B side includes an uncredited 'Keep On Moving'

Bob Marley & The Wailers – Trenchtown /
Bob Marley & The Wailers – Dub In Trenchtown
MML 1934A/B released in a black/silver Tuff Gong sleeve.

OTHER RE-PRESSES: 7" SINGLES

Listed below is a sampling of the re-pressed Bob Marley & The Wailers tunes that are largely without authorization from the Estate. Bunny Lee's 'Mr Chatterbox' is often around but usually re-pressed without the spoken intro. Recently I've seen expensive re-presses, from Japan, of 'Selassie Is The Chapel' and 'Adam & Eve'. Most re-presses can readily be avoided as they add nothing and line someone else's pockets.
All the JAD releases are via 55 records (France)
*indicates a 'Jamaican' or 'Soul Mix' from the world-renowned musician Bruno 'no over-dubs' Blum.

Rock To The Rock* / Rock To The Rock (a cappella)
JAD BB001

Nice Time* / Nice Time (a cappella)
JAD BB002

Rocking Steady* / How Many Times
JAD BB03

Gonna Get You / Touch Me
JAD BB005

Feel Alright / Rhythm
JAD BB006 *matrix is JAD BB014

Satisfy My Soul Babe / Version
JAD BB006

Selassie Is the Chapel / M. Planno – A Little Prayer
JAD BB007

Satisfy My Soul Jah Jah / version
JAD BB008

Mellow Mood* / Chances Are*
JAD BB009

Wisdom / Adam & Eve
JAD BB010

Pour Down The Sunshine / Comma Comma
JAD BB011

What Goes Around Comes Around / Version
JAD BB012

Reggae On Broadway / Oh Lord I've Got To Get There
JAD BB013

All the 'Impact' releases come from an 'enterprising' dealer!
Also available in coloured vinyl.

Bus Dem Shut (Pyaka) / Lyrical Satirical I
Impact BM 45 3273A / 73B

Pound Get A Blow / Burial
Impact WIRL 3673-1 / WIRL 3673-2

Sugar Sugar / Don't Rock My Boat
Impact Randys # 1056A / 56B

All the Ascension releases come from Australia.

I Know A Place / I Know A Place Dub
Ascension ANS I 01

Who Colt The Game / Who Colt The Game Dub
Ascension ANS I 02

Below are a couple of re-presses that turned up recently from JA and come with out of period Beverley's labels:

Judge Not / Skatalites – Snowboy
Beverley's SR 147

One Cup Of Coffee / Skatalites – Snowboy
Beverley's SR 147

PROMOTIONAL & OTHER RELEASES

This chapter features mainly UK-released promotional records from Island Records; undoubtedly there were promotional releases from Island around the world but those are beyond the scope of this book.
In Jamaica the release of 'Blank' labels were effectively promotional releases, although they were actually sold – but mainly to Sound System operators across the Island. I have only been able to discover one Jamaican single that is stamped ' COMPLIMENTARY' – it's from 1970, a Leslie Kong production of 'Soul Shake Down Party'.

ISLAND UK
Every Island release during Bob's career can be found with a 'DJ Copy Only' stamp on the 'push-out' centre of an otherwise standard release. These are fairly common.

1973
The Wailers – I Shot The Sheriff /
The Wailers – Pass It On / Duppy Conqueror
IDJ2 A 'DJ Album Sampler' for 'Burnin''

1974
Bob Marley & The Wailers – So Jah Seh
WIP 6212
A one-sided promo that comes in a pink sleeve, stickered 'One Sided Promo'

1975
Bob Marley & The Wailers – Trenchtown Rock /
Bob Marley & The Wailers – I Shot The Sheriff
IDJ 7
Promotion for 'Live At The Lyceum', label states 'Limited Pressing Only' & 'Not For Sale DJ Copy). Also on white label

1976
Bob Marley – Promotional Advert /
Bob Marley – Promotional Advert
WIP 6402 IDJ
Promotional message from Bob Marley for 'Exodus', featured on the deluxe edition of 'Exodus', on CD.

1977 – 12" SINGLE
Bob Marley & The Wailers – Exodus /
Bob Marley & The Wailers – Exodus
(Instrumental version)
IDJ 26 (IPR 2000).
'Special Disco Cut' – It's the 'IPR 2000' issue with a different label

1978
Bob Marley & The Wailers – Satisfy My Soul /
Bob Marley & The Wailers – Smile Jamaica
WIPX 1822-1U / WIPX 1823-1U
White label issue of WIP 6440
Circa 1986
Bob Marley – Get Up Stand Up / blank
BMRM 1
Promo Copy only – Not For Sale

Bob Marley & The Wailers – Rat Race /
Bob Marley & The Wailers – So Much Trouble In The World
BMRM 2
Promo copy only Not For Sale, picture label on B-side

Bob Marley & The Wailers – Zimbabwe /
Bob Marley & The Wailers – War & No More Trouble
BMRM 3
Promo copy only Not For Sale, picture label on B-side

Bob Marley & The Wailers –
No Woman, No Cry & Mix Up, Mix Up /
Could You Be Loved & I Shot The Sheriff
MPEP3
For Promo Use Only – Not For Sale

12" SINGLE
Bob Marley & The Wailers – Get Up, Stand Up /
Bob Marley & The Wailers – Get Up, Stand Up (Live)
12 BRMRM 1
Promo Copy only. Released in 'Rasta flag, with Rasta boy,' sleeve.

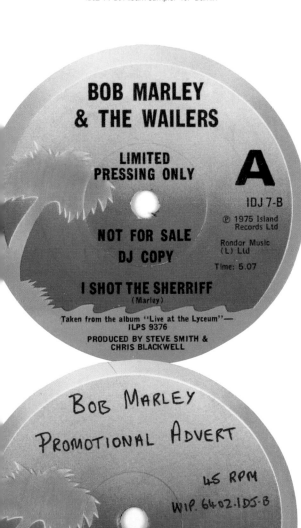

The Now Sound Reggae: Radio Station Promo
(Island IXP 5) USA
Features Stir It Up, I Shot The Sheriff and tracks from the soundtrack to 'The Harder They Come' and assorted other Island reggae artists. Released in a 'Babe in a wet T shirt' cover.

1978
Island Record Shop Sampler
RSS 1
Is This Love, Kaya, Misty Morning / Robert Palmer – Every Kind of People, You Overwhelm Me,
Best Of Both Worlds
Released in a plain white sleeve

OTHER ITEMS
1975
Bob Marley & The Wailers – Natty Dread (US)
Columbia Records, Terre Haute, Ind. ILPS 9281. A test pressing of 'Natty Dread', with test artwork printed out flat.

1976
Bob Marley & The Wailers – Rastaman Vibration
(US) Promotional box
A hessian box with the central image from the album as an inlaid cut-out. The box holds: the US album, the 'Marley Scrapbook 1976' (black & white press cuttings in a colour cover), a fold-out reproduction of an article from 'People Weekly' and a black & white promo 8 x10" photo of Bob (with Don Taylor's details on) and a full-size hessian sack with the image from the album printed on.
Many boxes are missing something – beware!

1977
Wailers – Exodus Trident Studios (UK)
No matrix number. A 7", one-sided, acetate

Bob Marley & The Wailers – Exodus /
Bob Marley & The Wailers – Exodus instrumental version
Island (US) IXP-7. Promotional copy – released in art sleeve

1980
Bob Marley & The Wailers – Could You Be Loved (US)
Island (US) PRO-A-902   Promotional copy – one sided, released in an Island 'naked woman / man' sleeve

1992
Bob Marley – Songs Of Freedom
Island TGCS 1
A 15-track CD, in a standard jewel case,
to promote the 'Songs Of Freedom' 4 CD box set.

1996
Bob Marley & The Wailers
The Complete Wailers Volume 1 (UK)
Housed in a wooden box, with Bob's image on are: The triple CD, a four-track promo CD single and a Bob T-shirt. The 'Complete Wailers' project was from an idea by Bruno Blum and Roger Steffens to bring together all the material from 1967 to 1972. It was made real by Bruno & myself, with Roger doing the sleeve notes.

OTHER ALBUMS
1973
Pop Spectacular featuring 'In Concert'
BBC Transcription services 133425/6-s
Slave Driver, Stop That Train, War – No More Trouble,
400 Years, Midnight Ravers, Stir It Up, Concrete Jungle,
Get Up Stand Up, Kinky Reggae, Rastaman Chant.
Comes in a plain ochre fold-out sleeve. It is the 'Old Grey Whistle Test' concert at The Paris Theatre that has been bootlegged often. Later reissued by the BBC on its 'Rock Goes To College' label. Both are non-commercial releases.

POSTERS
Bob's image appears on millions of posters across the world. The only posters with value to collectors are original promotional ones, which often have Island's name on; likewise Jamaican Tuff Gong posters.

A SAMPLING:
Uprising 1980 (23" x 23")
Confrontation (22" x 24")
Bob Marley – Island No 101 (20" x 30")
Bob Marley & The Wailers – Rastaman Vibration Island No 50 (20" x 30")
Exodus (20" x 30")
Kaya – Babylon By Bus – World Reggae Party (US) (25" x 38")
Survival (25" x 38")
Reggae Lives – with 5 lines from 'Africa Unite' (Tuff Gong JA) (13" x 17")
Bob's image on hessian (25" x 31") – Promo for Survival?
Bob on the Cover of Rolling Stone (US) (18" x 20")

A poster of Bob came free with initial copies of 'Live'; they carry the Island number 42 and of course are always folded.

ALBUMS
1973
It's Island (eye-land) Month
(Island SPRO-6619) USA
Features 'Rock It Baby' and 'Stir It Up' on this Island compilation, which also has tracks from Free, Traffic, Mike Harrison, John Martyn and Amazing Blondel.
The cover calls the Wailers album ('Catch A Fire') 'Jamaican Underground Music'. John Rabbit Bundrick is on the Free and the Marley tracks!

1975
Radio Sampler ISS 3
Lively Up Yourself, Kinky Reggae, No Woman No Cry, /
Get Up, Stand Up, I Shot The Sheriff, Stir It Up, Natty Dread
Released in a white sleeve with the title stamped on in a black box. Originally sent out with a 'Promo Press Pack' that included; A letter from Clive Banks (on Blue Island stationery), photocopies of 'Melody Maker' & 'NME' articles (6 pages, glossy A4, black & white), single pages from 'The Guardian', 'The Times', 'Morning Star', 'The Evening Standard' & two pages from 'Time Out' (all A4, glossy b/w). Watch out for modern photocopies!

THE WAILERS ON HARMONIES
including Rita Marley at Studio 1.

THE WAILERS ON HARMONIES AT STUDIO 1
In true entrepreneurial style Coxsone Dodd kept Bob, Bunny, Peter and Rita busy at Studio 1 and had them providing harmonies for other artists. Peter cut a few tunes as a solo artist and Rita had her own group, The Soulettes.

WAILERS ON HARMONIES
tracks in brackets do not feature the Wailers

Bob Andy & The Chorus – I Wouldn't Be A Fool /
Crime Don't Pay
Musik City blank CS DODD 96 / 98

Bob Andy – I've Got To Go Back Home /
Wailers – Climb The ladder
Coxsone CN 3602 / FC 6159-1 & CN 3608-1 / FC 6159-1

Bob Andy – I've Got To Go Back Home /
(Melodians – Lay It On)
Coxsone CSD 161 / CC Dodd 49

Ken Boothe – The Train Is Coming / Part 2
Studio 1 SC 126A / SC 123B

Delroy Wilson – Jerk All Night /
(Delroy Wilson – Here Comes The Heartache)
Studio 1 WIRL CS 1088-1 / WIRL CS 1210-1

Delroy Wilson – I Want Justice /
(Delroy Wilson – Low Minded Hypocrites)
Studio 1 FC 6567 / FC 6512

Jack Sparrow – Beggars Have No Choice /
(Roy Richards – Double Trouble)
Studio 1 FC 6766 / FC 6917

Jack Sparrow – Ice Water /
(Roland Alphonso – Ska-Culation)
Studio 1 CS 70 / CSD 195

Jackie Opel – The Mill Man /
(Jackie Opel – Don't Let Me die)
Studio 1 CSD 43 / CSD 45

Jackie Opel – I Didn't Want Her /
(Soul Boys – Rudie Get Wise)
Muzik City WIRL CS 1794 / CS DODD 137

Lee Perry – Pussy Galore* /
(Roland Alphonso – Provocation)
Studio 1 FC 6869 / CS 0010
*Also released with the following B-sides;
(Clue J & his Blues Blasters – Shufflin' jug)
& (Monty & the Cyclones – Summertime)
  Studio 1 KD 45 112 & Coxsone Blank FDR 577

Lord Brynner – Where's Sammy gone /
(Lord Brynner – Josephine)
Roland & Powie C DODD 117 / C DODD 118)

Bob was the musical director or coach for The Soulettes and thus the Wailers can be heard on several releases:

Rita Marley & The Soulettes – A Deh Pon Dem* /
(Jackie Opel – Don't Laugh At Me)
Blank CS DODD 75-006 / CS DODD 138
*features Bunny, Peter, Constantine 'Dream' Walker
& Marlene Gifford on harmonies

The Soulettes – La La Lover* /
(Roland Alphonso – Something Special)
Coxsone CS 0023 / CS 021
*Bob can be clearly heard in the mix

The Soulettes – One More Chance* /
(Roland Alphonso – Dick Tracy)
Studio 1 CSD 54 / CSD 50
*Bob, Peter & Bunny harmonies

Rita Marley – Friends & Lovers* /
I'm Sorry For You Baby
Studio 1 CS DODD 73-009 / CS DODD 76-007
*features Bunny, Peter & Constantine 'Dream' Walker
on harmonies

The Soulettes* - Oh My Darling /
(Hamlins – Trying To Keep A Good Man Down)
Muzik City DIR CD 2007-B 1H / WIRL CS 1010
*is actually a duet between Marcia Griffiths and Bob Marley

RITA MARLEY AT STUDIO 1
Rita Marley recorded under her own name, with her group The Soulettes, who were Constantine 'Dream' (aka 'Vision') Walker, Marlene 'Precious' Gifford and Rita. In 1966 when Bob went to the States and worked in the Chrysler car plant, 'Dream' joined the Wailers and cut some five tracks with them. The group also provided backing vocals to other artists, and these are listed separately below:

Rita Marley – Come to Me /
(Soul Boys – Blood Pressure)
Blank CS DODD 25 / WIRL CS 1857-1

Rita Marley – Friends & Lovers /
I'm Sorry For You Baby
Studio 1 CS DODD 73-009 / CS DODD 76-007

Rita Marley – You Lied /
(Soul Brothers – Cray Fish)
Studio 1 CS DODD 87 / WIRL CS 1790-1

Rita Marley – You Lied /
(Lee Perry – Sugar Bag)
Blank CS DODD 87 / CS DODD 119

Rita Marley & The Soulettes – A Deh Pon Dem/
(Jackie Opel – Don't Laugh At Me)
Blank CS DODD 75-006 / CS DODD 138

Rita & Jackie Opel – You Are My One Love /
(Don Drummond – Man In The Street)
Studio 1 FC 6521 / CSD 40

Rita & Bunny (Wailer) Bless You /
(Roland Alphonso – Beard Man Ska)
Studio 1 CSD 192 / CS 73

Rita & Bunny (Wailer) Bless You /
(Dennis Lovelock – Ificially Scorcher)
Coxsone CSD 192 / FCD 7805-A

Peter* & Rita – It's Only Time /
(Roland Alphonso – Tall in the Saddle)
Studio 1 CS 0001 / CS 0012
*Peter Austin of The Clarendonians, not Tosh

Rita Marley – Time to Turn /
Peter Tosh & The Chorus– Can't You See
Supreme WIRL CS 1477-1 / CC DODD 64

Girl Wonder* – Chopping Wood /
Girl Wonder – Mommy, Out De Light
Port O Jam FC 6957 – F / FC 6958
*aka Rita Marley. 'Chopping Wood' is a Mento number

AS THE SOULETTES
The Soulettes – Don't Care What People Say / Tighten Up
Studio 1 WIRL CS 1143-1 / CS 1144-1

The Soulettes – Hey Senorita /
Rita Anderson – Spring Is Coming
Studio 1 FC 6926 / FC 6927

The Soulettes – I Love You Baby* /
(Skatalites – instrumental)
Studio 1 CS 77 / CSD 196
*written by Bob Marley

The Soulettes – I Want To Be /
(Roland Alphonso – Sufferer's Choice)
Blank CS 0024 / CS 0025

The Soulettes – Oh My Darling /
(Hamlins – Trying to Keep a Good Man Down)
Muzik City DIR CD 2007-B 1H / WIRL CS 1010

The Soulettes – One More Chance /
(Roland Alphonso – Dick Tracy)
Studio 1 CSD 54 / CSD 50

The Soulettes – King Street / Satisfaction
Studio 1 WIRL CS 1310 / WIRL CS 1211

The Soulettes – La La Lover /
(Roland Alphonso – Something Special)
Coxsone CS 0023 / CS 021

The Soulettes   Opportunity /
(Johnny Moore – Sudden destruction)
Muzik City FC 6480 / FC 6479

AS BACKING VOCALISTS
Lee Perry & The Soulettes – Please Don't Go /
(Lee Perry & The Dynamites – By Saint Peter)
C&N CSD 47 / CSD 49

King Perry & The Soulettes – Rub & Squeeze /
(Soul Brothers – Here Comes The Minx)
Studio 1 WIRL CS 1369 / WIRL CS 1215

Tony Gregory & The Soulettes – Baby Come On Home /
(Tony Gregory – Maria Elana)
Supreme FC 6653-F1 9/6/65 / FC 6648-7

Soul Brothers – Sugar & Spice* /
(The Setbacks – Get Out Of My Life)
Coxsone WIRL CS 1105-1 / WIRL 1106-1
*features an intro & chorus from a girl group, reportedly The Soulettes

RHYTHM-WISE
And I Love Her
Horns cut, Senor Alphonso – And I Love Her /
(Lord Creator – March Jamaicans March)
Supreme FC 6720/21

JAILHOUSE
Harmonic cut, Roy Richards – Green Callie /
(Marcia Griffiths – You're No Good)
Coxsone CS1368 / CS1079

PUT IT ON
Organ Cut, Jackie Mittoo – Put It On /
(Chinese Chicken)
Blank FND 7306/CA 010 420

King Perry & The Soulettes – Rub & Squeeze /
(Soul Brothers – Here Comes The Minx)
Studio One WIRLCS 1369 / CS 1215
Rude Boy
King Perry – Pussy Galore /
(Roland Alphonso – Provocation)
Studio One FC 6869 / CS 0010

DISCOGRAPHY

Non-Single
Cry To Me
The version of 'Cry To Me' appears on the album 'Mellow Dub' (Studio 1)

Dancing Shoes
Al Capone's 'Dancing Version' is a DJ cut to 'Dancing Shoes' that uses the original rhythm track, with some of the original vocals left in. It's on 'Forever Version' (Studio 1)

NB The song 'Charley Marley' by the Gaylads (Coxsone) is an old folk / mento song that uses the biblical 'House Upon Sand' parable as its basis. Nothing to do with Bob!

THE WAILERS, WITH LEE PERRY, AT RANDY'S ON HARMONIES
The Wailers performed harmony duties on several Perry productions of other artists, but were only credited on one (Rass Dawkin's 'Picture On The Wall'). Below is the full listing of Jamaican releases; most have UK & US counterparts (not listed).

Dave Barker – Sound Underground /
Dave Barker - Don't Let The Sun Catch You Crying* /
Upsetter (NPT&C) DYNA KG 2269/70
*The Wailers sing the strong harmonies

Dave Barker – What a Confusion* /
Upsetters – version
Upsetter DYNA L Perry 3630/32
*Bunny Wailer provides the harmonies

Glen Adams – Never Had A Dream Come True* /
Upsetters – Version
Upsetter (NPT&C) FLP 3348/49
*features the Wailers on harmonies

Rass Dawkins & The Wailers – Picture On The Wall V/3 /
Righteous Upsetters – Picture On The Wall V/4
Upsetter Records DYNA LP 4149/56
Carl Dawkins – Heavy Load* /
Upsetters – Down the Road

Upsetter (NPT&C) GPW 9/10
*features the Wailers on harmonies

Eccles & Neville* – All Over /
Rightious Souls – Mount Zion
Supreme (UK) SUP 217 – no known JA issue.
*Clancy Eccles and Bunny 'Neville Livingston' Wailer on this track that sounds like it was cut at the 'Dreamland' session.

U-Roy – Rightful Ruler* /
Upsetters – Handy Cap
Upset DYNA Upsetter 718-1 / WIRL LP 4203
*Peter Tosh is featured in the tune that also samples The Sons Of Negus single 'Ethiopian National Anthem' (Zion Disc)

Little Roy – All Africans* /
(U-Roy – Copasetic)
Blank DYNA LP 3562/61
*Peter Tosh played guitar and Bunny Wailer played the Kette drum.

RHYTHM-WISE
The following records use original Upsetters/Wailers rhythms as the basis for new tracks. No Wailers vocals are included:

Brand New Second Hand
Owen Gray & Slim Smith – Sincerely / version
Blank (Sir Nephew) FNR 7482A/B

Junior English – Too Young To Be My Lover /
(Gene Rondo – Happy Birthday)
Blank (FUD?) FEC1714A/B

Mike Elliot – Milk & Honey /
(Harvey & Errol – Burst A Shirt)
Ackee ACK 151 (UK)

Soul Rebels – Judgment Day Is Near /
(Various – Solid As A Rock)
Count Shelly CS 001 (UK)

DREAMLAND
U-Roy – Rhythm Land / Out Of This World
Blank (Trojan) PW 1A/B
Bunny Wailer used the rhythm when he re-cut 'Dreamland' for his own Solomonic imprint in 1973 and for a DJ cut, Istan's 'Vision Land' (Solomonic 1975). When he re-cut 'Dreamland' again, for Island in 1975/6, he adapted the 'Peanut vendor' rhythm for the track.

DUPPY CONQUEROR
Dave Barker – Conqueror version 3* /
Upsetters – My Mother Law*
Upsetter US 348A / 348 B.
*released in UK as, 'Upsetting Station' / 'Dig Your Grave'.
Dave Barker deejays and sings snatches of The Temptations' 'Runaway Child, Running Wild'.

Lee Perry / The Upsetters – Big Joke /
(Gaylads – If You Don't Mind (aka 'I Wear My Slanders'))
Upsetter & High Note DYNA LP 253 / DYNA LP 3334 – 1
Big Joke is a horns cut to 'Duppy Conqueror' that features a joke shop 'laughing bag'.

KEEP ON MOVING
Big Youth – Mooving Version /
(The Upsetters – Crummy People)
Justice League DSR 6568 / LP + 3

Dennis Alcapone – Rasta Dub /
Upsetters – Rasta version
Upsetter SCR+18/17

SMALL AXE
Dave (Barker) & The Upsetters – Small Axe V/S 2* /
(The Upsetters – Fresh Up)
Spinning Wheel DYNA LP 1551 /US 258A *aka Shocks '71

SOUL REBEL
Glen Adams – Rebel Version /
Upsetters – Rhythm version
Capo DYNA CB 3030/40
A piano cut to 'Soul Rebel'

Joe Gibbs also had use of this rhythm track later in the decade ('75) and Jacob Miller cut 'I'm A Natty' over the rhythm (Reflections (JA)) and I Roy deejayed it as 'Knotty Knots' (Town & Country (JA)).

VARIOUS RHYTHMS
Upsetters- Copasetic* /
(Little Roy – Don't Cross The Nation)
Upsetter (UK) US 361 & Upsetter (US) LP 007
*a dub medley of 'Bend Down Low', 'Nice Time', 'One Love', 'Simmer Down', 'It Hurts To Be Alone' and 'Lonesome Feelings' with a spoken intro by U-Roy. (some say it's Lord Comic)

Joe Gibbs re-cut the 'Duppy Conqueror' rhythm as 'Ghost Capturer', which is a faithful horns cut to the original. Released in 1970. There is also a vocal cut, 'Ghost Walk', which uses the Duppy Conqueror rhythm, but is a different take and is not so faithful to the original.
Joe Gibbs All-Stars – Ghost Capturer /
(Caly Gibbs – Seeing Is Believing)
Jogib Records DYNA JG 3151/48

Above: The I-Threes – looking great and sounding fine. From left: Judy, Rita, Marcia.

THE WAILERS AND JAD

The US star Johnny Nash set up a new company (JODA) with Danny Sims: and in 1963 Johnny toured Jamaica and fell in love with the place. JODA released singles by white soul boy Johnny Daye, the first release from Gloria Gaynor and from R&B star (much loved in Jamaica) Roscoe Gordan. In 1965 they moved to Jamaica and stayed with Ken Khouri, JODA's licensee and friend. A house in Russell Heights was the base of operation from which Johnny Nash recorded his *Hold Me Tight* album that featured rocksteady guitar maestro Lynn Taitt, as a musician and arranger.

Johnny Nash came across Bob Marley at a grounation, which he was taken to by Neville Willoughby (a local journalist and musician) and by early 1967 Bob, Peter Tosh and Rita Marley were signed up to JAD as songwriters and performers (JAD reflecting the fact that producer Arthur Jenkins had joined the label).

JAD had their eyes on the international market for Johnny and also the other artists signed to JAD: Lloyd Price (a big star from the previous decade with whom the young Johnny had toured and been a label mate), Howard Tate

(the up coming soul star whose albums for Verve and Atlantic are sought after) and local star Byron Lee. Jamaica provided a cheap place to record these artists, then, using the kudos of having Johnny Nash on the label, the material was released in the US (via Epic), the UK (via CBS and Major Minor), Holland (via Philips), France (JAD through a label deal with CBS) and Canada (JAD).

Very little Marley product was released as can been seen from the main discography. The focus was on launching a US career, via major company support. Bob was also signed to JAD's publishing arm – 'Cayman' music, where much of Bob's songwriting catalogue can be found that now belongs to the Estate. In 1984, Danny Sims brought a court case against Bob's Estate as Bob had sometimes assigned songs to other people, to avoid Cayman claiming ownership. The case was lost, as over 8 years had elapsed and the matter was now beyond the Statute of Limitations. Following Bob's death JAD released, via a deal with Warners, an album *Chances Are* and a single 'Reggae On Broadway'. The project featured added production and was much criticized at the time but it's interesting how remixing of Bob's work is now commonplace.

SINGLE
UK 1981
Bob Marley
Reggae On Broadway / Gonna Get You
WEA K79250 *comes in a picture sleeve

ALBUM
Bob Marley
Chances Are
WEA K99183
Reggae On Broadway / Gonna Get You / Chances Are / Soul Rebel / Dance Do The Reggae / Mellow Mood / Stay With Me / Soul Rebel /

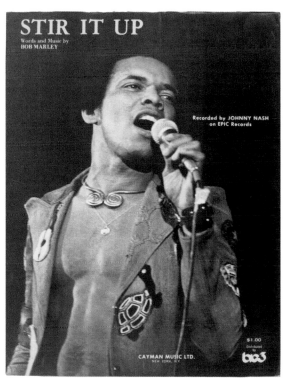

JAD artists ranged from the pop styling of The Cowsills to the blue-eyed Soul of Johnny Daye (who also recorded for Stax). Gloria Gaynor released her first single on Jocida and then signed to MGM (as did The Cowsills).

His credits from this period include 'The Fish & The Alley of Destruction' and 'Yellow House'.

'Rabbit' went on to join Free, released two solo albums for Island and currently plays with The Who.

JAD also signed up the purveyor of hits from the streets to the Uptown Jamaicans and tourists, the extraordinary Byron Lee, who still does the same thing today but has focused on Soca music.

On the 1969 album they cut for JAD *Bryon Lee & The Dragonaires* (UK, Major Minor & US, JAD) Bob's huge Jamaican hit 'Nice Time' was covered and was also released as a single.

Below are listed some of the Johnny Nash songs on which Bob or Peter got songwriting credits:

Bob Marley
Stir It Up, Guava Jelly, Rock it Baby (Baby We've Got a Date), You Poured Sugar On Me, and Comma Comma.

Peter Tosh
Love and You Got to Change Your Ways

These songs appeared on UK singles on Major Minor & CBS, in the US on JAD and CBS, in Jamaica on Federal and in Holland on Philips.

Johnny Nash also recorded the traditional gospel song 'Go Tell It To The Mountain', that the Wailers recorded with Lee Perry, on the album 'Prince of Peace' (US JAD 1001). Both these albums plus 'Love & Peace' (JAD JS 1003) & 'Soul Folk' (JAD JS 1006) were recorded in Jamaica, with the JA single release 'Hold Me Tight' c/w 'Cupid' carrying an 'arranged and conducted' credit to Arthur Jenkins and Lynn Taitt'.

Johnny Nash said of this period when interviewed in 1975 (by Tony Cummings, published in *Black Music*). 'I'd recorded a lot of things in Jamaica written by a super talent called Bob Marley. The first thing that English CBS put out on me was Bob's 'Stir It Up'. It was a hit here and I was getting somewhere again.'

Bob Marley said of this period when interviewed in 1973 (published in *Swing* 'In the beginning, I really thought the guy (Johnny Nash) was interested in helping Jamaicans with international exposure, but I find that I have helped him much more than he has helped me.' He continued 'He has made my music popular in the United States, and has made a lot of money, so it's time I got some'.

Another player in the Bob story was also a songwriter for JAD; John 'Rabbit' Bundrick, who famously was to provide the keyboard overdubs for 'Catch a Fire'. A Texan, like Johnny Nash, he lived as part of the JAD team and his story of living with Danny, Bob and various others, in Sweden, should be read as it's a good tale; it can be found in the *Songs Of Freedom* booklet.

Bryon Lee & The Dragonaires
Nice Time (Bob Morley) / Pupalick
JAD 75-100

Danny & Johnny brought in top session guys such as: Bernard 'Pretty' Purdie (drums), Eric Gale (guitar), Paul Martinez (bass), Richard Tee (piano), Hugh Masekela (horns). Songwriter Jimmy Norman and producer Arthur Jenkins (the 'A' in JAD) completed the US contingent. Local musicians used included Ernest Ranglin, Lyn Taitt, Paul Khouri and backing vocalists Winsome Dixon and Dawn Penn.

The core of the JAD writing team was Jimmy Norman and Al Pyfrom who focused on R&B. This team wrote some of the Marley recordings, which first surfaced on 'The Complete Bob Marley & The Wailers'.

There are lists of tracks that Bob Marley had registered, in the States, as being written by him for JAD that included tracks such as 'Rock To The Rock' that surfaced in 1999; how many more will ever appear remains unknown.

Bernard Purdie appeared on Gil Scott-Heron's *Pieces of a Man* (Philips) and *Free Will* (Flying Dutchman). Eric Gale was the producer of the *Negril* (Micron (JA) & Klik (UK), a jazz-reggae album. It featured Kingston heavyweights: Peter Tosh, Family Man, Cedric Brooks and Joe Higgs as well as 'Stuff' band mate and JAD session man Richard Tee. Gale became an occasional JA resident.

JAD

NOT FOR SALE
J-211-B

Time: 2:12
Cissi Music-BMI

Engineer:
Richard Alderson

MELLOW MOOD
(Bob Morley)
BOB, RITA & PETER
Produced by Johnny Nash & Arthur Jenkins in Jamaica, WI
Arr. by Arthur Jenkins

DANS LA SÉRIE ROCK STEADY

JOHNNY NASH	LLOYD PRICE
HOLD ME TIGHT	TAKE ALL
CUPID	LOVE, LOVE, LOVE
45 T. MAXI série Gémini 17508	45 T. JAD série Gémini 17516

BOB, RITA and PETER	BYRON LEE AND THE DRAGONAIRES
BEND DOWN LOW	EVERY DAY WILL BE LIKE A HOLIDAY
MELLOW MOOD	SLOW RUN
45 T. JAD série Gémini 17519	45 T. JAD série Gémini 17514

Above: Bob Marley & The Wailing Wailers record at the home of Johnny Nash and Danny Sims, in Kingston. JAD producer Arthur Jenkins holds the microphone.

DISTRIBUTED AND PRODUCED BY TUFF GONG 1970-1981

127, KING STREET 1970-1975

This period saw individuals within the group release solo work on the Tuff Gong label but most importantly establish their own labels – Peter Tosh's 'Intel-Diplo HIM', Bunny Wailers 'Solomonic', Family Man's 'Fams' & 'Cobra', Judy Mowatt's 'Ashandan' and, of course, Rita continued to record under her own name and with The Soulettes on the 'Wail 'N Soul 'M imprint that made a brief reappearance. Tuff Gong distributed all these releases and a poster for a U-Roy single at the time caught the vibe when it proclaimed 'Bob Marley & His Gang'. Just over 40 tunes from 'His Gang' carry the 127, King Street address. The shop appears to have been taken over by Bill Hutchinson and his 'Rocking Time' imprint, which released a track called 'King Street Special.' 'Rocking Time' singles have some great Tubby's Dub mixes on.

PETER TOSH

Tosh not only released singles on Tuff Gong & Intel-Diplo but also cut tunes for such producers as Joe Gibbs. Always active as a solo artist, he continued to record a whole range of material, ranging from ballads ('Little Green Apples', at Randy's) to Black Power & Rasta-inspired tunes ('Black Dignity' at Joe Gibbs) once the Wailers left Studio 1.

1971
Peter Tosh & The Wailers – Once Bitten /
(no credit)   Version
Tuff Gong DSR PT 7736-1/37-1

Peter Tosh & The Wailers – Lion /
(no credit) – Version
Tuff Gong DSR PT 7740-1/41-1

Peter Tosh – Here Comes the Sun /
Version
Blank (Tuff Gong) FPT 7898A/B

1972
Peter Tosh – Dog Teeth /
Peter Tosh – Version*
Intel Diplo HIM PPTD 2135 / WIRL BM 3707 – 2
*act. 'Steppin' Razor, Wail 'N Soul 'M cut. Probably released late 1971

Peter Tosh – No Mercy /
Peter Tosh – Version
Intel Diplo HIM PT 2260A / 2261B

Peter Tosh – Can't Blame The Youth /
Peter Tosh – Version
Intel Diplo HIM PT 1155 / 1156

1973
Peter Tosh & The Wailers – The Mark of the Beast /
Peter Tosh – Version
Intel Diplo HIM PT 4615A / PT 777

Peter Tosh & The Wailers – Burial /
Peter Tosh – Version
Intel Diplo HIM 001A / 4225B. & TC 9808A / 9809B
& Intel A / Intel B

Peter Tosh – What You Gonna Do /
Peter Tosh – Version
Intel Diplo HIM PT002A / PT D Intel

1974
Peter Tosh – Brand New Second Hand /
Peter Tosh – Version
Intel Diplo HIM PT 5084 / 5085

BUNNY WAILER

Bunny's records during this period were to form part of his classic 'Blackheart Man' album and he was in tremendous form artistically but, typically, he released a low number of singles and recorded for no one else.

1972
Heat Air Water – Searching For Love /
Uncredited (act. 'Searching for Love' version)
Solomonic NL 7759 / NL 7760

Bunny Wailer – Search For Love /
Bunny Wailer – Bide Up
Solomonic NL 7759 / FNL 7652A

I'ony & Big Youth – Bide /
Big Youth – Black On Black
Solomonic BL 5075A / 5076B
DJ cuts to 'Bide Up' and Youth rides the 'Bide Up' rhythm on' Black On Black'.

1973
Wailers – Life Line /
Wailers – Version*
Solomonic 2093 / FBM 7762
*act. Version to Craven Choke Puppy

Wailers – Pass It On /
Wailers – Trod On
Solomonic NL 1684 / 1683

Wailers – Dreamland /
Wailers – Dubd – Version*
Solomonic # 2649A / #2650B
*some copies labelled 'Wailers All Stars – Version 1'

1974/5
Bunny Wailer – Rasta-Man /
Istan – Vision Land
Solomonic BW 2733A / 2733B

Wailers – Arab Oil Weapon /
Wailers – Dubd – Version
Solomonic BW 3668 – 2 – 3675 / BW 3676
Bunny Wailers – Battering Down Sentence /
No credit – Version
Solomonic TC 2729A / TC 2729B & 'Talent A & B'.

The first pressings of Bunny Wailer's classic album, 'Blackheart Man', carries the 127, King Street address (matrix BL 001A/B). This was released in 1976 and must be the last piece of vinyl to carry the original Tuff Gong address. Both Peter & Bunny would shift distribution of their imprints to Tommy Cowan's Talent Corp. in Oxford Road following the demise of King Street Tuff Gong.

'Battering Down Sentence' has two matrixes, which both imply Tommy Cowan involvement but carry the King Street address – maybe old labels were being used up. The second pressing of 'Blackheart Man' has Tommy Cowan's 'Talent Corp.' as distributor (matrix BW 3263A/B)

RITA MARLEY

Since the early days of Studio 1, Rita recorded as a solo artist and as part of The Soulettes; The Soulettes were now Hortense Lewis and Cecile Campbell (sister to Cornell) and Rita. She continued cutting romantic ballads ('I Do' & 'I've Been Lonely') and funky Soul /Reggae ('Bring It Up', 'Gee Whiz'), especially with Lee Perry with whom she had worked at Studio 1. She also recorded for other producers during this time: with The Soulettes providing backing for a Lloyd Wilks album ('Jamaica Magic' FRM, 1970) for producer Ted Powder which was aimed at the tourist market and also various tracks for American Ted Binns. This period also saw the emergence of the I-Threes who were to support Bob with superb harmonies and such style during his years of international fame.

1971
The Soulettes – Bring It Up /
The Soulettes – My Desire (aka 'Got To Have Your Loving')
Tuff Gong DYNA Bob Marley 3515-1/3502-1 both sides are produced by Lee Perry

Rita Marley – Hallelujah Time / Version
Blank (Tuff Gong) 4919 / 4920 'Screwface' is TG 4915

1972
Rita & The Soulettes – I Do /
(No Credit) – Version
Tuff Gong RM 1332/33

Rita & The Soulettes – I've Been Lonely /
Rita & The Soulettes – I've Been Lonely – Version
Tuff Gong RM 7101-1 / 00-1
red on yellow & green on orange labels

1974
Esete* – Gee Whiz / *Rita Marley
(No credit) – Version
Wail N Soul RM 4702A / 4703A

JUDY MOWATT

Judy had a career previously as part of The Gaylettes And, once in the Tuff Gong camp, set up her own Ashandan imprint.

1974
Judy Mowatt – Mellow Mood /
Orthodox Revelation – Addis
Tuff Gong DSR SC 8465/66
blue on blue & red on yellow labels,

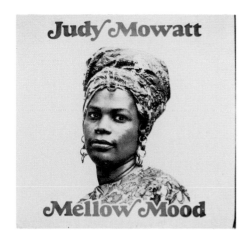

Top: Promotional poster for U-Roy's DJ cut of 'Trench Town Rock' (1971).

Judy Mowatt – Mr Big Man / Big Man
Ashandan AC 1330 / 1331
produced by Alan 'Skill' Cole, red/gold/green design

Judy Mowatt & The I-Threes – What An Experience /
Judy Mowatt – Version
Ashandan FC 22A/B

Judy Mowatt & The I-Threes – You Pour Sugar On Me /
(No credit) - Pour Sugar (Version)
Ashandan SCD 79112-A/ 79112-B & NVM

THE I-THREES
1974
Marcia, Judy & Rita – Medley /
(No credit) – Medley Version
Wail 'N Soul 'M* TG 1470 / 1471, *two different label
designs
It was mastered at the same time as Bob Marley & The
Wailers' 'Rebel Music'
(whose matrix is TG 1469) and was probably recorded at
the same session.

'FAMILY MAN'
Family Man was busy over this period and produced and
arranged for several other imprints as well as joining a
cruise ship for a while during Bob's sojourn in Sweden
with Danny Sims & Johnny Nash.

1971/2
Family Man & Knotty Roots – Distant Drums /
Family Man & Knotty Roots – Version
FAM'S AB 5009A / 5010B

1973
Wailers – Trouble Dub /
Wailers – Dub Feeling
FAM'S AB 2648 / 2649
A one-a-way piece from Wailers bassist, Aston
'Family Man' Barrett, where he revisits two old Bob Marley
and The Wailers tracks: 'Trouble is On the Road and
'Feel Alright' and gives them the remix treatment.

Family Man & The Rebel Arms – Eastern Memphis /
Rebel Am I – Version
Cobra – FM 3890 / 3891
look out for the full red/green/gold label!

Maria Anderson – Woman In Love /
(No credit) – Version
Cobra AB #4551A /#4552B
produced by Fams. Maria Anderson is not Rita Marley

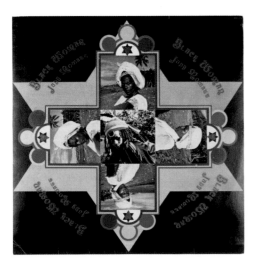

Vivian Jackson & The Defenders – Love Thy Neighbours /
No credit – Version
Defenders AB 4584/5
One of Yabby You foundation pieces, which uses the
Produced by Fams, it's Yabby You vocal to 'Distant Drums'
(see above)

The singles below carry the King Street address as
distributor, undoubtedly as a result of the Family Man link.

Horace Andy Family Man All Stars – Earth Must Be Hell /
Winston Jarrett & Family Man All Stars – Slaving In
Babylon*
Corporative Sounds WJ RF 2111/ 12 (1975)
*act. 'Let The Music Play'

The Righteous Flames – Slaving in Babylon /
Bus Dem Shut Version
Danger Zone WJ 5143/44

These tracks have formed the basis of such albums as:
'Horace Andy, Winston Jarrett & The Wailers – Earth
Must Be Hell' (Atra LP 1001 1988) and Wailers Band
– Tribute to 'Carly' Barrett (ATRALP 1008)

PRODUCTIONS OF OTHER ARTISTS
The Tuff Gong operation in King Street also produced and
released a few singles by other artists such as Pipe & The
Pipers (The Wailing Souls) and some DJ cuts to their own
Tunes, using the likes of Johnny Lover, Big Youth & U-Roy.

1971/2
Johnny Lover – Sun Is Shining DJ cut* /
Bob Marley & The Wailers – Sun Is Shining version
Tuff Gong DYNA Bob Marley 3360-1/ 3359-1. NPT&C
*known as 'Psalm 2' as that psalm provides the lyrics for
'Heathens Rage' as the opening lines are 'Why do the
heathens rage?' It briefly features Peter Tosh.

Big Youth – Craven Version Do Good /
Bob Marley & The Wailers – Thank The Lord*
Tuff Gong DSR RM 7103-1 / WIRL 3086-1
*the Wai I'N'Sou I'M cut from 1968 – 'Thank You Lord'
U-Roy & Bob Marley Kingston 12 Shuffle /
Wailers All Star Band – Ammunition
Tuff Gong DSR AC BM 4811-1/12-1

Pipe & The Pipers* – Harbour Shark /
Wailers All Stars – Shark
Tuff Gong DSR BM 4412/13
*aka The Wailing Souls

Pipe & The Pipers – Back Biter(s)* /
(No credit) - Version
Tuff Gong FBM 7730-A/ 7762-B
*some labels as 'Back Biters'

1974
A. Hudson – Got To Leave This Place /
(No credit) – Dynamite Hudson*
Tuff Gong RRS 2094 SC / DSR NL 7760
*act. the version to Bunny Wailer's 'Searching For Love'
Also comes labelled as 'Wailers – Live Line' / 'Wailers –
Version' on 'Solomonic' and also with a Tuff Gong label
on one side and a Solomonic label on the other side. The
obscure A. Hudson was a Twelve Tribes bredren of Bob's.

Leroy Smart – Pride and Ambition /
(No credit) – Pride version
Tuff Gong Gussie + Puppy Records
#0012 A 1768 rrs / # 2054 B RRS

UK ISSUES OF KING STREET, TUFF GONG
PRODUCTIONS
Just a few tracks surfaced:

Don Hutchinson – What You Gonna Do* /
Don Hutchinson – Version
IMF Pep 7001 PEP 001A/B
*act. A. Hudson's 'I've Got To Leave This Place'
This is a remixed version to the JA release & carries a
version, unlike the JA release. This tune was picked up by the
UK Coxsone, where it became a favourite and was also
known as 'Can An Ethiopian Change His Spots' and a dub
cut also appears on Sir Coxson Sound's 'King of The Dub
Rock' as 'It's Reggae Time Dubb Rock.'

The Soulettes – My Desire / Bring It Up
Jackpot JP 766
both sides produced by Lee Perry

Tuff Gong All-Stars – You Should Have Known Better /
Tuff Gong All Stars – Known Better
Punch PH114
*act. The Wailing Souls/ Pipe & The Pipers - 'Back Biter'

The Wailing Souls – Harbour Shark /
The Wailing Souls – Harbour Shark Version
Green Door GD 4014

Judy Mowatt – Pour Sugar On Me /
Judy Mowatt – What An Experience
EMI EMI 2469 (released 1976)
an Ashandan JA release (1974), but label states
'Produced by Alan Cole and Bob Marley for Tuff Gong'

A few Tuff Gong productions surfaced in the US on the
short-lived US arm of Tuff Gong. See 'US, Barbadian &
Canadian releases' section, page 160.

56, HOPE ROAD: 1976- 1981
This section covers vinyl released between 1975 and Bob's
death in early 1981. It covers the artists as King Street and
includes a short 'Distributed by' section. Bunny Wailer and
Peter Tosh continued to run their independent set-ups –
'Solomonic' and 'Intel-Diplo' respectively – and collaborated
on the splendid 'Anti-Aphartied', which had Peter blowing
melodica over Bunny's classic Amagideon rhythm. The third
I-Three, Marcia Griffiths, had no records put out by Tuff Gong,
but worked with Bunny Wailer's 'Solomonic' imprint from the
late 1970s. Together they had a hit in the US with 'Electric
Boogie', which even had its own 'Electric Slide' dance, in the
early 1980s. She cut the Wailers 'Dreamland' and 'Hurting
Inside' for Sonia Pottinger's 'High Note' label in 1977/8. I
have been unable to trace either 'Naturally' or 'Steppin'" on
Tuff Gong, both of which are said to exist. By 1984/85 Tuff
Gong had bought the old Federal plant at 220, Marcus
Garvey and all subsequent releases, and re-releases, carry
that address. The Federal manufacturing plant was renamed
'Ziggy's'. Several new imprints such as 'Rita Marley Music'
and 'Ghetto Youths' appeared and the Tuff Gong logo
changed design, briefly, in the early 1980s.

RITA MARLEY
Rita continued her solo career with a slew of singles towards
the end of the decade, as Bob spent more time abroad and
was frequently in London. Rita had the biggest hit of her
career in 1981 with the weed anthem 'One Draw' that was
released on Tuff Gong (with a new style logo) on both 7 & 12-
inch singles. The 12" Disco also came on red vinyl.

1978
Rita Marley – Thank You Lord /
No Credit – Version
Tuff Gong FRM 2001A/B

Rita Marley - (A) Jah Jah /
No Credit - Version Or Bob Marley – Jah Version
Tuff Gong DSR 6187A/B & Tuff Gong DSR 5090A/B
Matrix shows that 'Jah, Jah' may have been released in 1977.

1979
Rita Marley – Man To Man /
No Credit – Man To Man Version
Tuff Gong FRM 7626A/B

Rita Marley – That's The Way (Jah Planned It) /
Rita Marley – Jah Plan
Tuff Gong RM 003A/B

1980
The Beauty Of God's Plan /
Version
Tuff Gong DSR 0373/74

1981
Tuff Gong Music – Play Play /
Tuff Gong Music – Play Dub
Tuff Gong RM 3453A/B

1980: ALBUM
Who Feels It Knows It, Tuff Gong DSR 1278/79.
A Jah, Jah, That's The Way, Who Knows It Feels It,
I'm Still Waiting, Thank You Jah c/w Good Morning Jah,
Man To Man, Play Play, Jah Jah Don't Want, Easy Sailing

JUDY MOWATT

Judy released her first solo album on Tuff Gong and just
one single. Her Ashandan imprint remained active and was
distributed by Tuff Gong until Bob's death, when it moved
to Sonic Sounds.

1976
Judy Mowatt – We've Got To Leave The West /
Judy Mowatt – Leave The West
Tuff Gong JM 3379A/B

ALBUM: 1975
Mellow Mood, Tuff Gong JM 001A/B.
Mellow Mood, Love Seed, I'm Alone, What An Experience,
Mr Big Man c/w Pour Sugar On Me, You Were Too Good
For Me, First Cut, Just A Stranger Here, Rasta Woman Chant

Ashandan label. The early labels have no 'distributed by'
information on. By 1979 the 'Tuff Gong' name appears.

1975
Pablove Black – Flippings / Middle East Crisis
Ashandan MIC 2781/82
The artist credit is a 'best guess' as it carries track titles but
no artist credit. Black was the multi-instrumentalist who
worked for the Twelve Tribes, often live as opposed to
studio work. He had terrific musical ability and only the
relatively small amount of his recorded music prevents him
from being better known.

1975/76
Judy Mowatt – Only A Woman /
Judy Mowatt – Version
Ashandan MM 7744A/B

1977
Judy Mowatt – Black Woman /
Joy Tulloch – Black Beauty
Ashandan DSR 4585/86 two label variants.

1978
Judy Mowatt – Put It On /
Judy Mowatt – Put It Jah
Ashandan DSR 7842/43

Judy Mowatt – Change Is Gonna Come /
Judy Mowatt – Part Two
Ashandan DSR 6925/26

1979
Judy Mowatt – Slave Queen /
(No credit) – Slave Woman version
Ashandan DSR 9526/27

Light Of Love* – Warning /
Briggidare Jerry** – Warn Dem
Ashandan DSR 8627/28 two label variants
*a group which toured with Judy & included Joy Tulloch.
**Shows Judy's link with the Twelve Tribes organisation,
as partner Freddie McGregor is producing, and Brigadier
Jerry (great label spelling) was a Twelve Tribes member.
Judy also appears on a Twelve Tribes compilation album.

1980
Judy Mowatt – You're My People /
No Credit – Peoples version
Ashandan My People A / B

1979: ALBUM
Black Woman, Ashandan JM 1000A/B
Strength To Go Through, Concrete Jungle, Slave Queen,
Put It On, Zion Chant c/w Black Woman, Down In
The Valley, Joseph, Many Are Called, Sisters Chant.
This album stands perhaps as the most feminist of all
reggae albums ever released. Certainly it was a radical
position for a Rasta woman, in the late 1970s. Released by
Island in the UK, on the Grove Musik imprint. The JA issue
has two different covers, both of which are different from
the UK press, which has great Dennis Morris pictures.

I-THREES

Just a couple of singles surfaced credited to the I-Threes.
Later in the 1980s they would record an album for Tuff
Gong. The I-Threes get a credit on the Fred Bryan-
produced 'Bucket A Well' by Bunny & The I-Threes. The
'Bunny' is neither 'Wailer' nor 'Rugs', to my ears, but is
probably connected to the Fred Bryant who recorded
several gospel / reggae singles on Love-Link and various
other labels. Some of these tunes sound very much like
the I-Threes are involved (but not credited). Another Fred
Bryan single 'Don't Let The Children Suffer' (Welcome)
carries a 'High Threes' credit. The Disco 45 of 'Peaceful
Negotiation' / The Councillors – 'Talk About Love' (Lovelink
JA) is well worth looking out for. 'Talk About Love' is great
funky/pop/reggae whilst 'Peaceful Negotiation' is good
crossover reggae/ gospel/pop. The music is clearly played
by a very able set of musicians –Third World?

1975
I-Threes & The Wailers – No Woman No Cry /
I-Threes & The Wailers – No Woman No Cry Version
Tuff Gong MIC 2243A/B

1979
I-Threes – Many Are Called /
(No credit) – Chosen
Tuff Gong DSR 5260A/61B
Recorded at the Black Ark by Lee Perry

I-Threes – Precious World /
I-Threes – Precious Dub
56 Hope Road DSR 0280/81

1979: Disco 45
I-Threes – Music For The World /
I-Threes – Many Are Called
Tuff Gong TG 085A/B
*released in the US, with great picture cover, in the early
1980s. The Black Ark 'Many' has no dub on the US release.

In 1985 the I-Threes issued the single below as a tribute
to Bob. It's a picture disc:

I-Threes & The Wailers – He's A Legend /
The Wailers – Instrumental version
Tuff Gong / Rita Marley Music XW0095A/b

'FAMILY MAN'

Family Man continued to be involved in some work
outside the Wailers, in fact much of his best work is found
on a series of JA singles that had nothing to do with the
Wailers. A few pieces surfaced via Tuff Gong label or
distribution.

1975
Sena – Children Of The Ghetto / version
Fams FM 3017A/B also released on 'One Way Sound'

1976
The Wailers* – Work /
The Wailers – Guided Missile
Tuff Gong FAM MAN 1494A/AAA
*despite the credit, these are Fams instrumental tracks

1980
Sena - Natural Woman /
Tuff Gong All Stars – Natural Woman
Fams DSR 0402A/B.

1981: DISCO 45
Aston 'Family Man' Barrett – Well Pleased / Cobra Style
Fams TG 1982A/B Fine Fams instrumental

In 1981 'Family Man' released the 'Juvenile Delinquent'
album (Clappers US), which featured the Sena (aka Senya
or Olive Grant) tracks 'Natural Woman', and a re-recorded
'Children Of The Ghetto' in 'vocal plus dub 'showcase style'
with two Sonia Higgs tracks on Side 2.

MELODY MAKERS

Starting off with four of Bob's children, the Melody Makers'
first releases were on Tuff Gong singles (check out the picture
sleeve below). Their releases continued after Bob's death.

1979
Melody Maker – Children Playing In The Street /
Melody Maker – Dubbing In The Streets
Tuff Gong DSR 8723/24

1980
Melody Makers – Sugar Pie /
(No credit) – Version
Tuff Gong TG 1986A/B

Melody Makers – Trodding /
Melody Makers – Trod It
Tuff Gong DSR 0417/18
released in a b/w picture sleeve

DISCOGRAPHY

TUFF GONG IMPRINTS: HIGHLIGHTS

Outside of Bob Marley & The Wailers' activity, the imprint only released a few other artists. Towards the end of the 1970s and following Bob's death the imprint and others, like 56 Hope Road, became more active. Bob's mother, Cedella Booker, released ' Stay Alive' c/w 'Redemption Song' on the traditional Tuff Gong label, in 1982.

TUFF GONG LABEL

All circa 1979.
Dillenger – Cornbread Earl & Me / Corn Bread Dub
Tuff Gong DSR 1963A/64B
Dillenger's toast was inspired by the film ('Cornbread Earl and Me'), which starred a young Laurence Fishburn, about a top black athlete killed by the police in a case of mistaken identity (1975). The film also starred Jamaican actress Madge Sinclair (whom 'Swing' magazine liked to photograph).

The Meditations – Miracles / version
Tuff Gong DSR 7607A/B
The Meditations provided harmonies on 'Rasta Man Live It Up' and 'Blackman Redemption' singles.

Sheena Spirit & The Third Eyes – Reggae Pounding / Sheena & Blue – Reggae Street
Tuff Gong DSR 7608/09

The classic 'Arise' album by The Abyssinians (Virgin UK) was pressed on the Tuff Gong label (1978); it came in the UK sleeve (DSR 9005/06 Tuff Gong Records).
Ken Boothe's 'Reggae For Lovers' album appeared on the imprint. It looks like a 'pressing & distribution' deal, as Tuff Gong have no other credits (GEN 3010 Tuff Gong). Tuff Gong also released Aswad's Island albums in JA.

56 HOPE ROAD IMPRINT

Started in the late 1970s and utilising the Hope Road Studio, it featured a variety of artists (in the usual JA style) that included several of the new wave of Dancehall artists like Early B & Eek a Mouse. The label saw the first releases of child star Nadine Sutherland – whom Tuff Gong kept under their wing as she grew up – and who released her first album on the classic 'Tuff Gong' label in 1985. Something over 60 singles were released on the Hope Road imprint before the end of the 1980s.

Half a dozen of the best 56 Hope Road releases
(all circa 79/80):
Jah Stone & The Elect Of Elders
 – Wah Go Home / Golden Jubilee
56 Hope Road DSR 1454/55
A heavy Rasta tune!'

Papa Michigan & General Smiley
 – One Love Jamdown / Dub-Down
56 Hope Road DSR 0415A/16B 1980
One of the new generation of Dancehall DJs pays homage to Bob's 'One Love' ideal, with this piece that looks back to the 'Peace & Love' fashions of the mid/late 1970s. By now DJs chatted over slow & heavy rhythms and talked of diseases, connections and the ghetto runnings of guns and soldiers. It was released on a UK Tuff Gong Disco 45 (Island IPR 2035), and worthy of mention is the flip: Freddie McGregor's 'Joggin' (56 Hope Road), which is a great tune.

Mighty Diamonds – Don't Want War / Dub Wise
56 Hope Road DSR 0103//04
A Tommy Cowan production

Mystic M – Feeling Happy / Version
56 Hope Road DSR 8350A/B
features the production, and Black Ark Studio, of Lee Perry

Oku Onuora – Reflections in Red / Reflections in Dub
56 Hope Road DSR 8459/60.
released in a two-sided picture cover
First release from the Dub Poet, who was often featured in *Swing* Magazine.

Soul Power & Sound – Yard Music / Yard Music Dub
Fifty Six Hope Road DSR 3343/44.
Produced by T. C. McLaughlin & Andy Cherton

Freddie McGregor's 'Rastaman Camp' album (Observer) was also pressed up on the 56, Hope Road imprint with a different cover and simply called 'Freddie McGregor'.

RELATED RELEASES

Various other tunes appeared with Tuff Gong connections. The pair below are little gems with such links:

Donald Palmer – Cool It Youthman / version
Vibes Label DSR 2351A/52B 1980
Great poppy reggae, with lyrical reference to the popular 'tracksuit' style of the time.

Viceroys – Shaddai Children / Version
Victorious Steppers DSR 1264/65 1980/1

Tommy Cowan worked with the Twelve Tribes on their commercial recordings, which were issued on the likes of 'Jah Love Music' and 'Jahmikmusic' imprints. The 'Orthodox' label singles and albums were aimed at Twelve Tribes members only. Israel Vibration, who were first recorded by the Twelve Tribes, later worked with Tommy Cowan at the Tuff Gong Studio. Both the albums and 12" Disco 45, listed below, carry the Tuff Gong name. The Barrett Brothers played on the album, and Tuff Gong Art Director, Neville Garrick, looked after the artwork.

Israel Vibration – Unconquered People
Israel Vibes, 1980
The album carries the Tuff Gong logo and was recorded and mixed at the Studio. There is also a dub version of the album.

Israel Vibration – Crisis* / Crisis In Dub
Positive Vibe, Disco 45 *featuring Augustus Pablo

DISTRIBUTED BY TUFF GONG

Few singles, outside of the band members', were distributed by Hope Road during Bob's life. One early single that has surfaced is by a very obscure deep roots / Rasta outfit called the Almighty Stones. Almighty Stones – Clean Hands and A Pure Heart / Almighty Hands
Bird Label AS 082 A/B (1976)

From a similar time comes the single below, which has the Hope Road address and carries a 'Wailers' credit on the flip. Jimmy (Martin) Riley certainly recorded with 'Family Man' around this time. Riley again recorded with The Wailers band in the mid-1980s.
Jimmy Riley – Hot Summer / Wailers – Version
Full Moon DSR 2833/34 (1976)

Once signed to Tuff Gong as 'Pipe & The Pipers', the Wailing Souls released a single on their own 'Massive' imprint that carried the Hope Road address.
McDonald & W. Mathews – Feel The Spirit / version
Massive DSR 8372A/73B (1979)

A co Jah Love Muzik & Tafari production of Twelve Tribes member, Fred Locks – 'Gun Court Affair' – carries the Hope Road address as distributor.
Fred Locks – Gun Court Affair / Gun Court Dub
Tafari DSR 7812A/B (1979)

Drummond later released a single, 'Inequity', that credited the Wailers band and had 'Family Man' as co-producer (Faithful African Tribe circa 1983).
Fitzroy Drummond & The Creative Explosion / Part Two
Faithful African Tribe DSR 1339A/B (1980)

The splendid deep roots reggae/jazz/nyahbinghi group The Light Of Saba released the album 'Sabee' on their own 'Universal Will Power – The Light Of Saba' label, which was manufactured and distributed by 'Tuff Gong, 56, Hope Road' (1979).

UNRELEASED TRACKS

Anyone familiar with Bob Marley & The Wailers' work will notice that there are various tracks not mentioned thus far that have appeared in the flood of posthumous releases. These have been culled from the following sources, or remain commercially unreleased.

1. DUB PLATES

Dub plates were an important part of a Sound System's armoury as they provided exclusive material that could only be heard at that Sound. Producers and groups sold directly to Sounds as it provided them with extra income. Originally these tracks would be supplied on two-track tapes and the Sounds would create their own specials. As the 1970s moved on, specials would be mixed on to plates or tape and then sold to Sounds. In the latter part of Bob Marley & The Wailers career, various mixes, straight from the studio mixing desk, would appear as Dub plates.

At the 1974 Notting Hill Carnival Bob Marley and the Barrett Brothers appeared on the Sir Lloyd Coxsone sound. Lloydie announced their presence and then said 'We just want you to know that all these Bob Marley dubs were specially made only for this Sound System…these tunes can only be played by this Sound, your number one station.'

Who mixed these tracks is often lost in the mists of time, especially on the early two tracks that were mixed several times over the years. But Dub plate mixes are a true part of the music, as they are what people heard when they went to Sounds.

Various Bob Marley tracks never made it past Dub plate release; these include:
Natural Mystic & Rainbow Country
(Perry/Black Ark circa 1975/76)
Pass It On (Tuff Gong, circa 1971)
Why Should I (Tuff Gong, circa 1971)
The rhythm tracks for the Wail'N Soul'M tracks 'Nice Time', 'Hypocrite' and 'Thank You Lord' were culled from 2 track Dub plates.
It appears that 'Jump Nyahbinghi' was constructed from a Dub plate called 'Dancing From Within.'
Dub plates were also cut as 'Sound Specials' and two Marley ones have surfaced on which Pablo blows over the Wailers rhythm track. From the mid-1970s they are:
Screw Face Pablo (over Screwface rhythm)
Keep on Pablo (over Keep On Moving rhythm)
These are a good example of how older favourites were recycled by newer artists. Likewise, older tracks would be remixed, especially as the technology developed. Such mixes include:
Brand New Second Hand, Man To Man, Hold On To This Feeling.

YET TO BE RELEASED:

Babylon Feel This One (Tuff Gong for the Twelve Tribes Sound, circa 1978)
Soul Shake Up Party (Tuff Gong, circa 1977)
My Woman (Tuff Gong, circa 1976)
There are a host of mixes that were created for Sound System play. From the mid-1970s onwards the mixing of these releases, compared to the radio-friendly Island issues, was far 'rootsier' and designed to be played through large and powerful amplifiers with huge speakers.
There are great mixes of:
Babylon System – raw Dub
Belly Full – two different Dub mixes (no vocals)
Is This Love – slower than the released cut & no I-Threes
Jah Live – vocal & Dub
Smile – Harry J cut Dub wise
Waiting In Vain – no multi-tracking on Bob's voice
Wake Up & Live – rhythm mix, no vocal
War – vocal & Dub

2. JAD TRACKS

When Bob Marley was signed to JAD many demos were recorded for projected albums that never saw the light of day. These vary from basic acoustic 'Bob & his guitar' pieces to almost finished tracks that JAD were waiting to send to the US for 'polishing'. Such tracks include: Chances Are, Dance Do The Reggae, Fallin in & Out Of Love, Gonna Get You, Hammer, How Many Times, I'm Hurting Inside, I'm Still Waiting, Love, Milk Shake & Potato Chips, Music Gonna Teach, One Love - True Love, Rocking Steady, Rock To The Rock, Soul Rebel, Splish For My Splash, Stay With Me, There She Goes, The World Is Changing, Touch Me, Treat You right, What Goes Around, Comes Around.

These tracks can be found on the JAD/Universal set 'Fy-ah, Fy-ah' & 'Grooving Kingston 12'

3. LEFT ON STUDIO TAPE

Various tracks ended up never being released and were found following Bob's death. Such tracks include:

STUDIO 1

And I Love Her (alternative take), Don't Ever Leave Me (alternative take), Dreamland (unreleased original, Bunny lead), I'm Gonna Put It On (alternative take), It Hurts To Be Alone (alternative take),
Nobody Knows (unreleased original, sans overdubs)
Playboy (alternative take)
Rocking Steady (alternative take)
Sinner Man (alternative take)
This Train (with Bunny lead vocal)
True Confession
Wages Of Love (acoustic rehearsal, with Bob on lead vocal)
Wages Of Love (Bob on solo lead, alternative take)
Where Is My Mother (demo version)
Wailers as background vocalists.
Joanne Dennis and the Wailers: Don't Cry Over me
Rita Marley & The Soulettes: That Ain't Right
These tracks can be found on the Heartbeat / Studio 1 CDs.

PERRY

I Know A Place*
Kaya version – with spoken intro
Keep On Skanking (Perry)
Long Long Winter (Perry/Marley)
More Axe – alternative take, with studio chat
Shocks Almighty, often known as Shocks Of (The Mighty), and there are two cuts, one with Lee Perry vocal. There is also a Dub plate with different lyrics.
Turn Me Loose – a Kaya re-cut
Who Colt The Game*
*It's claimed that Perry pressed these up on blanks to hawk around. I've never seen them to confirm this.
These tracks have surfaced on all kinds of albums.

POWDER

Thank You Lord (Ted Powder)
This Train (Ted Powder)
These two tracks were reportedly pressed up on a 'Tiger' or 'Dynamic' single and credited to 'Bob Marley Singers'. I've even seen it listed in a Dynamics catalogue but have found no trace of. They only appeared posthumously, so that's why I think it was from tape…but who knows.

TUFF GONG ISLAND

Various of these tracks have appeared as Dub plates (see previous page). Below is a 'complete' listing:
Babylon Feel This One – circa 1978
Jailhouse – circa 1977
Jingling Keys – circa 1979
Jungle Fever – circa 1980
She Used to Call Me Dada circa 1979 – for Cindy Breakspeare
Soul Shake Down Party – circa 1979
Uprising Theme – circa 1980

There are also some tapes of tracks from later Island albums in much rawer forms, before the harmonies and other later over-dubs were added. Some of these can be heard as Dub plates at Sounds. 'Sun Is Shining', from the *Kaya* album, is particularly well known. There is a full CD of these and they are straight from the mixing desk. (known as the Dennis Thompson tapes).

4. OTHER TAPES:

(i) John 'Rabbit' Bundrick Hotel tape – acoustic tape first seen on *Songs Of Freedom*
(ii) The 'Bedroom' tapes – some of Bob's final works – due to be released in 2005!
(iii) There are other private tapes that circulate of Bob out of the studio. Really only of interest to hard-core collectors.

5. LIVE AND REHEARSAL SETS

The BBC transcription disc (see Promotional items) of the concert that The Wailers did for the BBC at the Paris Theatre, In London, has been the source of many bootleg CDs.
Like many other major bands, there are in circulation many tapes (now CDs) of many concerts. Bob didn't change set lists that often, so many concerts carry the same set. Generally one for the collectors, though the following are of interest:
(i)The Wailers last concert, at which Stevie Wonder appeared, is a highly atmospheric concert, with Bob & Stevie together on 'I Shot The Sheriff' and Bob singing 'Simmer Down' – which is a rarity in itself. Low-fi style! There are two recordings.
(ii) The full set from 'The Record Plant' (see 'Talkin' Blues') and has a great vibe.
(iii) From rehearsal tapes there are still tracks such as 'Can't Bow Ina Babylon', 'Can't Take Your Slogans No More' and 'Russian Invasion'.

ABOUT THESE TRACKS
1. DUB PLATES

Natural Mystic – is the original to the Island *Exodus* album cut. It's much rougher, as it was cut for Dub plate play. The released vinyl versions are from tape and aren't the same as the Dub plate cuts. The version sides on the vinyl are just rhythms, whereas the Dub plates had Dub mixes. (same for Rainbow Country). Rainbow Country – was cut as the same time as Natural Mystic and finds Bob in metaphysical mood, as he sings 'I'm a rainbow too'. Remixed by Funk Star Deluxe, as a follow-up to their smash mix of 'Sun Is Shining'. Pass It On – is an absolute little gem as Bunny leads on this, his own composition, that he re-cut for *Burnin'*. The lyrics are different on the first verse and it's a Bunny *tour-de-force*. Why Should I – usually you know why a track doesn't appear on vinyl, but not in this case. It easily stands alongside the other Tuff Gong productions from the early 1970s. Great.

YET TO BE RELEASED:

Babylon Feel this One – with its pedigree of being cut for the Twelve Tribes you'd hope it would be a roots gem, but no. It's of its time – Bob was very busy!

Soul Shake Up Party – a bit of fun as Bob revisits 'Soul Shake Down Party'.

My Woman – a typical Tuff Gong production of its time. Never fully finished.

2. JAD TRACKS

All the tracks from JAD are pretty much pure pop songs and have no great interest as songs.

3. LEFT ON STUDIO TAPE
STUDIO1

Dreamland – this unreleased original, with Bunny on lead, was cut following a suggestion by Dodd, who introduced Bunny to the original. A great bit of Wailers history.

PERRY

Shocks Almighty – Bob and Lee give 'Soul Almighty' the Dave Barker 'Shocks Of Mighty' treatment. Dave Barker worked with Perry and had a very American soul sound and did the 'Shocks' tracks, which featured 'soul shouting'. There is one cut that has just Bob singing the lyrics and one with Bob and Lee sharing the lead. The Dub plate cut has alternative (but similar) lyrics and even has Dave Barker adding various shouts like 'Mercy!' or 'Good Gosh!' and the vibe is great.
Long Long Winter – from late 1971, it's another Curtis Mayfield track that Bob recorded with Lee Perry, after his return from Sweden.
Keep On Skanking and Turn Me Loose were cut when Lee Perry opened his Black Ark Studio. Marley voiced over old rhythms: Leo Grahams', 'Black Candle' for 'Keep On Skanking' and Turn Me Loose is 'Kaya' re-cut. UK journalist Chris Lane was at the session and even took pictures. Chris also joined in, on bongos, on the Dub cut and then took it to Tubby's to have it cut on to acetate!
I Know A Place and Who Colt The Game – were both recorded in the Black Ark in 1978. Who Colt The Game uses dominoes as a metaphor for the troubles of the world. Whilst I Know A Place finds Bob yearning for a better place in a song full of deep pathos and loneliness. Not the same as 'I Know'.

POWDER

Thank You Lord and This Train are both re-cuts of the Wail 'N Soul'M classics, in an 'Uptown' style, that did little at the time and now are a footnote.

SINGLE RELEASES 1973–1980
CATALOGUE DETAILS

1973
Bob Marley & The Wailers –
Baby Baby We've Got A Date
Bob Marley & The Wailers – Stop That Train (instrumental)
Blue Mountain BM 1021

The Wailers – Concrete Jungle
The Wailers – Reincarnated Souls
Island WI 6164

1974
The Wailers – Get Up, Stand Up
The Wailers – Slave Driver
Island WIP 6167

Bob Marley & The Wailers – Natty Dread
Bob Marley & The Wailers – So Jah Say
Island WIP 6212

1975
Bob Marley & The Wailers – No Woman, No Cry
Bob Marley & The Wailers – Kinky Reggae
Island WIP 6244
both Live at the Lyceum, released in picture cover

1976
Bob Marley & The Wailers – Jah Live
Bob Marley & The Wailers – Concrete
Island WIP 6265
produced by Bob Marley & Lee Perry

Bob Marley & The Wailers – Johnny Was
(Woman Hold Her Head & Cry)
Bob Marley & The Wailers – Cry To Me
Island WIP 6296

Bob Marley & The Wailers – Roots, Rock, Reggae
Bob Marley & The Wailers – Them Belly Full (But We Hungry Now)
Island WIP 6309

1977
Bob Marley & The Wailers – Exodus
Bob Marley & The Wailers – Exodus (instrumental version)
Island WIP 6390 UK No 14, 9 weeks

12" Disco
Bob Marley & The Wailers – Exodus*
Bob Marley & The Wailers – Exodus (instrumental version)
Island IPR 2000 * is a 7'38" mix

Bob Marley & The Wailers – Waiting In Vain
Bob Marley & The Wailers – Roots
Island WIP 6402 UK No 27, 6 weeks

Bob Marley & The Wailers – Jamming
Bob Marley & The Wailers – Punky Reggae Party*
Island WIP 6410 UK No 9, 12 weeks
released in picture sleeve

12" Disco
Bob Marley & The Wailers – Jamming
Bob Marley & The Wailers – Punky Reggae Party*
Island IPR 2005
*produced by Lee Perry & isn't The 'Wailers' band

1978
Bob Marley & The Wailers – Is This Love
Bob Marley & The Wailers – Crisis (version)
Island WIP 6420 UK No 9, 9 weeks
released in picture sleeve

Bob Marley & The Wailers – Satisfy My Soul
Bob Marley & The Wailers – Smile Jamaica*
Island WIP 6440 UK No 21, 10 weeks
*produced by Lee Perry. Released in a picture sleeve

Bob Marley & The Wailers – Stir It Up
Bob Marley & The Wailers – Rat Race
Island WIP 6478
both sides taken from 'Babylon by Bus'

12" Disco
Bob Marley & The Wailers –
War/No More Trouble
Bob Marley & The Wailers – Exodus
Island IPR 2026 released in a picture sleeve
both tracks from 'Babylon By Bus'

Bob Marley & The Wailers – No Woman, No Cry*
Bob Marley & The Wailers – Jamming**
Island 12 WIP 6244 *released in a picture sleeve
*taken from 'Live!' ** from 'Babylon By Bus'

1979
Bob Marley & The Wailers –
So Much Trouble In The World
Bob Marley & The Wailers – So Much Trouble (instrumental)
Island WIP 6510 UK No 56, 4 weeks
released in a picture sleeve

Bob Marley & The Wailers – Survival
Bob Marley & The Wailers – Wake Up & Live
Island WIP 6553

Bob Marley & The Wailers – Zimbabwe
Bob Marley & The Wailers – Survival
Island WIP 6597 released in a picture sleeve

12" Disco
Bob Marley & The Wailers – Zimbabwe & Africa Unite
Bob Marley & The Wailers – Wake Up & Live Island
12 WIP 6597

1980
Bob Marley & The Wailers – Could You Be Loved
Bob Marley & The Wailers – One Drop
Island WIP 6610 UK No 5, 12 weeks

Bob Marley & The Wailers – Three Little Birds
Bob Marley & The Wailers – Every Need Got An Ego To Feed
Island WIP 6641 UK No17, 9 weeks

12" Disco
Bob Marley & The Wailers – Could You Be Loved
Bob Marley & The Wailers – One Drop & Ride Natty Ride
Island 12 WIP 6610

Bob Marley & The Wailers – Redemption Song
Bob Marley & The Wailers – Redemption Song (band version)
Island WIP 6653 released in a picture sleeve

Bob Marley & The Wailers – Redemption Song
Bob Marley & The Wailers – Redemption Song (band version)
& I Shot The Sheriff (Live)
Island 12 WIP 6653 released in a picture sleeve

A BUYER'S GUIDE TO BOB MARLEY & THE WAILERS ON CD

All the music that Bob made is almost fully available on good quality CDs, there is no need to buy the cheap CDs that clutter the racks as they offer nothing new, are often of poor audio quality, have incorrect track titles and the Marley Estate receives not a penny from them.

CAREER OVERVIEW

The best career overview remains the million-selling *Songs Of Freedom* 4 CD set, that is now housed in a CD sized slip case, not the long box style as originally released, but still includes the fine booklet.
Disc One: Judge Not / One Cup Of Coffee / Simmer Down / I'm Still Waiting / One Love/People Get Ready (original) / Put It On / Bus Dem Shut (Pyaka) / Mellow Mood (original) / Bend Down Low / Hypocrites / Stir It Up (original) / Nice Time / Thank You Lord (original) / Hammer / Caution / Back Out / Soul Shake Down Party / Do It Twice / Soul Rebel / Sun Is Shining / Don't Rock My Boat / Small Axe / Duppy Conqueror / Mr Brown
Disc Two: Screw Face / Lick Samba / Trench Town Rock / (alternative mix) / Craven Choke Puppy / Guava Jelly / Acoustic Melody / I'm Hurting Inside (alternative mix) / High Tide Or Low Tide / Slave Driver / No More Trouble / Concrete Jungle / Get Up Stand Up / Rastaman Chant / Burnin' And Lootin' / Iron Lion Zion / Lively Up Yourself / Natty Dread / I Shot The Sheriff (live)
Disc Three: No Woman No Cry (live at the Roxy) / Who The Cap Fit / Jah Live / Crazy Baldheads / War / Johnny Was / Rat Race / Jammin' (12" mix) / Waiting In Vain (advert mix) / Exodus (12" mix) / Natural Mystic / Three Little Birds (alternative mix) / Running Away / Keep On Moving (London version) / Easy Skanking / Is This Love (horns mix) / Smile Jamaica / Time Will Tell
Disc Four: Africa Unite / Survival / One Drop / One Dub / Zimbabwe / So Much Trouble In The World / Ride Natty Ride (12" mix) / Babylon System / Coming In From The Cold (12" mix) / Real Situation / Bad Card / Could You Be Loved (12" mix) / Forever Loving Jah / Rastaman Live Up / Give Thanks And Praise / One Love/People Get Ready (12" mix) Why Should I / Redemption Song (live in Pittsburgh)

CATALOGUE
STUDIO 1 (1964 TO 1966)

Over the past few years almost the complete canon of Wailers work at Studio 1 has appeared on Heartbeat releases that all feature quality sleeve notes (by the lovely Roger Steffens and / or Leroy Pierson) and fine audio reproduction.

OVERVIEW COLLECTION

The one for the casual purchaser. All the others below can only be recommended for the serious collector!

GREATEST HITS AT STUDIO ONE

Heartbeat CD261
One Love, I'm Gonna Put It On, Simmer Down, Treat Me Good, Who Feels It Knows It, Cry To Me, It Hurts To Be Alone, Dreamland, Let Him Go, Sinner Man, Jailhouse, Love and Affection, Maga Dog, I Am Going Home, I Need You So, I'm Still Waiting, And I Love Her, Sunday Morning

COLLECTORS' COLLECTIONS
One Love

Heartbeat CD HB 111/112
Disc One: This Train (previously unreleased) / Simmer Down / I Am Going Home / Do You Remember / Mr. Talkative / Habits / Amen / Go Jimmy Go / Teenager In Love / I Need You / It Hurts To Be Alone (previously unreleased alternative take) / True Confession (previously unreleased) / Diamond Baby / Playboy (previously unreleased alternative take) / Where's The Girl For Me / Hooligan / One Love / Love And Affection

Disc Two: And I Love Her (previously unreleased alternative take) / Rude Boy / I'm Still Waiting / Ska Jerk / Somewhere To Lay My Head / Wages Of Love Rehearsal (previously unreleased) / Wages Of Love / I'm Gonna Put It On / (previously unreleased alternative take) / Cry To Me / Jailhouse / Sinner Man (previously unreleased alternative take) / Who Feels It Knows It / Let Him Go / When The Well Runs Dry / Can't You See / What Am I Supposed to Do / Rolling Stone / Bend Down Low / Freedom Time / Rocking Steady
Also released as two separate discs: *Simmer Down At Studio 1* CD HB 171 and *Wailing Wailers At Studio 1* CD HB 172

Destiny: Rare Ska Sides from Studio 1

Heartbeat 11661-7691-2
Destiny / Wages Of Love / Do You Feel The Same Way Too / Your Love / Don't Ever Leave Me (take 1) / Don't Ever Leave Me (take 2) / I Need You So / Rock Sweet Rock / Another Dance / I Stand Predominate / Where Is My Mother (acoustic version) / Where Is My Mother (band take) / Dance With Me / What's New Pussycat / Treat Me Good / Jerking Time (aka Jerk In Time) / Do It Right / Let The Lord Be Seen In You / White Christmas

Wailers and Friends

Heartbeat 11661-7701-2
I've Got To Go Back Home (Bob Andy & The Wailers) / Jerk All Night (Delroy Wilson and The Wailers) / That Ain't Right (Rita Marley and The Soulettes, with The Wailers) / The Train Is Coming (Ken Boothe and The Wailers) / Oh My Darling (Bob Marley & Marcia Griffiths) / One More Chance (Rita Marley and The Soulettes, with The Wailers) / Tell Them Lord (Bob Marley & The Wailers) / Where's Sammy Gone (Lord Brynner and The Wailers) / Ice Water (Jack Sparrow and The Wailers) / Friends and Lovers (Rita Marley and The Soulettes with the Wailers) / Rude Boy (Bob Marley and The Wailers) / Pussy Galore (Lee 'Scratch' Perry and Wailers) / Bless You (Bunny Livingston and Rita Marley) / A Time To Cry (Jackie Opel and The Wailers) / A Deh Pon Dem (Rita Marley and The Soulettes with The Wailers) / I Want Justice (Delroy Wilson and The Wailers) / The Mill Man (Jackie Opel and The Wailers) / Don't Cry Over Me (Joanne Dennis and The Wailers)
Showcases The Wailers' backing vocal duties at Studio 1.

Climb The Ladder

Heartbeat 11661-7751-2
Dancing Shoes / (I'm Gonna) Put It On / Lonesome Track / Climb The Ladder / Love Won't Be Mine This Way / Dreamland / Lemon Tree / Nobody Knows / Wings Of A Dove / Sinner Man / Ten Commandments of Love / Sunday Morning / I Made A Mistake / I Don't Need Your Love / Donna / The Jerk / Just In Time

1967-1972 ERA

The legal and moral spaghetti that surrounded Bob's recording career after he left Studio 1 and before he signed to Island has dogged the releases of material from this period. There are quite literally hundreds of CDs that cover this period but none pay royalties to the Estate of Bob Marley, Peter Tosh or Bunny Wailer. Below are the 'official' releases that cover this period.

OVERVIEW COLLECTIONS

Universal Masters series:

Classic Bob Marley & The Wailers:

19 tracks, from the 200 plus that Bob Marley & The Wailers recorded between 1967-72.
Nice Time / Mellow Mood / Dreamland / Small Axe, Concrete Jungle / Satisfy My Soul / Trench Town Rock / Lively Up Yourself / Kaya / Play Play / Stir It Up / Steppin' Razor / Duppy Conqueror / Soul Shake Down Party / Sugar Sugar / Redder Than Red / Who Is Mr Brown / Black Progress / Selassie Is The Chapel

Original Cuts features all original recordings of songs that Bob would later record during his Island period. It also includes the previously unreleased cut of 'Pass It On'.
Trench Town Rock / Small Axe / Don't Rock My Boat / Bend Down Low / Lively Up Yourself / Sun Is Shining / Kaya / Stir It Up / Man To Man / Stop The Train / 400 Years / Duppy Conqueror / Concrete Jungle / Pass It On / Versions: Grooving Kingston 12 / Axe Man / Live / Sun Is Shining version / Kaya version / Nicoteen / My Sympathy / Duppy Conqueror version / Ammunition / Pass It On version

Wail 'N Soul 'M Single Selecta:

Pulls together all the first ten singles released on the label.
Bend Down Low / Freedom Time / Stir It Up / This Train / Nice Time / Hypocrite / Mellow Mood / Thank You Lord / Bus Dem Shut / Lyrical Satirical I / Funeral / Pound Get a Blow / Steppin Razor / Hurtin Inside / Play Play / Them Have Fi Get a Beatin' / Fire Fire / Don't You Rock My Boat / Chances Are / The Lord Will Make A Way Somehow / Bonus Tracks; Hypocrites – vocal channel / Thank You Lord – vocal channel / Studio Chat

127 King Street:

Captures the music that was released on the Tuff Gong label from 1970 to 1972.
Lively Up Yourself / Screwface / Lick Samba / Satisfy My Soul Jah Jah / Guava Jelly / Rock My Boat / Concrete Jungle / Redder Than Red / Sun Is Shining / Satisfy My Soul Babe / Lovelight / Pour Down The Sunshine / Send Me That Love / Run For Cover / Screwface (alternative) / Hold On To This Feeling / Big Youth – Do Good / Johnny Lover – I Like It Like That / U-Roy – Kingston 12 Shuffle / U-Roy & Peter Tosh – Kingston 12 Shuffle version / Johnny Lover – Heathen's Rage

Ammunition: Dub Collection:

24 tracks of early 'version' sides, which were becoming 'dubs'. UK Sound Systems mixed some tracks a few years after release.
Nicoteen (Dub plate mix) / Ammunition / Red (dub plate mix) / Long Long Winter version / Satisfy version / Kaya Scat version / Zig Zag / Lovelight version / Faceman / Pass It On (dub plate mix) / Dracula / Soul Rebel version / Axe Man / Dreamland version / Grooving Kingston 12 / Samba / Live / Babe version / Black Progress / Keep On Moving version / Downpressor version / Soul Almighty version / Choke / Nice Time (71) version

Lee Perry recordings: the original albums *Soul Rebels*, *Soul Revolution Part II* and *Upsetter Revolution Rhythm* are all available as budget albums with bonus tracks. As is the Wailers album with Leslie Kong *Best Of*.

THE FULL STORY

These three box sets, with 10 CDs in all, cover all the currently known material from this period.
Grooving Kingston 12: A three-CD long box that tells the story of 'Funky Kingston' and the Wailers leading role in the music culture of Kingston. Full of period shots and rich in images, light on words.
Music is from the Tuff Gong label, Lee Perry and the later JAD material
Fy-ah, Fy-ah: A three-CD long box that tells the story of The Wailers after they left Studio 1 and signed with Danny Sims and Johnny Nash's JAD set-up. Full of period shots and rich in images; light on words.
Music is from The Wail 'N Soul 'M period, the Leslie Kong period and the JAD earlier period.
Man To Man: The third box completes the story. It covers the rest of the Lee Perry material, the various tracks recorded for other producers and a CD of alternative and Sound System Dub plate mixes.

PETER TOSH

During the period 1967-72 Peter recorded for several producers. This material is gathered together on two CDs, which feature his solo recordings and his tracks with Bob Marley & The Wailers on which he took lead vocal duties.

Black Dignity: Black Dignity/ Steppin' Razor / Stop The Train / Soon Come / Oppressor Man / Burial / Dem a Fi Get a Beatin' / Downpressor / Mark Of The Beast / Dog Teeth / Second Hand / No Mercy / Four Hundred Years / No Sympathy / Pound Get A Blow / Can't You See / Fire Fire / Funeral / Once Bitten

You Can't Blame The Youth features a mix of solo material recorded with Joe Gibbs, the rest of his material with the Wailers and his melodica pieces: Can't Blame The Youth/ Arise Blackman/ Lion / Maga Dog / Go Tell It To The Mountain / Here Comes The Judge / Four Hundred Years / Soon Come / Here Comes The Sun / Little Green Apples / Them A Fi Get A Beatin' / You Can't Fool Me again / Leave My Business / Love / A Little Love version 4 / We Can Make It Uptight / Evil Version / My Sympathy

RITA MARLEY
Play Play: collects all Rita's recordings from 1967-72, for assorted producers as a solo artist, as The Soulettes and with The Wailers.
Play Play (Rita & The Wailers) / Bring It Up (The Soulettes) / Lonely Girl (Rita & The Wailers) / This World (Justice Leagues) / Why (Rita & The Soulettes) / Give Her Love (Rita & The Wailers) / My Desire (The Soulettes) / Give Me A Ticket (Rita & The Wailers) / When The Festival Is Over (Rita Marley) / Friends & Lovers Forever (Rita & The Soulettes) / Let It Be (Rita & The Soulettes) / I've Been Lonely (Rita & The Soulettes) / Rainbow Island (Rita Marley) / Sylvia's Mother (Rita & The Soulettes) / I Do (Rita & The Soulettes) / Put Your Hand In The Hand (Rita Marley)

THE ISLAND ERA
The past few years have seen Tuff Gong reissue the entire CD catalogue with quality mastering, additional tracks and extra information and pictures in the booklets. Key releases have enjoyed the full 'Deluxe Edition' treatment with good results especially with *Catch A Fire* that presents, for the first time ever, the original album that Bob & Co delivered to Island in the UK and the released album side by side.
All albums have also been issued as top quality vinyl, in reproduction original sleeves, but with no additional tracks. The *Catch A Fire* deluxe edition is highly recommended.
All track listing as albums with only bonus tracks listed.

Catch A Fire: Bonus tracks: High Tide or Low tide / All Day & All Night

Burnin': Bonus tracks: Reincarnated Souls / No Sympathy / The Oppressed Song

Natty Dread: Bonus track: Am-A-Do

Live!: Bonus track: Kinky Reggae

Rastaman Vibration: Bonus track: Jah Live

Kaya: Bonus track: Smile Jamaica (version)

Uprising: Bonus tracks: Redemption Song (band version) / Could You Be Loved (12" mix)

Survival: Bonus track: Ride Natty Ride (12" mix)
Confrontation: Bonus track: Buffalo Soldier (12" mix)

Rebel Music: Bonus track: Wake Up & Live (parts 1 & 2)

Talkin' Blues: Bonus tracks: Lively Up yourself / Stop That Train / Bend Down Low (all live at the Record Plant, San Francisco)

Legend: Bonus track: Punky Reggae Party

DELUXE EDITIONS
Catch A Fire: The extra disc contains the album as delivered to Island by Bob. Hear what Chris Blackwell did and judge for yourself.
Burnin': The second disc features material recorded live in Leeds in 1973. Disc one bonus gives some singles and unreleased alternative takes.
Disc One: Burnin', as album, plus bonus tracks: Reincarnated Souls, No Sympathy, The Oppressed Song, Get Up, Stand Up – two unreleased takes.
Disc Two: Live at Leeds, 1972. Unreleased: Duppy Conqueror / Slave Driver / Burnin' & Lootin' / Can't Blame The Youth / Stop The Train / Midnight Ravers / No More Trouble / Kinky Reggae / Get Up, Stand Up / Stir It up / Put It On / Lively Up Yourself.

Exodus: The classic crossover album with a host of extra material, including live material and some later Perry productions
Disc One: Exodus, as album, plus bonus tracks: Roots / Waiting In Vain (alternative version) / Jamming (long version) / Jamming (version – previously unreleased) / Exodus (version)
Disc Two: Live at the Rainbow 1977, previously unreleased: The Heathen / Crazy Baldhead / Running Away / War / No More Trouble / Jamming / Exodus: Sessions with Lee Perry 1977: Punky Reggae Party (A side of JA 12" single) / Punky Reggae Party (dub) (b Side of JA 12" single) / Keep On Moving (previously unreleased original mix) / Keep On Moving (dub) (previously unreleased original mix) / Exodus Advertisement

Rastaman Vibration: The original album comes with a whole host of unreleased mixes aswell as live recordings from the 'Rastaman Vibration' tour
Disc One: Rastaman Vibration album, as released, plus bonus tracks: Jah Live (original mix) / Concrete (B side of WIP 6265) / Roots, Rock, Reggae (unreleased single mix) / Roots, Rock, Dub (unreleased single dub mix) / Want More (unreleased alternative mix) / Crazy Baldhead (unreleased alternative mix) / War (unreleased alternative mix) / Johnny Was (unreleased alternative mix)
Disc Two: Rastaman Vibration Tour (Live At The Roxy), Introduction / Trenchtown Rock / Burnin' and Lootin' / Them Belly Full (But We Hungry) / Rebel Music (3 O'Clock Road Block) / I Shot The Sheriff / Want More / No Woman No Cry / Lively Up Yourself / Roots, Rock, Reggae / Rat Race. Plus: Smile Jamaica Part One (A-side WIP 6376) / Smile Jamaica Part Two (B Side WIP 6376)

Legend: The all-time seller gets a CD of remixes to go with it. Horrible to my ears, but I'm told it sells in the USA.
Disc One: Legend, as album, plus bonus track: Punky Reggae Party
Disc Two: One Love/People Get Ready (remixed by JM) / Waiting In Vain (remixed by JM) / Jamming (remixed by PGS) / Three Little Birds/Three Little Birds Dub (remixed by JM) / Could You Be Loved (remixed by EB & AS) / No Woman No Cry (remixed by EB & AS) / Coming In From The Cold / (remixed by ET) / Buffalo Soldier (remixed by ET) / Jamming (remixed by ET) / Waiting In Vain (remixed by ET) Exodus (remixed by ET) / Lively Up Yourself (remixed by ET) / One Love/People Get Ready (remixed by GL)
Key: JM = Julian Mendelsohn, PDS = Paul 'Groucho' Smykle, EB & AS = Errol Brown & Alex Sadkin, ET = Eric Thorhgren, & GT = Godwin Logie
Disc Two: features remixes from when *Legend* was first released in 1984 and previously only available in the US (thankfully). Avoid.

OTHER WAILERS RELATED RELEASES
BUNNY WAILER
Bunny Wailer's *Blackheart Man* remains one of the best ever reggae albums. The current CD edition has been remastered but no bonus tracks. His catalogue has not been updated to meet current CD standards. His 'Rock & Groove' and 'Sings the Wailers' are fine albums. His tribute to Bob, 'Time Will Tell', is also worth investigating.

PETER TOSH
His classic 'Legalize It' remains a good place to start. Of his later period the *Talking Revolution* CD collection (Pressure Sounds) is worth checking out. There's a great compilation waiting to be made. His life is the subject of the film *Stepping Razor: Red X.*

ASTON 'FAMILY MAN' BARRETT
Family Man, indeed the 'Barrett Brothers', magnificent playing can be heard on the following albums (not all Wailers related)
Yabby You: King Tubby's Prophesy Of Dub (Blood & Fire CD BASFCD 005)
Simply one of the best Dub albums of all time
Keith Hudson: Pick a Dub (Blood & Fire BAFCD 003)

Excellent Dub album with Fams co-producing and he and Carlton driving the rhythms.
Family Man's own productions can be heard on the album(s) below but they are a very 'curate's egg' brace of albums. His instrumentals such as 'Cobra Style' and the drum machine (or rhythm box) -driven pieces like 'Guided Missile' or 'Work' are top drawer. The productions of various 'Roots Dawtas' are not. It is the only place to find these tracks on CD.
Aston Family Man Barrett: Cobra Style & Family Man In Dub (Heartbeat 7657 & 7659)

RITA MARLEY
Rita has released various albums over the years but her best work remains on singles. A single career overview compilation is needed from Studio One onwards.

JUDY MOWATT
Her 'Black Woman' album is a classic of reggae and stands as a pinnacle of women's voice in reggae.

MARCIA GRIFFITHS
Two late 1970s albums 'Naturally' (High Note) and 'Steppin' (High Note) are both fine albums. Her 1993 album 'Indomitable' (Penthouse) shows just how ably Marcia Griffiths was able to work with the completely new reggae idiom.

FURTHER READING
The biography is by Timothy White and the latest edition has lots extra on reggae politics, Ziggy and the Marley family. *Catch A Fire* (Omnibus) is a great read but it's style of using conversations between the main characters in the story makes it far more 'faction' than biography.

Bob Marley: Songs of Freedom by Adrian Boot and Chris Salewicz (Bloomsbury) is the large format book with loads of pictures. It tells the whole story but it's very heavy with Island period photographs. Not surprising as Adrian Boot was the long-time Island photographer.

People Funny Boy by David Katz is the definitive biography of Lee 'Scratch' Perry.
For a wider look at reggae there is no better place than *The Rough Guide To Reggae* (Penguin) by Steve Barrow and Peter Dalton. It combines a guide to CDs available with the story from Mento to current Dancehall.

The fanzine *Distant Drums* will be publishing the definitive discographies of Bunny Wailer, Peter Tosh, Judy Mowatt, Rita Marley and Family Man over the next few issues.
www.DistantDrums.org

Above: Marcia Griffiths. Like Judy Mowatt, Marcia had a successful solo career before and after her time with Bob.

Note: BMW = Bob Marley & The Wailers

1945

FEB 6   Bob is born Robert Nesta Marley

1950

Bob's father, Norval, sends for him. Bob's placed in the care of an elderly lady for 18 months, until his mother, Cedella, fetches him back.

1957

Bob moves to Kingston with his mother who's set up house with Thaddius (Taddy) Livingston, Bunny's father.

1962

Bob's mum Cedella marries Edward Booker. They move to Delaware, USA the following year.
Bob, now 17, records 4 sides for Leslie Kong. The two singles released are failures.
Chris Blackwell releases his first UK single on the 'Island Label'. It's 'Independent Jamaica' by Lord Creator.
Bob and close friends Bunny Livingston and Peter Tosh are tutored by Joe Higgs in his Trenchtown yard.

1963

DECEMBER   The Wailers are signed to Coxsone Dodd's Studio One. They release over 70 tracks of Ska, R&B, Gospel and Pop over the next three years.
The group includes Bob, Bunny & Peter as well as Junior Braithwaite, Beverly Kelso and occasional member Cherry Green.
Island's single number WI 088 is Robert Marley's 'Judge Not'.

1964

SPRING   'Simmer Down' is a huge hit in Jamaica and sells 60,000 copies.
Bob helps Coxsone Dodd by coaching new signings 'The Soulettes', whose lead singer is Cuban-born Alpharita Anderson.
'It Hurts to Be Alone', with Junior Braithwaite on lead vocals, is a hit.
The group perform at some of Coxsone Dodd's Downbeat Sound System Dances.
Junior Braithwaite leaves for America.

1965

The Wailers, now down to Bob, Peter & Bunny, record several classics, such as 'One Love', 'I'm Gonna Put It On', 'Rude Boy' and 'I'm Still Waiting'. Covers range from 'What's New, Pussy Cat' to 'White Christmas'.
Beverly Kelso and Cherry Green quit the group.
Island records have now released over 250 singles and over a dozen albums of Jamaican music (from Easy Listening to Comedy).

1966

FEB 10   Bob Marley marries Alpharita Anderson.
FEB 11   Bob goes to Wilmington, Delaware to visit his mother and works in the Chrysler car factory.
The group continues with Constantine 'Dream' or 'Vision' Walker joining. Hits include 'Let Him Go', 'Dancing Shoes' and 'I Stand Predominate'.
APRIL 21   Emperor Haile Selassie visits Jamaica. He's met by a massive excited crowd. Riots break out. Selassie is non-plussed by this reaction.
OCTOBER   Bob returns from the US. The group quit Dodd's Studio One, but record their first independent single at his Studio.

1967

JANUARY   The first single is released on their new Wail 'N Soul 'M imprint: Bob Marley & The Wailing Wailers: 'Bend Down Low / Freedom Time'.
The group release a series of fine rocksteady singles on the label, many of which are popular hits and become the basis for re-records in the future.
Bob, Peter, Bunny & Rita sign simple heads of agreements with JAD. Recording with JAD continues, on & off, for the next 5 years.
JUNE   Bunny goes to jail for 18 months on cannabis charges.

1968

MARCH   Bob, Peter and Rita sign full contracts with JAD. Bunny's still in jail & never signs a full contract. They are signed as performers and songwriters.
They start recording tracks aimed at the US Soul / Pop market. BMW are free to record for the JA market, but international explotation is JAD's.
Bob buys a car (a Hillman Minx) with some of the JAD money. He's arrested along with Mortimer Planner, who was driving. A night in jail follows.
The group release their first (& last) single with JAD, which is released in JA (as 'Bob plus two') and in the US and France as 'Bob, Peter & Rita'.
'Selassie is the Chapel' is recorded, with Mortimer Planner. It's the rarest and most overtly Rastafarian song that Bob has recorded.
SEPTEMBER   Bunny's released from jail.

1969

Island stop releasing Jamaican music on singles – over 450 have been released.
BMW record four tracks for uptown producer Ted Powder.
SUMMER   Bob goes to visit his mother In Delaware, with Rita and the kids.
It's the quietest year that the group have ever experienced.
AUTUMN   Bob Leaves the US when he gets served Vietnam draft papers. The group 'reforms' and links up with Lee Perry late in the year.

1970

Bob Marley checks out 'Family Man' and records an ode to James Brown: 'Black Progress'. They then work with Lee Perry.
BMW begin recording with Lee Perry: The album Soul Rebels appears in JA & The UK.
They have JA hits with 'Duppy Conqueror' (late 1970) and 'Mr Brown' and 'Small Axe' (in 1971). Perry continues to release singles until 1972.
BMW record an album project with Leslie Kong: The Best Of The Wailers.
They also record several tracks for themselves and various other producers.
Peter records 'Black Dignity' for Joe Gibbs; he would cut several more sides with Gibbs over the next three years.

1971

Late in 1970, or early in 1971, BMW establish Tuff Gong, based at 127, King Street. It is their base until 1975 when they move to 56, Hope Road.
They have hits with 'Trench Town Rock', 'Lively Up Yourself', 'Screw Face', 'Sun Is Shining' and 'Craven Choke Puppy'.
The Lee Perry-produced album Soul Revolution is released in Jamaica, as is Upsetter Revolution Rhythm (Trojan, in the UK, decline both sets).
Bob Marley flies to Sweden to work on the JAD film project: Love Is Not A Game.
Bob Marley flies to the UK; Sims arranges for Peter, Bunny & the Barretts to join him. A rather unusual set of gigs at schools & clubs takes place.
BMW record several tracks for JAD, at CBS's studio in London; these are not released until 1997. (Complete Wailers - JAD).
Bob sees Soul Rebels in UK record shops and is livid. He also sees the 'Maroon' issue of the album in Jamaica. Bob & Perry have a stand-up row.
SEPTEMBER   Alan 'Skill' Cole is announced as Bob Marley & The Wailers' manager.

1972

Bob tours the UK supporting Johnny Nash, for JAD.
MAY   JAD/CBS release a solo single from Bob 'Reggae On Broadway / Oh, Lord I Got To Get There'. It plummets without a trace.
Bob Marley is signed to Island Records. The first album is recorded, with Bunny & Peter, in Jamaica. Island have a tape by the end of the year.
Bunny Wailer establishes his own label, Solomonic, and releases 'Searching For Love'.
Peter Tosh establishes his own label, Intel-Diplo, and releases 'Dog Teeth'. Both labels are distributed by Tuff Gong.

1973

MAY   Catch A Fire is released. Chris Blackwell gets western musicians to over-dub rock friendly guitar and keyboard pieces.
FROM APRIL   BMW tour the UK and US in support of the album (from April to December). Bunny quits the tour in the US (June).
Bob Marley is presented with an award, sponsored by Red Stripe, for sale of 30,000 copies of 'Trench Town Rock' at the Swing awards in Kingston.

In the UK Bob sees the Trojan re-issues of *Soul Rebels* and *African Herbsman* (*Soul Revolution*) on sale and is, once again, furious with Perry.

OCTOBER *Burnin'* is released, as 'The Wailers'.

DECEMBER Bob, Peter and Bunny, with the Barrett Brothers are the opening act for a Marvin Gaye gig in Kingston, organised by Don Taylor.

DECEMBER By the end of the year both Peter and Bunny have quit the group.

1974

JANUARY Lee Perry opens the doors to his new studio, the Black Ark. Bob is an early visitor and cuts 'Turn Me Loose' & 'Keep On Skanking'. Trojan re-issue *Soul Rebels* as *Rasta Revolution* (& slightly alter the track listing) to exploit all the publicity that Island are generating.

OCTOBER The album *Natty Dread* is released, with the band's name reverting to the pre-Island 'Bob Marley & The Wailers'. No touring, as the album was being recorded.

The album introduces the I-Threes on harmonies: Rita Marley, Judy Mowatt and Marcia Griffiths. Don Taylor becomes part of the Tuff Gong team and encourages Bob to tour.

Island House, at 56, Hope Road is sold to Bob Marley by Chris Blackwell.

Chris Blackwell has invested over £300,000 in the group by now (that's £1.5m at today's prices).

1975

56, Hope Road becomes the base for Bob Marley & The Wailers. Peter and Bunny develop their own careers.

FROM JUNE BMW tour the US & UK in support of *Natty Dread*. The I-Threes make their stage debut.

JUNE 21 BMW concert at The Manhattan Center in New York is filmed. The funky-reggae set has never been released and remains in a vault.

JULY 17/18 BMW record the *Live!* album at the Lyceum Ballroom, London.

OCTOBER Bob, Bunny & Peter play together for the last time, at the National Stadium in Kingston. Bob duets with Stevie Wonder on two songs.

DECEMBER Bob Marley & The Wailers *Live!* is released, to great acclaim. It remains in 'Top Tens' of all-time great live albums to this day.

1976

MARCH Island launch a 'Ghetto Rockers' promotional campaign for Jamaican reggae. Virgin launch their 'Front Line' imprint and associated marketing.

APRIL *Rastaman Vibration* is released, with a strong marketing campaign.

FROM APRIL BMW tour to support *Rastaman Vibration*.

AUGUST To mark the death of Haile Selassie, Bob and Lee Perry record 'Jah Live'.

Bob appears on the cover of *Rolling Stone* magazine.

AUTUMN Bunny Wailer's *Blackheart Man* and Peter Tosh's *Legalize It* albums are released.

DECEMBER 3 Bob Marley, Don Taylor (his then manager) and Rita are shot when the Hope Road compound is raided by gunmen.

DECEMBER 3 Bob plays the 'Smile Jamaica' concert despite his injuries.

1977

Bob goes into exile from Jamaica, following the shooting. Lives mostly in London with 'one of my girlfriends' aka 'Miss World' Cindy Breakspeare.

MAY The album *Exodus* is released, bringing album chart (UK - No 8 & US - No 20) and single success (UK - No 14).

Bob hurts his toe playing football in Paris, aggravating an old injury.

FROM MAY BMW start tour to support album. The European and UK legs of the tour go OK, but Don Taylor cancels the US leg, due to Bob's toe injury.

JUNE The gig at London's Rainbow is filmed.

JULY Lee Perry records 'Punky Reggae Party' and 'Keep On Moving' in London. He later re-records Bob's vocals and remixes it for JA release (November).

1978

MARCH The album *Kaya* is released, to very mixed reviews

APRIL BMW play the 'One Love Peace Concert' in Kingston. On stage, Bob links the hands of Michael Manley & Edward Seaga.

MAY BMW tour the UK, Europe and the US and Canada. The tour ends in September.

JUNE Bob receives the first 'Third World Peace Gold Medal' in New York, from Mamada Johnny Seka, on behalf on the peoples of West Africa.

SEPTEMBER The live album, *Babylon By Bus* is released, to the poorest reviews of Bob's career. Both Alan 'Skill' Cole and Danny Sims again become part of Bob's management team.

1979

APRIL/MAY BMW tour Japan, Australia and Hawaii.

OCTOBER The album *Survival* is released, seen as a return to Bob's 'roots'.

OCTOBER BMW start a major tour of the US, that ends in the middle of December.

NOVEMBER Stevie Wonder joins Bob on stage, at the Black Music Association, for 'Get Up, Stand Up' and 'Exodus'.

1980

JANAURY Don Taylor is fired.

APRIL BMW play the Zimbabwe Independence Concert, in Salisbury. The first gig is cancelled as riots break out. The concert 'continues' the next day.

MAY The album *Uprising* is released.

JUNE/JULY BMW tour Europe and the UK.

SEPTEMBER Bob collapses, whilst out running, on the US leg of his tour. His old toe injury has led to cancer.

Bob, along with Alan 'Skill' Cole and Doctor Pee Wee Frasier stay with Danny Sims in New York, whilst treatment for Bob's cancer is sought.

NOVEMBER Bob is baptised into the Ethiopian Orthodox Church. He takes the name 'Berhane Selassie' – 'Light Of The Trinity'.

Bob goes to the German clinic of Doctor Josef Issels for treatment.

1981

FEBRUARY Bob Marley is awarded the 'Order Of Merit' by the Jamaican Government.

MAY 11 Bob loses his battle with cancer, which has spread throughout his body.

MAY 21 A State funeral is held for Bob. He is buried at his birthplace of Nine Mile, St Ann's. His funeral draws massive crowds.

MAY A commemorative set of postage stamps is issued by the Jamaican Government of Edward Seaga

1984

Danny Sims launches a legal claim against the Estate of Bob Marley. When contracted to 'Cayman' music publishing Bob was encouraged to credit songs he wrote to other people to avoid breaking his contractual obligations to Cayman. Sims loses as the Statute of Limitations on these offences has run out.

The trial uncovers the darker side of the reggae business.

1986

JULY As Bob died without making a will, years of litigation begin between various musicians, record companies and the family.

1987

Peter Tosh (and others) are shot dead by armed intruders.

Long time Wailers' drummer, Carlton 'Carly' Barrett is shot dead. His wife and her lover are charged.

1991

Bob's birthday is proclaimed 'Bob Marley Day' in Jamaica.

1994

Bob Marley is inducted into the 'Rock and Roll Hall of Fame'.

2002

A settlement is reached between Bunny Wailer, The Estate of Peter Tosh and The Bob Marley Estate.

2004

Rumours emerge that Bob's body will be 'returned' to Ethiopia, as a final resting place.

Bob Marley & The Wailers: Live

1962-1969

This first Jamaican section is probably no more than a sampling of the gigs that the group played. Bands played at Sound Systems dances where they might just make a 'Personal Appearance', or perform as part of large, multi-act bills, in a large venue. Some groups also played support to films at cinemas – in fact an early advert for the Hippy Boys (Family Man's band) doing just that, appeared in the *Jamaica Gleaner*.

1963 - Montego Bay, Jamaica
1963 - Capri Theatre, May Pen, Jamaica
1964 - Ward Theatre, Kingston, Jamaica
1964 - Palace Theatre, Kingston, Jamaica
1964 - Majestic Theatre, Kingston, Jamaica
1965 - Ward Theatre (Battle Of The Groups Contest), Kingston, Jamaica
1965 - The Glass Bucket, Kingston, Jamaica
1966 - State Theatre, Kingston, Jamaica – opening for American R&B acts.
1968 - June – State Theatre – Elimination Contest for Festival Song contest
1969 - Psychedelic Shop, Jamaica
1969 - Queens Cinema, Jamaica

1970 - 1972

During this period the appearances in Jamaica are probably only a sampling. Bob Marley & The Wailers made their first appearances outside of JA with gigs in the US & the UK.

1970 - Sombrero Night Club, Kingston, Jamaica
1970 - Negril, Jamaica
1970 - Skateland, Kingston, Jamaica
1970 - The Glass Bucket at Crossroads, Jamaica
1970 - The Silver Slipper (Forest Roads), Jamaica
1970 - The Prime Time, Jamaica
1970 - VIP Club, Jamaica
1971 - August - The Ferry Inn (with The Soulettes), supporting the
        Fabulous Five - Jamaica
1971 - Brooklyn, New York City, USA
1971 - New York, New York City, USA
1972 - January, Bronx, New York City, USA
1972 - January, Manhattan, New York City, USA
1972 - January, Pennsylvania, Philadelphia, USA
1972 - January, Queens, New York City, USA
1972 - Delaware, USA
1972 - As part of Michael Manley's 'Victory Bandwagon'
1972 - Ward Theatre, Kingston, Jamaica
1972 - May, Birmingham, England
1972 - June, California Ballroom, Dunstable, England
1972 - July, Shades Club, Northampton, England
1972 - July, Commonwealth Social Club, Croydon, England
1972 - August, Telegraph, Brixton, England

1973

Now signed as The Wailers to Island Records in the UK, the group played a large number of dates in the UK and the US. The tours were in support of both the *Catch A Fire* and the *Burnin'* albums. In June of this year Bunny quit the group and was replaced on tour by Joe Higgs. By the end of the year both Bunny Wailer and Peter Tosh had effectively left the group.

April 27 - Coleman Club, Nottingham, Derbyshire, England
April 28 - Lancaster University, Lancaster, England
April 29 - Mr. B's, Peckham, England
May 1 - *Old Grey Whistle Test* TV & *Top Gear* Radio (BBC radio programme)
May 2 - Hatfield Polytechnic, England
May 4 - York University, England
May 5 - Manchester University, Manchester, England
May 6 - 67 Club, Wolverhampton, England
May 8 - Essex University, Colchester, England
May 9 - Boobs, Bristol, England
May 11 - North Staffs Polytechnic, Stoke, England
May 12 - Middleton St. George College, Teesside, England
May 13 - Mr. B's, Peckham, England
May 15 - Speakeasy, London, England
May 16 - Speakeasy, London, England
May 17 - Speakeasy, London, England
May 18 - Speakeasy, London, England
May 19 - Town Hall, Hitchin, England
May 20 - Greyhound Pub, Fulham Palace Road, Hammersmith, England
May 22 - Fantasia, Northampton, England
May 23 - Leicester Polytechnic, Leicester, England
May 24 - *In Concert* (BBC Radio), Paris Theatre, London, England
May 25 - Rolle College, Exmouth, England
May 26 - Bamboo Club, Bristol, England
May 27 - Edmonton, Hitchin, Herts, England
May 28 - Birmingham Top Rank, England
May 29 - Coach House, Southampton, England
July 11 - Paul's Mall, Boston, Massachusetts, USA
July 12 - Paul's Mall, Boston, Massachusetts, USA
July 13 - Paul's Mall, Boston, Massachusetts, USA
July 14 - Paul's Mall, Boston, Massachusetts, USA
July 15 - Paul's Mall, Boston, Massachusetts, USA
July 18 - Max's Kansas City, New York City, New York, USA
July 19 - Max's Kansas City, New York City, New York, USA
July 20 - Max's Kansas City, New York City, New York, USA
July 21 - Max's Kansas City, New York City, New York, USA
October - The Wailers play 5 nights as support to Sly & The Family Stone:
        - Homestead, Florida
        - Tampa, Florida
        - Lexington, Kentucky
        - Denver, Colorado
        - Las Vegas, Nevada

Tour Guide 1962-80

October 16 - Bijou Café, Philadelphia, USA
October 19 - The Matrix Club, San Francisco, California, USA
October 20 - The Matrix Club, San Francisco, California, USA
October 22 - Colorado University, Colorado, USA
October 24 - Rehearsal Session for Capitol Records, Hollywood, California, USA
October 29 - The Matrix Club, San Francisco, California, USA
October 30 - The Matrix Club, San Francisco, California, USA
October 31 - KSAN Broadcast, Record Plant, Sausalito, California, USA
Late October - Sundown Edmonton, The Ethiopian Famine Relief Fund, Canada
November 19 - Nottingham, Derbyshire, England
November 20 - Bradford, England
November 21 - Birmingham, England
November 22 - Stafford, England
November 23 - The Locarno, Blackpool, England
November 24 - Liverpool, England
November 25 - Doncaster Outlook, Doncaster, England
November 26 - *Top Gear*, Kensington House, Shepherds Bush, London, England
November 27 - Leeds Polytechnic, Leeds, England
November 28 - Manchester, England
November 30 - Northampton, London, England

1974

This was the quietest touring year that the group ever had. Bob, Bunny and Peter played two gigs in Jamaica as support to Marvin Gaye. Tapes of the gig circulate and there exists film footage of the concert. The majority of the year is taken up with recording
May 28 - Wailers with Marvin Gaye, Carib Theatre, Jamaica
May 31 - Wailers with Marvin Gaye, National Arena, Kingston, Jamaica

1975

This year saw extensive touring of the US & UK in support of the *Natty Dread* album, the first without Bunny or Peter. The original line-up did play two gigs during the year, with the October date being the last time the group performed on stage together. This tour also marked the first live appearance of the I-Threes. The London concert at the Lyceum was recorded for the *Live!* album.
March 8 - Wailers with Jackson Five, National Heroes Stadium, Kingston, Jamaica
June 5 - Diplomat Hotel, Miami, Florida, USA
June 7 - Agora Theatre, Cleveland, Ohio, USA
June 8 - Toronto Massey Hall, Toronto, Ontario, Canada
June 9 - Quiet Knight Club, Chicago, Illinois, USA
June 10 - Quiet Knight Club, Chicago, Illinois, USA
June 14 - Showcase Theatre, Detroit, Michigan, USA
June 18 - Schaeffer Music Festival, Wohlman Skating Rink, Central Park, New York City, New York
June 20 - The Spectrum Theatre, Philadelphia, Pennsylvania, USA
June 21 - Manhattan Center, New York City, New York, USA
June 22 - Hartford, Connecticut, USA
June 23 - Paul's Mall, Boston, Massachusetts, USA (2 shows per night)

June 24 - Paul's Mall, Boston, Massachusetts, USA (2 shows per night)
June 25 - Paul's Mall, Boston, Massachusetts, USA (2 shows per night)
June 26 - Paul's Mall, Boston, Massachusetts, USA (2 shows per night)
June 27 - Paul's Mall, Boston, Massachusetts, USA (2 shows per night)
June 28 - Paul's Mall, Boston, Massachusetts, USA (2 shows per night)
June 29 - Paul's Mall, Boston, Massachusetts, USA (2 shows per night)
Early July - CBS Studio City, Hollywood, California, USA
July 4 - Boarding House, San Francisco, California, USA
July 5 - Boarding House, San Francisco, California, USA
July 6 - Boarding House, San Francisco, California, USA
July 7 - Boarding House, San Francisco, California, USA
July 8 - Paramount Theater, Oakland, California, USA
July 9 - Roxy Theater, Los Angeles, California, USA
July 10 - Roxy Theater, Los Angeles, California, USA
July 11 - Roxy Theater, Los Angeles, California, USA
July 12 - Roxy Theater, Los Angeles, California, USA
July 13 - Roxy Theater, Los Angeles, California, USA
July 17 - The Lyceum Ballroom, London, England
July 18 - The Lyceum Ballroom, London, England
July 19 - The Odeon, Birmingham, England
July 20 - The Hard Rock, Manchester, England
August 29 - National Arena, Kingston, Jamaica
October 4 - Wailers Wonder Dream Concert, Kingston National Stadium, Kingston, Jamaica
On the album *King Tubby Surrounded by Dreads In The Arena* (Fay, 1976/Studio 16, 1978) the notes say that King Tubby entertained the audience that was at the National Arena to see The Wailers on September 26. Perhaps this was a rehearsal for the October 4 gig. The album features tracks that Tubby played that night – no Wailers though.

1976

In support of the *Rastaman Vibration* album Bob toured the US & the UK. The year ended with the 'Smile Jamaica' concert, at which Bob performed despite carrying a wound from a murder attempt before the concert.
April 23 - Tower Theater, Upper Darby, Pennsylvania, USA
April 26 - Boston, Massachusetts, USA
April 30 - Beacon Theater, New York City, USA (Early Show)
April 30 - Beacon Theater, New York City, USA (Late Show)
May 1 - Beacon Theater, New York City, USA (Early Show)
May 1 - Beacon Theater, New York City, USA (Late Show)
May 5 - Convocation Hall, Toronto, Ontario, Canada (Early Show)
May 5 - Convocation Hall, Toronto, Ontario, Canada (Late Show)
May 8 - Auditorium Theater, Chicago, USA
May 13 - Orchestra Hall, Minneapolis, Minnesota, USA
May 20 - Houston, Texas, USA
May 25 - San Diego, California, USA
May 26 - Roxy Theater, Hollywood, California, USA
May 29 - Paramount Theater, Oakland, California, USA
May 30 - Paramount Theater, Oakland, California, USA
May 31 - Santa Barbara County Bowl, Santa Barbara, California, USA

1976 Continued

June 9 - Hamburg, West Germany
June 13 - Jaap Edenhal, Amsterdam, Holland
June 14 - Paris, France
June 15 - Hammersmith Odeon, London, England
June 16 - Hammersmith Odeon, London, England
June 17 - Hammersmith Odeon, London, England
June 18 - Hammersmith Odeon, London, England
June 19 - West Coast Rock Show, Ninian Park, Cardiff, Wales
June 20 - Civic Hall, Wolverhampton, England
June 22 - The Odeon, Birmingham, England
June 23 - Colston Hall, Bristol, England
June 24 - Stardust Club, Exeter, Devon, England
June 26 - Leeds University, Leeds, England
June 27 - Bellevue, Manchester, England
December 5 - Smile Jamaica Concert, National Heroes Park, Kingston, Jamaica

1977

The tour in support of *Exodus* took in several European gigs. Bob's ability to relate to new audiences meant that he attracted a strong following in all the countries that he played.

The touring schedule was cut short due to recurring problems that Bob had with a toe injury, so there were no US concerts.

May 11 - Brussels, Belgium
May 13 - Paris Pavilion, Paris, France
May 14 - Den Haag, Netherlands
May 15 - The Circus Krone, Munich, Germany
May 16 - Rhein-Neckar-Hulle, Heidelberg, Germany
May 17 - The CCH, Hamburg, Germany
May 18 - The Eissporthalle, Berlin, Germany
May 19 - Gottenburg, Scandinavia
May 20 - Gronalund, Stockholm, Sweden
May 22 - Falconer Theatre, Copenhagen, Denmark
May 31 - Rehearsal, London, England
June - *Top Of The Pops* TV Programme, London, England
June 1 - Rainbow Theatre, London, England
June 2 - Rainbow Theatre, London, England
June 3 - Rainbow Theatre, London, England
June 4 - Rainbow Theatre, London, England

1978

A massive touring schedule in support of *Kaya* started with two gigs in JA. The second, the 'One Love Peace Concert' has gone down in history, as Bob united the warring political leaders, Michael Manley & Edward Seaga, on stage in a three-way hand clasp.

February 26 - National Heroes Stadium, Kingston, Jamaica
April 22 - One Love Peace Concert, Kingston, Jamaica
May 18 - Hill Auditorium, Ann Arbor, USA
May 19 - Music Hall, Cleveland, Ohio, USA
May 24 - Veteran Memorial Hall, Columbus, Ohio, USA
May 25 - Orpheum Theater, Madison, Wisconsin, USA (Early Show)
May 25 - Orpheum Theater, Madison, Wisconsin, USA (Late Show)
May 27 - Uptown Theater, Chicago, Illinois, USA
May 29 - Performing Arts Center, Milwaukee, Wisconsin, USA (Early Show)

May 29 - Performing Arts Center, Milwaukee, Wisconsin, USA (Late Show)
May 30 - Northrup Auditorium, Minneapolis, Minnesota, USA
May 31 - Rehearsals, Miami, Florida, USA
June 1 - Waldorf Astoria, New York City, New York, USA
June 2 - Stanley Theater, Pittsburgh, Pennsylvania, USA
June 3 - Landmark Theater, Syracuse, New York, USA
June 4 - Masonic Temple, Detroit, Michigan, USA
June 5 - The Spectrum, Philadelphia, Pennsylvania, USA
June 8 - Music Hall, Boston, Massachusetts, USA (Early Show)
June 8 - Music Hall, Boston, Massachusetts, USA (Late Show)
June 9 - Maple Leaf Gardens, Toronto, Ontario, Canada
June 10 - Forum Concert Bowl, Montreal, Quebec, Canada
June 11 - Shea Stadium, Buffalo, New York, USA
June 12 - Civic Center, Poughkeepsie, New York, USA
June 14 - Pinecrest Country Club, Shelton, Connecticut, USA
June 16 - Capital Center, Landover, Maryland, USA
June 17 - Madison Square Garden, New York City, New York, USA
June 18 - Music Inn, Lennox, Massachusetts, USA
June 22 - New Bingley Hall, Staffordshire, England
June 25 - Unknown Location, Paris, France
June 26 - Paris Pavilion, Paris, France
June 27 - Unknown Location, Paris, France
June 28 - Plaza De Toros, Ibiza, Spain
June 30 - Gronalund, Stockholm, Sweden
July 1 - Roskilde Festival, Roskilde, Denmark
July 2 - Horten Festival, Horten, Norway
July 7 - Ahoy Hallen, Rotterdam, Holland
July 10 - Unknown Venue, London, England
July 14 - Queen Elizabeth Theatre, Vancouver, British Columbia, Canada
July 15 - Paramount Theater, Seattle, Washington, USA
July 16 - Paramount Theater, Portland, Oregon, USA
July 18 - Civic Centre, Santa Cruz, California, USA (Early Show)
July 18 - Civic Centre, Santa Cruz, California, USA (Late Show)
July 21 - Greek Theater, University of California at Berkeley, Berkeley, California, USA
July 22 - State Amphitheater, San Diego, California, USA
July 23 - Santa Barbara County Bowl, Santa Barbara, California, USA
July 24 - Starlite Bowl, Los Angeles, California, USA
July 25 - Roxy Theater, Los Angeles, California, USA
July 27 - Music Hall, Houston, Texas, USA
July 28 - The Tarrant County Convention Center, Fort Worth, Texas, USA
July 29 - Paramount Theater, Austin, Texas, USA (Early Show)
July 29 - Paramount Theater, Austin, Texas, USA (Late Show)
July 30 - The Warehouse, New Orleans, Louisiana, USA
August 1 - Fox Theater, Atlanta, Georgia, USA
August 5 - Jai Alai Fronton, Miami, Florida, USA

1979

The tour supporting the *Survival* album was Bob's first truly international adventure. In typical style he made legions of new fans in Japan, Australia and New Zealand.

April 5 - Shinjuku Kouseinenkin Hall, Tokyo, Japan
April 6 - Shinjuku Kouseinenkin Hall, Tokyo, Japan
April 7 - Shibuya Public Hall, Tokyo, Japan
April 10 - Nakano Sun Plaza Hall, Tokyo, Japan
April 11 - Kosei Nenkin Main Hall, Osaka, Japan

April 13 - Festival Hall, Osaka, Japan
April 16 - Auckland, New Zealand
April 18 - Brisbane, Australia
April 20 - Adelaide, Australia
April 23 - Perth, Australia
April 25 - Festival Hall, Melbourne, Australia
April 27 - Sydney, Australia
May 5 - Maui, Hawaii
May 6 - Waikiki Shell, Honolulu, Oahu, Hawaii
May 20 - Seattle, Washington, USA
June 23 - Ahoy Hallen, Rotterdam, Netherlands
July 7 - Reggae Sunsplash II, Jarrett Park, Montego Bay, Jamaica
July 21 - Amandla Festival, Boston, Massachusetts, USA
September 24 - National Heroes Arena, Kingston, Jamaica
October - Boston, Massachusetts, USA
October - Madison Square Garden, New York City, New York, USA
October 25 - Apollo Theater, Harlem, New York, USA (Early Show)
October 25 - Apollo Theater, Harlem, New York, USA (Late Show)
October 26 - Apollo Theater, Harlem, New York, USA (Early Show)
October 26 - Apollo Theater, Harlem, New York, USA (Late Show)
October 27 - Apollo Theater, Harlem, New York, USA (Early Show)
October 27 - Apollo Theater, Harlem, New York, USA (Late Show)
October 28 - Apollo Theater, Harlem, New York, USA
October 31 - Colgate University, Hamilton, New York, USA
November 1 - Maple Leaf Gardens, Toronto, Canada
November 2 - The Forum, Montreal, Quebec, Canada
November 3 - Ottawa, Canada
November 4 - Burlington, Ontario, Canada
November 7 - Black Music Association, Penn Hall, Philadelphia,
    Pennsylvania, USA
November 10 - Detroit, Michigan, USA
November 11 - Dane County Coliseum, Madison, Wisconsin, USA
November 12 - Milwaukee, Wisconsin, USA
November 13 - Uptown Theater, Chicago, Illinois, USA
November 15 - Northrup Auditorium, Minneapolis, Minnesota, USA
November 17 - Edmonton, Alberta, Canada
November 19 - Paramount Theater, Portland, Oregon, USA
November 20 - Seattle, Washington, USA
November 21 - Vancouver, British Columbia, Canada
November 23 - UCLA, Pauley Pavilion, Los Angeles, California, USA
November 24 - San Diego Sports Arena, San Diego, California, USA
November 25 - County Bowl, Santa Barbara, California, USA
November 27 - Sugar Ray Robinson Foundation Benefit,
            Roxy Theater, Los Angeles, California, USA
November 30 - Oakland Coliseum, Oakland, California, USA
December 1 - Freeborn Hall on UC Davis Campus, Sacramento, California, USA
December 2 - The Civic Auditorium, Santa Cruz, California, USA (Early Show)
December 2 - The Civic Auditorium, Santa Cruz, California, USA (Late Show)
December 5 - Denver University Arena, Denver, Colorado, USA
December 6 - Hoch Auditorium, The University of Kansas, Lawrence, Kansas, USA
December 8 - Nashville, Tennessee, USA
December - Tampa, Florida, USA
December 12 - Fox Theater, Atlanta, Georgia, USA
December - Queens Park, Savanna, Trinidad, West Indies
December 15 - Queen Elizabeth Sports Centre, Nassau, Bahamas

1980

In what turned out to be Bob's last year of touring, he fulfilled a dream by playing in Africa. He also toured extensively in Europe, including Scandinavia, and was on the US section of the tour when his illness overtook him.

January 4 - Libreville, Gabon, Africa
January 5 - Libreville, Gabon, Africa
April 18 - Zimbabwe Independence Concert, Rufaro Stadium, Salisbury, Zimbabwe
April 19 - Zimbabwe Independence Concert, Rufaro Stadium, Salisbury, Zimbabwe
May 30 - Kallerstadion, Zurich, Switzerland
June 1 - Munich Festival, Horse Riding Stadium, Germany
June 3 - Palais des Sports, Grenoble, France
June 4 - Parc des Sports, Dijon, France
June 6 - Sporthalle, Cologne, Germany
June 7 - Crystal Palace, London, Germany
June 8 - Kaiserslautern Festival, Betzenberg Stadium, Germany
June 9 - Strasbourg, France
June 10 - Orleans, France
June 11 - Bordeaux, France
June 12 - Westfalen Stadium, Dortmund, Germany
June 13 - Reitstadion, Munich, Germany
June 14 - Hamburg, Germany
June 16 - Oslo, Norway
June 17 - Grona Lund, Stockholm, Sweden
June 18 - The Forum, Copenhagen, Denmark
June 20 - Waldbuhne, West Berlin, East Germany
June 21 - Kassel, Germany
June 22 - Forset National, Brussels, Belgium
June 23 - Ahoy Hallen, Rotterdam, Holland
June 24 - Lille, France
June 25 - Stade Mayol, Toulon, France
June 27 - San Siro Stadio, Milan, Italy
June 28 - Turin, Italy
June 30 - Plaza deTorros Monumental, Barcelona, Spain
July 2 - Nantes, France
July 3 - Le Bourget, Paris, France
July 4 - Dijon, France
July 6 - Dublin, Ireland
July 7 - Crystal Palace, London, England
July 8 - Brighton Leisure Centre, Brighton, England
July 9 - Brighton Leisure Centre, Brighton, England
July 10 - Apollo, Glasgow, Scotland
July 11 - Apollo, Glasgow, Scotland
July 12 - Deeside Leisure Centre, Deeside, Chester, England
July 13 - Stafford Bingley Hall, Staffordshire, England
September 13 - Down South Rehearsal, Miami, Florida, USA
September 14 - Rehearsal, Miami, Florida, USA
September 16 - JB Hynes Auditorium, Boston, Massachusetts, USA
September 17 - Meehan Auditorium at Brown University, Providence,
            Rhode Island, USA
September 19 - Madison Square Garden, New York City, New York, USA
September 20 - Madison Square Garden, New York City, New York, USA
September 23 - Stanley Theater, Pittsburgh, Pennsylvania, USA

Glossary/Footnotes

Below are listed various words and phrases that are common in the world of reggae but not so well-known outside of it. Many words now common in music started as reggae expressions, such as 'bad' (meaning good) or 'wicked'. Given the largely aural tradition and nature of much of Jamaican language, it's not uncommon for a word to have alternative spellings and therefore there's often no one definitive spelling. e.g. Pocomania or Pukumina.

Alpha Boys' School Run by Catholic nuns and presided over by the late and celebrated Sister Ignatius. Established in 1880, the school gave an excellent musical education to ghetto children. It produced disciplined musicians who could then find work in military or hotel bands. Old Boys include Studio One stalwarts Tommy McCook, Johnny 'Dizzy' Moore, Lester Sterling and Don Drummond, as well as 1970s artists like Leroy 'Horsemouth' Wallace and Leroy Smart.

Amharic The language of Ethiopia. Rastas used words and phrases in Amharic, as part of their identification with Ethiopia. Peter used it on tracks like 'Black Dignity'. The Bible was partly written in the early form of Amharic, called Ge'ez.

Babylon A term that comes from the place named in the Book of Revelation. It has come to mean a place of great luxury, sensuality and often vice and corruption.

Back-o-Wall/Back-a-Wall The shantytown in which many Rastas settled after the destruction of the Pinnacle Community in 1954. It was bulldozed in 1966 as part of a government plan to disperse the Rastas and destroy their community.

Beverley's Records Leslie Kong's record label on which he released many successful records. Desmond Dekker's 'The Israelites' sold, for example, 1 million copies.

The Bible Rastafarians focus on such books as Daniel, Deuteronomy, Isaiah, Leviticus and Numbers. There are also bibles that include 'lost' books, such as 'The Book Of Maccabees'. It's from The Apocrypha and was 'removed' from the official Bible. It's the base of the Jamaican saying 'the half that's never been told'. One bible is called the 'Black Bible' or 'Holy Piby'.

Calypso A music style from the Caribbean, especially Trinidad. Calypso bands use steel drums, to a greater or lesser extent, and the music has its origins in the mix of peoples in the Caribbean. The lyrics often deal with topical or humorous subjects.

Cut and re-cut A cut is a recording or take of a song. The reference is to it being cut into vinyl. A re-cut is when a previously recorded song is re-recorded at a later date. When an existing vocal was re-recorded as a DJ track, or an instrumental with a horn or bongo lead line, it was called DJ cut, horns cut, or bongo cut. Confusingly, they are also known as 'horns version', 'DJ version' etc.

Dub The instrumental track was initially issued on the flip side of the vocal, for DJs to talk over. These instrumentals (or 'versions') started to be remixed themselves in 1973/4 and created a whole new genre, in which the skill lay in the mixing of the track. King Tubby became the master of this art.

Dub plate The name for an acetate (vinyl over metal) that has been uniquely cut for play at a Sound System. Initially these were the same as the version released on vinyl but by the early to mid-1970s they started to feature exclusive mixes. Some caught live mixes direct on to acetate. They were important for Sounds as playing exclusive mixes or tracks was one of their ways of drawing a crowd. Few have labels, but carry markings so that the selector can identify the track.

Duppy is a Jamaican ghost. Believed to come from the Ashanti word 'dupe'. In folklore the Obeah man can manipulate Duppies to do harm. Also spelt 'Duppie' & 'Duppe'.

Grounation A meeting at which Rastas chant, dance, drum, discuss and smoke herb. These can go on for long periods of time. march 1958 saw the first Island-wide meeting of Rastas in Jamaica. Also spelt 'Groundation'.

Kebra Negast meaning 'Glory Of Kings' it is a fundamental book in Ethiopian culture, like the Old Testament is to Jews, or the Koran is to Muslims. All three books mention King Solomon and Queen Sheba (Saba) but the Kebra Negast establishes Ethiopia's link to the union of these two characters. It is this 'mythical' tale that Rastas believe in.

Mento Jamaican folk music that featured banjos, bamboo saxophones and rumba boxes (rather like an overgrown thumb piano). The music developed into Jamaican calypso that focused on the tourist market, so played up crude lyrics, delivered in a romantic manner. Mento was played at Sound Systems on 78s, along with American R&B. For a while 'calypso' was seen as the next 'Rock'n'Roll' in the USA and several Jamaican artists were signed up to major labels.

Nyabinghi Originally a religious and spiritual movement in Rwanda from the 1700s to the early 1900s. Some also link it to The Freedom Fighters in Colonial Kenya. It has come to have various meanings in Rasta: (i) A type of drumming and chanting used at Rastas grounations (ii) An orthodox and primarily religious faction of Rastas (iii) Similar use to 'Grounation'.

Rastafari Is a series of beliefs, spiritual and secular, based on the Coptic Church Of Ethiopia and its links to the Old Testament world. Emperor Haile Selassie is seen as divine and the fulfilment of a biblical prophecy. It's a long way from the organized Church of England model, rather it's a whole series of groups who have differing interpretations of arcane texts from The Bible. There are many of these groups, often with names such as 'The Divine Theocratic Order Of Nyabinghi'. It reflects the pattern of traditional religious groups in Jamaica. The wearing of dreadlocks, the smoking of ganja as a sacrament, and even the Divinity of Haile Selassie are not necessarily common beliefs, or actions, of all Rastas.

Rocksteady was the musical form that followed on from Ska, in which the beat was slowed down. It flowered briefly from late 1966 to late 1968.

Rude Boys / Rudies / Ruddies was the name given to rebellious and tough ghetto youths who caused trouble at Dances and other events during the 1960s. Several 'Rude Boy' songs were recorded, some for and some against. There was also a series of records on which judges were lampooned for imposing long sentences for Rude Boy crimes.

Runnings means the day-to-day stuff of business and the ghetto. These may be complex, in terms of how sessions get financed, who plays on the session and when and where the record gets played. The term reflects not just the business part of the process but all the social and personal dealings that need to happen before something can get going.

Ska the first modern music of Jamaica to find commercial success in the West. It's a mix of mento, boogie woogie and rhythm and blues. It was developed as supplies of R&B from New Orleans began to dry up, as American music changed. In this process there was a phase of Jamaicans playing and recording 'R&B', often called 'Shuffle' – some of these singles were released in the UK on the 'Blue Beat' label (as in Blues Beat).

Skank A reggae dance, which focuses on the drum and bass line. Jamaican folklorist, Louise Bennet, traces its origins to the 'weak-knee' steps called 'Yanga' that has African influences. Also used as a name for a 'con' or 'trick' to generate money.

Stamper is the name of the metal plate from which vinyl records are pressed. In the process of releasing a record it represents a relatively large investment. If stampers become broken, or lost, the re-pressing of an old tune may become uneconomical unless there is a large demand for it.

Tourists / Tourist Market From the 1930s Jamaica became a very fashionable place for the rich of the Western world to holiday. They provided a ready market for music, both live at the hotels in which they stayed and later on record. These were initially 78s pressed in the UK but by the end of the 1950s records began to be pressed in Jamaica. This remains a good market for live and recorded music.

Trenchtown (or Trench Town) was a Government-funded housing scheme in Kingston. Built in 1951, it replaced squatter camps destroyed by a hurricane. It was constructed without a sewage system, speaking volumes about Colonial Jamaica, and was home to many of the town's poor. It was located in the hottest part of the city where no cooling breezes relieved the oppressive heat.

Tuff: The JA way of saying 'tough', but with broader meanings. A tune or a person can be 'tuff'.

The Twelve Tribes One of many Rasta groupings. They had strong links with many successful reggae artists, including Bob Marley. They ran their own Sound called 'JahLoveMusik' which, uniquely, played only Rasta music. They were based near Hope Road and Tuff Gong helped with various record releases.

Version is an instrumental of the vocal side, usually released as a B-side. These tracks became 'Dub' versions. See 'Dub' and also 'Cut' (above).

A note on names

Many Jamaican musicians have their real name and at least one alter ego. Mento artists all took regal names, as a jibe, and a quick way to elevate themselves. Following on the jazz tradition ('Lady Day' and 'Duke Ellington') Jamaica gave us Lord Creator, Laro, Jellico, Fly, Flee, Lebby and Power and the Counts Lasher, Ossie, Owen, Machuki and Sticky.

Alphaharita Consticla Anderson is Rita Marley.

Cedella Booker is Bob's mother. Aka Mother Booker aka Ciddy aka Cedella Marley. One of Bob's daughters is also named Cedella.

Clement Dodd Early Jamaican music entrepreneur who recorded artists at his Studio One complex and ran a number of labels. Active from the early 1960s until his death in 2004. A dominant force in reggae in Jamaica. Also known as 'Coxsone' Dodd (because of his admiration for the English cricketer of that name). His Sounds were called 'Sir Coxsone Down Beat' or 'Sir Coxsone Round Beat'. His name is sometimes spelt 'Coxson' on labels and in adverts.

The I-Threes A group established in 1975 to provide harmonies for Bob Marley. It consisted of three of the best female vocalists in Jamaica: Rita Marley, Judy Mowatt and Marcia Griffiths.

Neville O'Reilly Livingston is Bunny Wailer aka Bunny Livingston aka Jah B.

Robert Nesta Marley is Bob Marley also known as 'Joseph', which was his Twelve Tribes name. Also as 'Skipper' or 'Tuff Gong'.

Winston Hubert McIntosh is Peter Tosh aka Peter Touch.

Rainford Hugh Perry is Lee Perry aka The Upsetter aka Lee 'Scratch' Perry aka lots of other names in the past decade. Lee Perry was a performer / producer / musician / writer / engineer who started out at Studio One. He built his own 'Black Ark' Studio, which he was to burn down some years later.

The Skatalites: The famous Ska band that also worked as the Studio One house band between 1963 and 1965. Tommy McCook – tenor sax, Roland Alphonso – tenor sax, Lester Sterling – alto sax, Don Drummond – trombone, Johnny 'Dizzy' Moore – trumpet, Jerome 'Jah Jerry' Haynes – guitar, Ernest Ranglin – guitar, Lloyd Brevett – bass, Lloyd Knibb – drums. Replaced by The Soul Brothers in 1965, which featured many of the same musicians.

The Soulettes The original group at Studio One, in 1964, consisted of Rita Anderson (Marley), Constantine 'Dream' Walker and Marlene 'Precious' Gifford. In the early 1970s Rita reformed the group with Hortense Lewis and Cecile Campbell (sister of the popular Jamaican singer Cornell Campbell).

INDEX OF SONG TITLES

INDEX OF SONG TITLES

Thank You Lord – UK 7" 153 (Powder)
The Box Set – 1982 140
The Jerk – UK 7" 152
The Lord Will Make A Way Somehow 41
The Toughest 29
(I Am) The Toughest – UK 7 152
The Vow 25
The World Is Changing – UT (JAD) 175/6
Them Belly Full (But We Hungry Now) – Natty Dread album 94
Them Belly Full (But We Hungry Now) – Island single 101
Them Belly Full (But We Hungry Now) – Live! album 97
Them Have Fi Get A Beatin' 41
There She Goes 25
There She Goes – UK 7" 152
There She Goes – UT (JAD) 175/6
This Train – original UT (Studio 1) 175/6
This Train 37
This Train – UK 7"152
This Train – UT (Powder) 175/6
Three Little Birds   Exodus album 110
Three Little Birds – Island single 132
Time Will Tell – Kaya album 116
To The Rescue – UK 7" 153
Top Rankin' – Survival album 122
Touch Me – UT (JAD) 175/6
Tread Along – see Trod Along
Treat Me Good 30
Treat Me Good – UK 7" 152
Treat You Right – UT (JAD) 175/6
Trench Town 159
Trench Town – Confrontation album 139
Trenchtown Rock 76
Trenchtown Rock – UK 7" 153
Trenchtown Rock – Live! album 97
Trod Along 41
Trouble Dub 172
Trouble Is On The Road Again 43
True Confessions – UT (Studio 1) 175/6
Try Me 51 (album track)
Turn Me Loose – UT (Perry) 175/6
Turn Your Lights Down Low – Exodus album 110
Uprising – Island album 130
Upsetter Revolution Rhythm – JA album 54
Wages Of Love 25
Wages Of Love – UT (acoustic rehearsal, Studio 1) 175/6
Wages Of Love – UT (alt. take (Bob), Studio 1) 175/6
The Wailing Wailers – album 30
Waiting In Vain – Exodus album 110
Waiting In Vain – Island single 112
Wake Up & Live – Survival album 122
Wake Up & Live – Island single 124

Walk The Proud Land – UT (Live) Talkin Blues album 141
Want More – Rastaman Vibration album 100
War – Rastaman Vibration album 100
War – Babylon By Bus album 118
War – Island single (Live BBB) 118
We And Dem (Them) – Uprising album 130
What Am I Supposed To Do 30
What Goes Around Comes Around – UT (JAD) 175/6
What's New Pussy Cat 27
What's New Pussy Cat – UK 7" 152
When The Well Runs Dry 30
Where Is My Mother 31 (v/a album track)
Where Is My Mother – UT (demo, Studio 1) 175/6
Where's The Girl For Me 26
Where Will I Find 27
Where Will I Find – UK 7" 152
White Christmas 27
Who Colt The Game – UT (Perry) 175/6
Who Is Mr Brown 47
(Who Is) Mr Brown – UK 7" 153
Who The Cap Fit – Rastaman Vibration album 100
Why Should I – UT (original Tuff Gong) 175/6
Why Should I – UT (Island remix) 141
Wings Of A Dove 31 (v/a album track)
Wisdom 59
Wisdom – UK 7" 153
Work – Uprising album 130
You Can't Blame The Youth – UT Talkin Blues album 141
Your Love 27
Your Love – UK 7" 152
Zig Zag 46 (Duppy Conqueror version)
Zimbabwe – Survival album 122
Zimbabwe – Island single 124
Zimmerman (Sinner Man) – UK 7" 152
Zion Train – Uprising album 130

*There are several unreleased takes, versions, mixes and live recordings of Island period tracks to be found on the CDs released in 2004/5 179

Alternative track names:
Angry Man – see Belly Full
Babylon's Burning – see Fire Fire
Burial – see Funeral
Flying Ska – see Wings Of A Dove
Fools Die – see Wisdom
Get Ready – see Freedom Time
Hey Happy People   see Soul Almighty (Perry)
I've Got The Action – see Try Me
I've Got To Cry Cry Cry – see My Cup
I Like It Like That – is an alternative cut of 'Don't Rock My Boat' – there is also a track 'Like It Like This' by Johnny Lover

Jail House – see Good Good Rudie
Power & More Power – see Satisfy My Soul Jah Jah
Pyaka – see Bus Dem Shut
Shocks of (The) Mighty – see Shocks Almighty
Six In One – see All In One
Soul Town Reporter – see Johnny Lover Like It Like This
Sun Is Shining V2 – see Heathens' Rage (Sun Is Shining DJ cut)
Who The Cap Fit – an Island track, but also can refer to Man To Man
You Can't Do That To Me – see The World Is Changing

'Cross The Nation' was credited to Bob Marley & The Wailers on a US release.
It's actually by Little Roy.

'You Should Have Known Better' is often credited to Bob Marley & The Wailers, as on its UK release it was credited to the 'Tuff Gong All Stars'. It's actually The Wailing Souls (as Pipe & The Pipers) 'Back Biter' (Tuff Gong).

ACKNOWLEDGEMENTS

Thanks...
To the dealers who have supplied my regular fixes and put up with endless questions about labels: Andrew @ Tradition, GregLocks, Steve @ Reggae Rhythms and Andy D of Reggae.co.uk & The Downbeat Sound System.

To those who have shared their passion & knowledge: The Dub Vendor Crew: John MacGillivary, Lol Bell Brown, Oxman and Chris Lane.

To all the musicians who have shared their experience: John 'Rabbit' Bundrick, Dawn Penn, Bunny Lee, Pauline Morrison, Larry 'Ethnic' Lawrence, Roland Alphonso, Lloyd Brevett and Lloyd Knibb.

To the photographers, Ossie Hamilton and Astley Chin, for their unique record of Bob Marley as a young man in his twenties.

To David Simmons at JAD for all the help and support.

To Danny Sims for all the conversations and insights.

Thanks to Dennis Morris, for his photographs from then and his passion now.

To Peter Murphy for his photographs and his work for Oxfam now.
Thanks to Colin Moore for his help and support. To Studio One Peter for helping with those gaps!

To Mike Cornfield for his help and skills on the Mac.

To all those at Universal Music International: Julian Huntley, Jessica Connor, Giancarlo Sciama and Simon Edwards.

To all those at Universal UK: Sir Daryl Easlea, Andy Street, Silva Montello.

To Island, and Christine Atkins, for their support of Distant Drums.

To Gabrielle, Karen and Auberon at Cassell.
To Ron Callow at Design 23.

To my lovely wife Rommy – 'Back to Back, Belly to Belly!'

To the Honourable Bob Marley OM, Peter Tosh, Rita Marley and Bunny Wailer for giving us such glorious music.

To all the other producers and musicians who helped along the way, especially Aston 'Family Man' Barrett, Carlton Barrett, Judy Mowatt, Marcia Griffiths.

To the writers of the following books:
The Rough Guide to Reggae: Steve Barrow & Peter Dalton,
Reggae & Caribbean Music: Dave Thompson
Bob Marley – The illustrated Disco/Biography: Observer Station
Roots Knotty Roots: Robert Sconfield
Coxson's Music – A Discography: Charlie Morgan
Complete Lyrics Of Bob Marley: Harry Hawke to whom a special vote of thanks for his help.
The Complete Guide to The Music Of Bob Marley: Ian McCann
Bob Marley – Songs Of Freedom: Adrian Boot & Chris Salewicz
Jamaica: Land of Wood & Water: Fernando Henriques
Reggae International: Stephen Davis
Catch A Fire: The Life Of Bob Marley: Timothy White
To all those collectors who have given their personal lists to aid this project over the years: Rodger Dalke and Olivier Albot.

To the magazines: *Swing, Blues & Soul, Black Music* and *Black Echoes.*
Respect to their writers: Carl Gayle, Steve Barrow, Chris Lane, Penny Reel, Dave Henley and Chris May.

To the *NME:* Respect to their writers Penny Reel and Neil Spencer.
To Richard Williams, at the *Melody Maker,* for his groundbreaking articles that took reggae seriously as music rather than as a novelty.

To Nick Kimberley @ *Pressure Drop* and Paul Bradshaw.

Websites
Bob Marley and the Wailers Definitive Discography – Leroy Jodie Pierson and Roger Steffens.
The 'Wailers A to Z', the 'wailers.co.uk', Gael Doyen and his 'Wailers Addict' site.

CD liner notes
The Wailers Studio 1 CD booklet liner notes (Heartbeat): Roger Steffens & Jodie Pierson

Distant Drums
The fanzine that is run, by fans, for fans. Issue 13 out now.
Check www.DistantDrums.org for full details.
To Glen Lockley who founded Distant Drums after listening to a 'Roger' road show. And welcome to Sam for his energy and help.

Photo Credits
Astley Chin: Jamaican Astley Chin was a photographer for National Jamaican Newspapers and was one of a very few professional photographers to take notice of the developing reggae scene. He has won several photography awards in Jamaica. Visit www.steppin.co.uk
Pages 16, 29, 35, 36, 38/39, 40/41, 42, 170 © copyright Traxonwax.net
Ossie Hamilton: A professional Jamaican photographer, Ossie Hamilton was a friend of Bob's and photographed Bob & The Wailers, as they became stars in Jamaica. His photos capture the spirit of Bob in his mid-twenties.
Visit www.steppin.co.uk
Pages: 4, 50, 53, 55, 62, 63, 64, 65, 72, 73, 77, 78, 86, 91, 95, 138, 148 © copyright Traxonwax.net
Chris Lane: Chris was the first music journalist in the UK to write about reggae on a regular basis and championed Bob Marley and the Wailers, as well as Lee Perry, King Tubby, Augustus Pablo and Lloyd Charmers in the early 1970s. The photos shown were taken when he stayed with Lee Perry for two weeks over Xmas / New Year 1973/4. Page: 80 © copyright Chris Lane
Dennis Morris: Dennis was a 14-year-old schoolboy when he first met Bob Marley at the Speakeasy Club. Dennis captured some of the most iconic images of Bob. Dennis is also known for his images of the Sex Pistols in their heyday and for his collection of photos taken of immigrant life in London's Southall. His photographs are regularly exhibited in London and have also been shown in Japan, Australia, Canada and the USA. See www.DennisMorris.com
Pages: 2, 11, 93, 98/99, 120/121, 131, 184/5 © copyright Dennis Morris
Peter Murphy: Peter photographed Bob as he toured the world as a superstar and worked at Hope Road. Peter's also known for his images of Peter Tosh, Burning Spear and Fela Kuti. Peter became fascinated by the cultures of Africa and the Caribbean and went on to make films in Africa. Currently he heads Oxfam's video unit. Visit www.steppin.co.uk
Pages: Endpapers, 1, 6, 8&9, 57, 88, 105, 107, 114/5, 119, 123, 125, 126/7, 129, 134/5, 137, 142, 143, 144, 168, 175, 179, 180/1, 182/3.

All other images from the Trax On Wax archive.

All Bob Marley songs are administered and controlled by Blue Mountain Publishing. The names 'Tuff Gong', 'Tuff Gong International' and '56 Hope Road,' are all controlled by The Estate and Family of Bob Marley.
The Official web site for merchandising and music is www.bobmarley.com